"The original *Flawless Consulting* was my consultant's bible many years ago. This new version is, again, an essential resource. Thank you Peter for going back to this work and gifting us with what you have learned along the way."

Margaret J. Wheatley, author of *Leadership and the New Science* and co-author of *A Simpler Way*

"Peter Block more than anyone has captured the spirit of consulting and has shown in specific detail how the consultant can learn the skills necessary to do an outstanding job in this complex profession."

Edgar H. Schein, Sloan Fellows Professor of Management Emeritus, senior lecturer, Mass

"In my 15 years in the profession, I have not read a more valuable book on effective consulting. This latest edition is practical wisdom for all consultants and the executives who hire them."

Susan Gretchko, partner Deloitte Consulting

"Peter Block gets to the heart matter, bringing earned wisdom and thoughtful balance to both the inner and outer dimensions of this most delicate craft."

Tim Gallwey, author of *The Inner Game of Golf* and *The Inner Game of Work*

"Peter Block's call for authenticity has long served as both beacon and gauntlet for staff professionals out to do meaningful work in a world seemingly set against it. The years of new wisdom included in the second edition reinforce the courage required and the benefits to be gained—for the head, hands, and heart."

Ken Murphy, senior vice president, human resources, Philip Morris USA

"Peter Block speaks to the heart of our work as consultants. He helps us discover how we can be our better selves while serving our clients. Peter's methods and stories kept reminding me why I love this work and find it so challenging."

Geoff Bellman, consultant author of *The Consultant's Calling*

"The values and beliefs underlying the concepts in *Flawless Consulting* and the practical examples are foundations used by internal consultants supporting Shell Exploration & Production Company's transformation."

Ann Burress, Shell Exploration & Production Company

"Worthy of more than one reading, Peter's second edition of *Flawless Consulting* is a seminal work for everyone who consults."

Jill Janov, consultant and author of
The Inventive Organization: Hope & Daring at Work

"It's so exciting to have this update! Peter is a major source of insight; infusing *Flawless Consulting* with his latest thinking adds immediate depth to consulting professionals and value to those we serve."

Blake Emery, senior organization development consultant,
Boeing Commercial Airplane Group

"The more deeply involved or affected by change, the more relevant and useful *Flawless Consulting* becomes. The second generation builds on the strengths of the original without detracting from it and represents a source of continuing professional development."

Cliff Bolster, consultant, Arthur D. Little, Inc.

"Peter's life is his teaching. *Flawless Consulting* in its new form has given new insights based on Peter's inspiring and trying moments. For us in Eicher Consultancy, our mission of Economic Development with spiritual enrichment has been made possible to a great extent because of what we have learned from his writings and his thoughts."

Anil Sachdev, managing director,
Eicher Consultancy Services Ltd., India

"*Flawless Consulting* presents a straightforward process that establishes successful consultative relationships within organizations. Peter Block's development of authentic communication skills increases the success for ownership of potentially difficult client relationships."

Harold B. Todd, Jr., executive vice president, retired
National City Corporation

"Peter Block captures the essence of what a consultant should be; namely a 'learning architect.' With the ever-increasing pace of change in the world, Peter's advocacy is as timely as it is thought-provoking."

Tom Garrihy, information services executive

"I have found the practical advice in Flawless Consulting invaluable. Its simple, logical approach gives trememdous insight into consulting for new and established consultants alike."

Andrew Rothery, director
Xerox Europe

To Dorothy, with love . . .

Also by Peter Block

Stewardship: Choosing Service over Self-Interest

The Empowered Manager: Positive Political Skills at Work

Contents

Preface
to the Second Edition

FOR SOME YEARS I have resisted revising this book. It has been very successful over the last twenty years, and I don't want to make it worse. It has done well around the world, and wherever I go people come up and tell me that the book has been of value to them.

It has even earned me some respect in the eyes of my brother, Jim. He was in a meeting a while back with some nuns in a Catholic service agency. One of the nuns asked him if he was Peter Block's brother and when he confessed that he was, the nun held up her copy of the book and proclaimed, "In my work, this book is my Bible!" He was impressed, and that is no small feat. So my concern is that in the enthusiasm to bring the book up to date, I will make it current but no better.

My other concern is that when I am often asked how my thinking has changed over the years, I struggle for an answer. The truth is that, in ways that are central to the book, my thinking has not so much changed as it has just gone deeper and wider into what I knew then. I hope that in going deeper into what I know, I can be clearer and stronger in what I say, and in that way add value.

On the other hand, much has changed over twenty years, and it seems worth the effort to bring the book into our current world. What was marginal in 1978 has become mainstream in 1998. The ideas in this book were born in the mid-Seventies when the vice president of management information services at an Exxon affiliate realized that 60 percent of the recommendations his group made to the line organization were never implemented. He knew his group's recommendations were well-conceived and relevant, but few clients used them.

He had attended a management training workshop conducted by our employee relations department and afterward invited us to design a consulting skills workshop for his systems group that would increase the implementation ratio of their recommendations. Neale Clapp and I worked on that project, and out of it came a successful consulting skills workshop that formed the basis for the book.

The idea that teams and personal relationships are critical to technical and business success was an innovative thought twenty years ago. Now the value of teams and relationships is more widely accepted, at least intellectually. We may not be any better at working together, but at least we know it matters and are willing to invest effort into building a more cooperative workplace.

The reason the ideas in this book have endured over the years is not so much because specific consulting skills are presented in such overconfident specificity; it is more because of the persistent emphasis given to the emotional and personal dimensions of our workplaces. Even now, with all the rhetoric given to relationships, personal development, and even spirituality, our institutions still operate as if strategy, structure, and technology are what really matter.

Relationships continue to be treated as a necessary inconvenience—as if relationships have to be endured and wherever there is an opportunity to automate a transaction or communicate electronically, we take it. We are reaching a point where most phone conversations involve a machine on one end, where learning from a television set or a computer terminal is considered an advantage, and where we encourage people to work at home, where human interaction is minimized in the name of serenity and a more balanced life.

What is difficult about managing relationships is that something is demanded of us that technology and automatic routines do not require—the need to know ourselves and be authentic. Authenticity is simply being honest with ourselves and being direct and honest with others. For whatever the reason, authenticity continues to be rare in our workplaces. Most interactions carry an element of role play, positioning, and strategy. All are reflections of our wish to control our environment and the people in it.

In some ways, this book is a long and detailed description of the landscape of authenticity. What has stood the test of time is that this rare act is not only good for the soul, but also works very well. An authentic consultant is not an oxymoron, but a compelling competitive advantage, if unfortunately a rare one.

What is difficult about authenticity is that it is a high-risk strategy. It swims upstream in a culture of control, which is where most of our organizations remain. It also demands some faith in ourselves: We have to be tuned into the feeling dimension of our connection with others. Most of us have spent our days developing our brain and have left our body and its feeling parts behind, to be reclaimed at night. So even when we decide to risk being authentic, we have trouble knowing how.

Valuing the relationship between consultant and client and defining how to manage that relationship is where this book has found its niche. The intent of this revision is to deepen and expand the white space between strategy, structure, and technology, which we label relationship.

One shift that has happened in recent years is the interest in thinking about organizations as human and living systems. Our workplaces are understaffed and shrinking, and organizations are in a continual search for new structures and practices. The need for speed and self-designed customized solutions has driven this shift. The importance of speed and on-the-spot decision making about service and product changes the role of the consultant. The days of long studies and expert-driven answers are passing. The task of the consultant is increasingly to build the capacity of clients to make their own assessments and answer their own questions. Plus, the shelf life of a solution is down to one minute. As soon as you implement a recommendation, you start the process all over again.

The self-managing aspect of change is dealt with in the last part of the book, in which I have added chapters on implementation, a subject I essentially avoided in the first writing. I have also added a new chapter on whole-system strategies. We now know how to involve larger numbers of people in rethinking their own workplace. I increasingly question whether the expert-driven model of change is ever useful and believe that, in most instances, giving recommendations simply breeds dependency and distracts from confronting clients with their own responsibility.

In the new chapters on implementation, I have tackled some of the conventional beliefs that unfortunately still interfere with our ability to help clients confront their challenges and decide how to proceed. Supporting all of those obstacles is a philosophy about change in human systems that I also question more and more. Is it ever legitimate to call ourselves "change agents"? It is common for consultants to talk about how to "intervene" in order to achieve change in an organization. It may feel fine for us to intervene in another's world, but which of us wants to be intervened upon? If we are change agents, who are we trying to change? We can claim we are trying to change systems, but systems are still people in various formations. The mind-set that we can change another is risky business. And what about the common phrase "change management"? Can change in fact be managed, and if it can, is it not someone else that we have in mind?

The alternative is to realize that a crucial part of implementation is the art of engagement, the ways to bring people together to create and plan how to make something work. This approach rests on the idea that shifts in the intangibles—relationships, commitment, accountability—are what make implementation succeed.

It is paradoxical that while we increasingly question the value of outsider answers, and cynicism about the value of consulting is as strong as ever, the world of external consulting has become widely commercialized. What once were the big six accounting firms have now become the bigger three consulting businesses. In the brief, but bright explosion of reengineering and the drive to become information-aged, change management and organization improvement consulting has become big business. The benefit of this is that the market for consulting has broadened and some of the softer aspects of consulting, such as process improvement, team building, and culture change, have been sold more effectively and thereby have gained wider acceptance.

The dark side of this commercialization of change is that client disappointments growing out of exaggerated consultant promises now take place on a much wider scale. The price we all pay for this is that each consultation that ends in disappointment breeds a cynicism that makes the next effort at change more difficult.

One of the things that has always haunted me about consulting is truly knowing whether we are making a difference. My concerns about whether either external or internal consulting really adds value grows out of some more profound changes in how I understand my own life and the work that I do. This is the attention I now give to understanding the shadow side of existence. There is a self-serving aspect to each act of service. Consulting at its best is an act of love: The wish to be genuinely helpful to another . . . To use what we know, or feel, or have endured in a way that lightens the weight on another.

The cost of our generosity, though, is that it carries within it our wish for dominance and gratitude. To be seen as wise and right, to be first with the insight, to claim credit for the changes in another are not gifts. They are subtle demands on a client to pay for our help with currency more costly than money.

I have deepened my understanding over the years of the extent to which consultants are high-control people. There is no inherent sin in this, except that the control is packaged in the form of care. Both internal and external consultants are prone to measure the value of their help by whether today's consulting service leads to a demand for more service tomorrow. The wish to continue to do more work for a line manager for a long period of time is really the commercialization of care.

Given these concerns and the exploitative potential of consulting, I have added a chapter on ethics and the shadow side of consulting. Included in this chapter are some thoughts about how we have commercialized our services and what it means to call ourselves a business. There needs to be a better way of thinking about our practice independent of asking how our client feels about us and whether our business is growing.

A final comment on what consultation means today: More and more line managers now define their role as consultative or facilitative. Managers have moved from command and control to more of a coaching function. In the movement to flatter, more flexible organizations, a boss in control has become too slow and too expensive. The core of consulting is about social contracting and managing in a self-managing world. It will take only minor shifts in language for line managers to apply most of the methods in the book to their own challenges of supervision.

Peter Block
July, 1999

Preface
to the First Edition

THIS BOOK IS FOR ANYONE who does consulting, even if you don't call yourself a consultant. You are consulting any time you are trying to change or improve a situation but have no direct control over the implementation. If you have direct control you are managing, not consulting. The consultant's lack of direct control and authority is what makes our task difficult and, at times, drives us crazy. This book is about having leverage and impact when we don't have direct control. Leverage and impact are what we want and what we get paid for. Leverage and impact mean that our expertise is used and our recommendations are accepted. This makes for job satisfaction for consultant and client alike. The path to having leverage and impact is what I immodestly call *flawless consultation.* This book is a guide to developing the skills to navigate that path.

I use the word *consulting* here in a very general sense, to cover many functions. Anyone doing "staff work" is consulting. So, this book is geared not just to people who consider themselves consultants but also to both technical and nontechnical staff people. My beliefs about consulting have grown out of what is now thirty years of full-time experience doing consulting, from positions both inside and outside organizations. The book grows even more directly from conducting scores of Staff Consulting Skills Training sessions. These workshops have been for engineers, purchasing agents, personnel and organization development people, lawyers, financial analysts and auditors, systems analysts, health service professionals, nurses, corporate staff and planners, and more—all people who have professional expertise, limited direct authority over the use of their expertise, and the desire to have some impact.

Most people do consulting work for organizations, rather than for themselves or consulting businesses. People doing staff work for an organization where they work full-time are called *internal consultants* (as opposed to external consultants). This book gives primary attention to internal consulting in its illustrative examples, case studies and exercises, and commentary on pitfalls. But the concepts apply to all consulting, and the dilemmas and guidance presented here should ring as true for the external as for the internal consultant.

I believe this book is unique in its attention to specific consultant behavior. Other books on consulting tend to provide theories for understanding organizations or theories for understanding the different types of consultant interventions. This is a how-to-do-it book: It tells you what to do and what to say in different consulting situations. At some points I get so carried away as to provide actual lines for you to say. I offer these lines and guidelines because they have worked for me and for hundreds of participants in the staff consulting skills workshops.

After working with consultants in both workshop and on-the-job situations, it is clear to me that most of us *understand* what is happening to ourselves and our clients; we just don't quite know what to *do* about it. When we get stuck with a client in a downward spiral, we know it's happening, but we feel lost about how to get out of the spiral. If after enduring the practical, what-to-do-next focus of this book, you still hunger for more conceptual understanding, I would suggest you read the books about the ways of thinking about change. Most of the best books come from outside the field of organizational change. They are listed in the bibliography and will broaden your way of thinking and being, a nice balance to all this discussion about ways of doing.

When I say the approach described in this book leads to "flawless consultation," it may sound somewhat audacious and arrogant. Many of us have a real aversion to perfection. The book, though, is in fact about flawless consultation, and the concept is a serious one, even if the practice is difficult. There is a way to manage yourself as you are consulting that maximizes your potential usefulness and directly deals with the resistance you encounter. This is within the reach of each of us, and to operate flawlessly, without error, is possible. Consulting flawlessly requires intense concentration on two processes.

1. Being as authentic as you can be at all times with the client

2. Attending directly, in words and actions, to the business of each stage of the consulting process

This book describes and gives examples of what authentic consulting behavior looks like. It also describes the business of each stage of the consulting process that must be attended to.

The strength of the book is that it is specific and literal. It is not so much a book of theory; it is a book of practice, for practitioners. It describes, even demonstrates, ways of behaving with clients. The leap of faith is that the practices and guidance presented here will result in more effective consultation. This has been borne out in my experience in doing consulting and conducting consulting skills workshops. I hope the book proves a useful guide to you.

The challenge for all of us is about having impact without control. This is true for both consultants and managers. For a manager, when you have thirty subordinates, how much control can you really exercise? Even for line managers who think they are still captains of the ship, the control they have is mostly an illusion. The inmates run the prison, the workers determine the quality of the work that they do, students are in charge of learning. So consulting in most cases is having impact on people who wish they had more control. Our real task is to help our clients learn how to better function in their world, which is permanently and elusively out of control. The fact that most clients seek from consultants a way to increase their own sense of control makes the consulting job more difficult. The resolution of this is to stay focused on the relationship with the client, for out of this comes the realization that clients can achieve the results they want without having to control those around them.

Peter Block

Acknowledgments

IT IS A TREAT to have an opportunity to formally express appreciation to people who have really created the concepts expressed in this book.

Conceptually, the role of interpersonal skills in organizations and the key role that authentic behavior plays was pioneered by Chris Argyris. What I learned as a student of his in the now famous Sixties is still powerful and relevant.

Most of us learn how to consult from watching someone who knows how to do it. I was lucky early in the game to follow around Barry Oshry, Roger Harrison, and Dick Walton. They are the best and gave support to us above and beyond the call of duty.

Tony Petrella, partner in crime from the beginning, and Marv Weisbord have so deeply contributed to my understanding of consulting skills that I can't begin to separate my thoughts from theirs. I can only express appreciation for a valued partnership that was enduring and priceless.

Neale Clapp contributed greatly in two ways. He has given unqualified support and friendship, and he recognized the value in the consulting skills workshop and theory long before I did. In conducting many of the early workshops, Neale contributed conceptually to the early sections of the book on the staff role and helped generously with the revision.

The section on "Resistance" was clarified by Jim Maselko. Through his skill and enthusiasm, Jim has helped give life to the approach to consulting the book represents.

The first attempt at writing the original version of the book was done collaboratively with Mike Hill. Although the book eventually took a different direction, Mike was the key to getting the thing started. His fingerprints remain in portions of the early sections.

The basic concepts on contracting are drawn from Gestalt psychology. These were crystallized in a workshop I attended run by Claire and Mike Reiker. Their ability to present them simply and powerfully was a great gift.

The cartoons in the book are by Janis Nowlan. I sent her a very primitive form of the manuscript to see whether she could enliven the copy with illustrations. I thought I had given her an impossible task. The drawings Janis sent back were incredible. Her light touch in visually expressing the concepts in many cases is much more perceptive than all the words I have put together. Janis has continued to support this effort with new illustrations and by updating some language and creating a new wardrobe for the old ones.

Thanks go to Ray Bard, who was my publisher when the book was begun. Ray believed a book was possible when I thought all I had were some notes for a workshop participant's workbook. Also thanks to Matt Holt and Jossey-Bass, whose patience and persistence, with a little nudge from Jerry Pavlov, got me going on the revision.

A continuing thanks goes to the participants in the Designed Learning Staff Consulting Skills Workshops we have conducted over the years. The bulk of the book documents the theory we have been presenting in the workshops. Most of the concepts have emerged as answers to questions from people learning about consulting. Thanks go to their patience when the concepts were confusing and to their willingness to help us articulate the consulting process out of their own experience.

As with the original edition, Leslie Stephen helped with the editing of this revision. This is the fourth book that she has helped edit with me. She supports my voice and gives structure, simple clarity, and deep understanding to whatever she touches. I only hope she outlives me so I don't have to face writing another book without her.

My thinking is always influenced by my connection with Joel Henning. The ideas about changing the conversation and the struggle with new language of commitment and barter are just a few of the areas where he keeps opening my thoughts. Look for the book he is writing on conversation that I hope is available soon.

The chapters on implementation in this edition were greatly influenced by my association with The Association for Quality and Participation's School for Managing and Leading Change. The School has been the laboratory where the new ideas were tested. My practice has been changed by my involvement with the faculty from the School. The thoughts about designing group experiences have been influenced by watching Jill Janov do her work so well. I am especially grateful to Kathie Dannemiller and her associates at Dannemiller-Tyson Associates. They understand something profound about the heartbeat of large assemblies. Also Dick and Emily Axelrod have created magic in their work with The Conference Model. Dick is writing his own book on engagement, and the material in this book grew out of many conversations with him that have changed my consciousness.

Finally, all of us who consult today owe a debt of gratitude to the work of Ed Schein. He was one of the early beacons of light who gave direction and insight to those of us who contemplated working in the field of organization change. He made understandable and explicit the process consulting path that later became a central part of how I operated, and for that I am very grateful.

Chapter 1
A Consultant by Any Other Name . . .

THE TERM "CONSULTANT" HAS BECOME MUCH MALIGNED AND IN DISREPUTE:

ANY FORM OF HUMOR or sarcasm has some truth in it. The truth in the prevailing skepticism about consultants is that the traditional consultant has tended to act solely as an agent of management: assuming the manager's role either in performing highly technical activities that a manager could not do or in performing distasteful and boring activities that a manager did not want to do. The most dramatic examples of consultants taking the place of managers is when they identify people or functions to be eliminated.

When you are asked directions and you tell someone to get off the bus two stops before you do, you are acting as a consultant. Every time you give advice to someone who is faced with a choice, you are consulting. When you don't have direct control over people

1

and yet want them to listen to you and heed your advice, you are face to face with the consultant's dilemma. For some of you, this may be your full-time predicament. Some of you may face it only occasionally, functioning part-time as managers (having direct control) and part-time as consultants (wanting to influence, but lacking authority to control).

Some Definitions and Distinctions

A *consultant* is a person in a position to have some influence over an individual, a group, or an organization, but who has no direct power to make changes or implement programs. A manager is someone who has direct responsibility over the action. The moment you take direct responsibility, you are acting as a manager.

Most people in staff roles in organizations are really consultants, even if they don't officially call themselves "consultants." Staff people function in any organization by planning, recommending, assisting, or advising in such matters as:

Personnel

Financial analysis

Auditing

Systems analysis

Market research

Product design

Long-range planning

Organizational effectiveness

Safety

Human resource development

and many more

The recipients of all this advice are called *clients*. Sometimes the client is a single individual. Other times, the client may be a work group, a department, or a whole organization. The client is the person or persons that the consultant wants to influence, without exercising direct control.[1]

In organizations, clients for the services provided by staff people are called *line managers.* Line managers have to labor under the advice of staff groups, whether they like it or not. But any staff function, by definition, has no direct authority over anything but its own time, its own internal staff, and the nature of the service it offers. This tension between the line manager (or client) who has direct control and the staff person (or consultant) who does not have direct control is one of the central themes of this book.

The key to understanding the consultant role is to see the difference between a consultant and a manager.

Listen to Alfred:

> It was a great four-month project. I headed the team from administrative services that installed the new management information system. We assessed the problems, designed the system and got Alice, the line manager, to let us install the system from top to bottom.

Alfred is very satisfied—but this is the line manager's satisfaction. He wasn't really acting as a consultant; he took over a piece of the line manager's job for four months.

This distinction is important. A consultant needs to function differently from a line manager—for the consultant's own sake and for the learning goals of the client. It's OK to have direct control—most of us want it in various forms of disguise. It is essential, though, to be aware of the difference in the roles we are assuming when we have it and when we don't.

---

[1]You will mainly see the terms consultant and client used throughout the rest of the text to reinforce this belief and—especially if you are in a staff role—to assist your thinking of yourself as a consultant.

Much of the disfavor associated with the term consultant comes from the actions of people who call themselves "consultants" but act as surrogate line managers. When you act on the behalf of or in the place of the manager, you are acting as a surrogate manager. When the client says, "Complete this report for me," "Hire this person for me," "Design this system for me," "Counsel this employee," or "Figure out which jobs stay and which jobs go," the manager is asking for a surrogate. The attraction of the surrogate manager role is that, at least for that one moment, you assume the manager's power—but you do the manager's job, not yours.

Your goal or end product in any consulting activity is some kind of change. Change comes in two varieties. At one level, we consult to create change in the line organization of a structural, policy, or procedural nature—a new compensation package, a new reporting process, a new safety program. The second kind of change is the end result that one person or many people in the line organization have learned something new. They may have learned what norms dominate their staff meetings, what they do to keep lower-level people in a highly dependent position in decision making, how to involve people more directly in setting goals, or how to conduct better performance evaluations.

In its most general use, consultation describes any action you take with a system of which you are not a part. An interview with someone asking for help is a consulting act. A survey of problems, a training program, an evaluation, a study—all are consultations for the sake of change. The consultant's objective is to engage in successful actions that result in people or organizations managing themselves differently.

I think of the terms staff work and consulting work as being interchangeable, to reflect my belief that people in a staff role really need consulting skills to be effective—regardless of their field of technical expertise (finance, planning, engineering, personnel, law). Every time you give advice to someone who is in the position to make the choice, you are consulting. For each of these moments of consultation, there are three kinds of skills you need to do a good job—technical, interpersonal, and consulting skills.

Here are the distinctions.

Technical Skills

Above all, we need to know what the person is talking about. We need expertise about the question. Either in college or in our first job, we were trained in a specific field or function. This might be engineering, sales, accounting, counseling, or any of the thousands of ways people make a living. This is our basic training. It is only later, after acquiring some technical expertise, that we start consulting. If we didn't have some expertise, then people wouldn't ask for our advice. The foundation for consulting skills is some expertise—whether it be very scientific, such as coke particle sizing, or very nonscientific, such as management or organizational development. This book assumes you have some area of expertise.

Interpersonal Skills

To function with people, we need to have some interpersonal skills. Some ability to put ideas into words, to listen, to give support, to disagree reasonably, to basically maintain a relationship. There are many books and seminars offered now to help us with these skills, in fact, there is a whole humanistic social movement devoted to improving these skills. Just like technical skills, interpersonal skills are necessary to effective consultation. Some authorities suggest that good consulting actually requires only good interpersonal skills. This is not true. There is a set of skills that is an essential part of consulting over and above technical expertise and interpersonal skills—these are *consulting skills.*

Consulting Skills

Each consulting project, whether it lasts ten minutes or ten months, goes through five phases. The steps in each phase are sequential; if you skip one or assume it has been taken care of, you are headed for trouble. Skillful consulting is being competent in the execution of each of these steps. Successfully completing the business of each phase is the primary focus of this book.

Consulting Skills Preview

Here is an overview of what is involved in the five phases of consulting.

Phase 1. Entry and Contracting

This has to do with the initial contact with a client about the project. It includes setting up the first meeting as well as exploring what the problem is, whether the consultant is the right person to work on this issue, what the client's expectations are, what the consultant's expectations are, and how to get started. When consultants talk about their disasters, their conclusion is usually that the project was faulty in the initial contracting stage.

Phase 2. Discovery and Dialogue

Consultants need to come up with their own sense of the problem. This may be the most useful thing they do. They also need skill in helping the client do the same. The questions here for the consultant are: Who is going to be involved in defining the problem? What methods will be used? What kind of data should be collected? and How long will it take?

**Phase 3.
Feedback and
the Decision
to Act**

The data collection and analysis must be reported in some fashion. The consultant is always in the position of reducing a large amount of data to a manageable number of issues. There are also choices for the consultant on how to involve the client in the process of analyzing the information. In giving feedback to an organization, there is always some resistance to the data (if it deals with important issues). The consultant must handle this resistance before an appropriate decision can be made about how to proceed. This phase is really what many people call planning: It includes setting ultimate goals for the project and selecting the best action steps or changes.

**Phase 4.
Engagement and
Implementation**

This involves carrying out the planning of the previous step. In many cases the implementation may fall entirely on the line organization. For larger change efforts, the consultant may be deeply involved. Some projects start implementation with an educational event. This could be a series of meetings to introduce some change. It may require a single meeting to get different parts of the organization together to address a problem. It may be a training session. In these cases, the consultant is usually involved in rather complicated design work and in running the meeting or training session.

**Phase 5.
Extension,
Recycle, or
Termination**

Phase 5 begins with an evaluation of what went on during engagement and implementation. Following this is the decision whether to extend the process to a larger segment of the organization. Sometimes it is not until after some implementation occurs that a clear picture of the real problem emerges. In this case the process recycles and a new contract needs to be discussed. If the implementation was either a huge success or a moderate-to-high failure, termination of further involvement on this project may be in the offing. There are many options for ending the relationship, and termination should be considered a legitimate and important part of the consultation. If done well, it can provide an important learning experience for the client and the consultant and also keep the door open for future work with the organization.

When you look at Figure 1, you will see a preview of some of the skills and topics covered for each consulting step. On the figure, the steps are grouped into *preliminary events* and the *main event*.

Preliminary events are the initial contacts, the planning meetings, the data collection, and feedback and decision-making meetings.

The main event is when you finally do something with enough impact to be noticeable to many people in the organization, and they have the expectation that noticeable change, or learning, will occur because of that event. One of my beliefs is that the preliminary events are in many ways more crucial for success than the main event. An understanding of consulting skills is really an understanding of preliminary events.

The Promise of Flawless Consultation

One reason consulting can be frustrating is that you are continually managing lateral relationships. As a staff person or consultant, you are working with a line manager in a context in which there is no clear boss-subordinate relationship between you. Vertical relationships are easier to understand: If your boss gives you an order, you know that he or she has the right to tell you what to do. If your client makes a demand, you don't necessarily have to obey. The power balance in lateral relationships is always open to ambiguity—and to negotiation. When we get resistance from a client,

Figure 1. An Overview of Consulting Skills

The Preliminary Events

Technical Skills	*Interpersonal Skills*	*Consulting Skills*
Specific to Your Discipline	**Apply to All Situations**	**Requirements of Each Consulting Phase**

• Engineering • Project management • Planning • Marketing • Manufacturing • Personnel • Finance • Systems analysis	• Assertiveness • Supportiveness • Confrontation • Listening • Management style • Group process	*Contracting* • Negotiating wants • Coping with mixed motivation • Dealing with concerns about exposure and the loss of control • Doing triangular and rectangular contracting *Discovery* • Surfacing layers of analysis • Dealing with political climate • Resisting the urge for complete data • Seeing the interview as an intervention *Feedback* • Funneling data • Identifying and working with different forms of resistance • Presenting personal and organizational data *Decision* • Running group meetings • Focusing on here and now choices • Not taking it personally

The Main Event

Engagement and Implementation

sometimes we aren't sure whether to push harder or to let go. This book is about managing this kind of ambiguity.

Taken as a whole, this book is about flawless consultation—consulting without error. It concentrates most on the preliminary events because I believe competence in contracting, discovery, and feedback create the foundation for successful outcomes in the implementation stage. I have deliberately avoided discussing and demonstrating consulting skills in an overall step-wise sequence of chapters because there are some concepts and competencies that must be brought to bear in every stage of a consulting relationship. So I have included chapters treating consulting assumptions, goals for a consulting relationship, and consultant role choices, as well as the requirements for flawless consultation, before the chapters that specify and illustrate the skills required for each of the preliminary events. I have also interspersed chapters on such issues as client resistance and the special considerations of the internal consultant's role to demonstrate the belief that successful consulting demands more than a methodical, step-by-step application of technical expertise.

My belief is that if you consult in the way this book describes, your consultation can be flawless and you will:

1. Have your expertise better utilized

2. Have your recommendations more frequently implemented

3. Become more in a partnership role with clients

4. Avoid no-win consulting situations

5. Develop internal commitment in your clients

6. Receive support from clients

7. Increase the leverage you have on clients

8. Establish more trusting relationships with clients

My using the term *flawless consultation* may sound presumptuous, but it is not accidental. A basic value underlying the book is that there is in each of us the possibility of perfection. There is a consulting "pro" inside of each of us, and our task is to allow that flawless consultant to emerge. On its surface, this book is about methods and techniques. But each technique carries a consistent message more important than any method—that each act that expresses trust in ourselves and belief in the validity of our own experience is always the right path to follow. Each act that is manipulative or filled with pretense is always self-destructive.

Working in organizations means we are constantly bombarded by pressure to be clever and indirect and to ignore what we are feeling at the moment. Flawless consulting offers the possibility to let our behavior be consistent with our beliefs and feelings and also to be successful in working with our clients. The focus here on techniques and skills in consulting is simply a way to identify the high self-trust choices we all have as we work in organizations. From the first day on our first job, each of us has struggled with the conflict between really being ourselves and conforming to the expectations we think our employers or clients have of us. The desire to be successful can lead us into playing roles and adopting behaviors that are internally alien and represent some loss of ourselves.

Consultants are especially vulnerable to this conflict because we are supposed to be serving our client's needs. Our projects also tend to be short-term and we work at the pleasure of the client. It is easier to terminate a consultant or staff person than to terminate a subordinate. In hard times, managers end consulting projects before they reduce their own work force. This sense of vulnerability can become a rationalization for consultants to deny their own needs and feelings and to not be authentic. This book offers an alternative. It says that trusting ourselves is the path that serves us well with clients and increases the chances that our expertise will be used again and again.

Chapter 2

Techniques Are Not Enough

MANY PEOPLE learning consulting skills look for techniques and procedural ways to be more effective as consultants. But there are special demands of the consulting role that transcend any specific methods we might employ and that contribute to our effectiveness no matter what our technical expertise. A unique and beguiling aspect of doing consulting is that your own self is involved in the process to a much greater extent than if you were applying your expertise in some other way. Your own reactions to a client, your own feelings during discussions, your own ability to solicit feedback from the client—all are important dimensions to consultation.

In acting as a consultant, you always operate at two levels. One level is the substance, the cognitive part of a discussion between yourself and the client. The client presents a certain organizational problem. Perhaps it's the need for training, improving the skills of people in an organization. Perhaps it's how the organization makes decisions. The problem may be one of furnace design—or financial controls.

The substance level is the problem-solving, rational, or explicit part of the discussion, where you are working on what I call the technical/business problem. At the same time and at another level, both you and the client are generating and sensing your feelings about each other—whether you feel accepting or resistant, whether you feel high or low tension, whether you feel support or confrontation. So, the relationship of the consultant to the client during each phase is a second level of data that needs attention.

Beyond Substance

There is much more to the client-consultant relationship than the simple substance of the problem or project the consultant is working on. Feelings are the *affective* side of the discussion and an important source of *data* for the consultant—data about the client's real problems and what the possibilities are for establishing a good relationship.

A major objective of this book is to encourage you to focus on and value the affective, or interpersonal, aspect of the relationship between the client and the consultant. Most of us have a great deal of experience working at the cognitive or substance level of discussion. We come to a meeting equipped with our expertise, and we feel quite comfortable talking about problems we know something about. There should be equal balance in the attention given to the substance of the client's problem and to the feelings you are having about the interaction that is taking place as you are talking to the client.

Once you value the affective side of the relationship as an important area of attention, the second step is to increase your comfort level in putting into words how you are feeling about the relationship as it's going on. The third step is to grow more skillful in putting your data about the relationship into words so you don't overly increase defensiveness on the part of the client.

There are four elements to the affective side of consultant-client interaction that are always operating.

Responsibility

To have a good contract with the client, responsibility for what is planned and takes place has to be balanced—50/50. In most cases, the client comes to you with the expectation that once you are told what the problem is, you provide the solution. Your goal is to act out the fact that it's a 50/50 proposition.

Just a small example: When you start a program, communication on the program is often required—when it is, what the arrangements are, why you're doing it. It's important that the client go to the trouble of writing the letter and doing this communicating, not because it's a task that only the client can do—in fact, the consultant might be in a better position to do it—but it's a way of visibly expressing to the organization that the client is taking at least 50 percent of the responsibility for the program. If the client wants the consultant to write a draft of the letter and to take care of all the administrative details, the client is saying that he or she wants to take a limited amount of responsibility. As a consultant, it makes sense at times to resist taking on this responsibility. This is a substantively small issue, but it's an example of what to look for in trying to decide in your own mind whether the responsibility is balanced.

Feelings

The second element that's always an issue is to what extent clients are able to own their own feelings. In a way, this is working on the responsibility. The consultant needs to constantly keep in mind how much the client is owning feelings versus talking as if just an observer of the organization. The consultant also has to keep in mind what his or her own feelings are about the client. If the consultant is feeling that the client is very defensive or very controlling, or doesn't listen or doesn't take responsibility, this is important data. However the consultant feels working with that client, the people inside the client's organization are going to feel the same way. It is equally important for you to pay close attention to your own feelings during the consultation, particularly during the early stages, and use these as valuable data on how the organization functions and how this person manages.

Trust

The third element is trust. Most of us go into a situation as a consultant and bring with us the prevailing image of the consultant as the expert and someone to watch out for. It is often useful to ask the clients whether they trust your confidentiality, whether they trust you not to put them down or to take things over. By doing this, you're working to build trust. The more the distrust is put into words, the more likely you are to build trust.

Your Own Needs

The fourth element on the affective side of the consultant-client relationship is that consultants have a right to their own needs from the relationship.

It's easy to fall into a service mentality, in which you see yourself charged with solving the client's problems and serving the client's needs—and it's possible to act in such a way that you, as the consultant, appear not to have any needs. The reality is that you do have needs. You may have organizational needs to have a client, so that your own organization feels that you're doing something worthwhile. You have needs for acceptance and inclusion by the client, and you require some validation that what you have is valuable and worth offering.

On a practical level, you have needs for access to that organization—to talk to people, to ask them questions. And you also have needs for support from that manager, and meeting the people in the manager's organization, and dealing with the kind of resistance that you're likely to get. You are entitled to have your needs met.

To sum up my beliefs about learning consulting skills, the beliefs that are the foundation for the rest of this book—pay close attention to your own style and your own feelings as important dimensions to the consulting relationship. Skill in consulting is not only skill in providing a program, a process, and procedures that respond to the client's needs. It's also your skill in being able to identify and put into words the issues around trust, feelings, responsibility, and your own needs.

The Consultant's Assumptions

Any view of what makes for effective consultation relies heavily on the assumptions the consultant has about what makes an effective organization. These assumptions will be implicitly or explicitly a part of any recommendation.

Each of us doing consulting ought to be very clear about our own beliefs. Our own consulting behavior should be consistent with the style of management we advocate to our clients. If we are recommending to our clients that they tighten up controls, be more decisive, and set clear goals, we will be undermining our credibility if we operate without controls, are indecisive, and aren't quite sure where we are headed. If we think our clients should work on being more participative and collaborative, we undermine ourselves if we keep tight control of our consulting projects and don't act collaboratively with the very clients we are trying to encourage to try collaboration.

You can begin by thinking about what your assumptions about good management might be. There are countless models to choose from.

Most organizations currently operate from a variation of the military/church model. Structurally, there is a great emphasis on the hierarchical pyramid and the clear separation of authority and responsibility. The cornerstone of hierarchical management is strong leadership. Leadership is seen as individual ability to plan work, organize people to do the work, maintain control of those people and their results, and then delegate responsibility to the right people to achieve results. The products of these leader-centered assumptions are individuals with an upward conforming and downward controlling orientation toward their roles.

The traditional emphasis on control and leadership qualities has shifted in the past twenty years (at least in the literature) to more collaborative or participative conceptions of organizations. Participative management is a theme that runs throughout most current assumptions about effective organizations.

Your assumptions about organizations determine in subtle ways your own consulting style and the skills you should be working on. Here is the set of assumptions that underlie the consulting approach presented in this book.[2]

---

[2]Chris Argyris has been at the leading edge of organization and consulting theory since the 1960's. I believe his clear way of defining what makes for an effective management process holds up a standard for effective consultant performance as well.

Problem Solving Requires Valid Data

Using *valid data* eliminates a major cause of confusion, uncertainty, and resulting inefficiency in problem solving. Valid data encompasses two things: (1) *objective data,* data about ideas, events, or situations that everyone accepts as facts, and (2) *personal data.* Personal data are also "facts," but they concern how individuals feel about what is happening to them and around them. If people feel they will not get a fair shake, it is a "fact" that they feel that way, and it is also a "fact" that this belief will have an effect on their behavior. To ignore this kind of "fact" is to throw away data that may be crucial to any problem-solving effort.

Effective Decision Making Requires Free and Open Choice

Making decisions is easy. Making decisions that people will support is not so easy. Organizations seem to work better when people get an opportunity to influence decisions that have a direct impact on their work. When people feel that something is important and they have some control, they will be motivated to exert the effort to make things work. When they believe that something is important but they can exert no control, the common tendencies are to become cautious or defensive, to play it safe, to withhold information, to protect themselves from blame.

Effective Implementation Requires Internal Commitment

People readily commit themselves to things they believe will further their interests. If no link is seen between what a person is asked to do and what a person wants to do, the probability of getting an all-out effort is not likely. You can order people to do things and ordinarily they will comply—at least while you are watching. But if you want them to apply themselves, internal commitment is required.

The Consultant's Goals

My assumptions about what contributes to effective consultant and manager performance lead to a set of preferred goals for each consulting job. Achieving each of these goals may not always be possible, but I can always be clear about my preference.

**Goal Number 1.
To Establish a
Collaborative
Relationship**

I believe there are two reasons for consultants to strive for collaborative relationships with their clients. One is that a collaborative relationship promises maximum use of people's resources—both the consultant's and the client's. It also spreads the responsibility for success or failure and for implementation, and it's a nice way to work. The second reason for consultants to act in a collaborative way is that, knowingly or not, they are always functioning as models of how to solve problems. The message contained in the way consultants act is much more powerful than their words. To talk collaboration and behave differently is confusing and self-defeating.

**Goal Number 2.
To Solve
Problems So
They Stay Solved**

It is possible to act in a way that only the immediate problem gets solved. If there is a problem with employees coming late to work, for example, actions can be taken to prevent it—station the boss at the door in the morning with a pencil and a black book, or have room checks at starting time each morning, or issue a policy statement about lateness, or have meetings with employees about the need for punctuality. This might reduce the problem of lateness. If internal (or external) consultants are involved in making these kinds of recommendations, they might have contributed to an increase in the present effectiveness of the organization. But this does not mean that the managers have learned anything about how to solve similar problems and thus become more competent.

The consultant's alternative is to work with line managers at another level of analysis—the way they handle lateness problems. For example, managers may not see lateness as being a symptom of discontent, or a symptom of inexperienced supervision at the first level, or any of the other possible root problems lateness could be signaling. Also, it is possible the consultant is being asked to solve problems line managers should be confronting themselves. Teaching the managers skills in solving the problem themselves next time requires that they understand that disturbing employee behavior is a symptom of more basic problems, and that they should not ask others to confront problems that belong to them.

Goal Number 3. To Ensure Attention Is Given to Both the Technical/Business Problem and the Relationships

Each situation has two elements: The technical/business problem that has to be resolved and the way people are interacting around that problem. In most organizations, primary attention is given to the technical/business problem. Consultants are in a unique position to address the people or process issues productively. As third parties, they have no vested interest in the process issues—no power to gain or lose, no territory to expand or contract, no budget to increase or decrease. Consultants can urge attention to the process issues, and line managers will listen to them in a way in which they would not listen to each other.

Developing Client Commitment— A Secondary Goal of Each Consulting Act

Because consultants or staff people have no direct control over implementation, they become very dependent on line managers for producing results. The line manager ultimately will decide whether to take action, and this choice will be based on how internally committed the line manager is to the concepts the consultant is suggesting. So the consultant needs to be very conscious of building internal commitment all during the consulting process. Effective consulting skills are those steps and behaviors that act to create internal commitment in managers. Each of us has seen examples of consulting projects where the study or report ends up on a shelf, despite its cost and relevance. When this happens, it often means that somewhere along the line, the consulting process lost the managers who had to decide to use the results of the study.

In flawless consulting, you move through the steps of a consulting process *designed* to build commitment and reduce the chance of losing the client along the way.

Client commitment is the key to consultant leverage and impact. We can't order the client to take action. (Sometimes we decide to go to the client's boss and urge him or her to direct the client to use our recommendations, but this is a risky proposition—particularly if we want to stay in the good graces of our client.) So our impact is determined by the client's commitment to our suggestions. Building this commitment is often a process of removing obstacles that block the client from acting on our advice.

We may cling to the fantasy that if our thinking is clear and logical, our wording is eloquent, and our convictions are solid, the strength of our arguments will carry the day. Clear arguments do help. But they are not enough. The client and his or her colleagues will experience doubts and dilemmas that block commitment.

Roles Consultants Choose

Having leverage requires confronting the doubts at each stage of the consulting process—during contracting, data collection, discovery, and while preparing for the feedback meeting. Waiting until the implementation phase to "overcome resistance" is too late.

Ed Schein has identified three ways consultants work with line managers[3]: in an *expert* role, a *pair-of-hands* role, or a *collaborative* role. The choice depends on individual differences in management style, the nature of the task, and the consultant's own personal preference.

As you consult in a variety of situations, it helps to become aware of the role you typically assume and to be able to identify situations

---

[3]These roles were first formulated by Ed Schein in the 1960s. He was one of the first to see the limitations of the expert role for consultants and defined and opened the door to the collaborative potential in the helping process. His recent book, *Process Consulting Revisited: Building the Helping Relationship,* more fully describes the power of Process Consultation as a vital capacity for those in a helping position. It is a book I would strongly recommend.

where this will help or hinder your performance. Only then can you make a conscious choice among alternatives. One discovery people often make in such self-analysis is that they begin to identify situations where they can operate more successfully in a collaborative mode. However, the realities of most organizations are such that there will be times when the pair-of-hands or expert roles are more appropriate and other times when they cannot be avoided.

Expert Role

One way line managers typically relate to staff specialists, as well as to external consultants, is client-to-expert. The staff person becomes the "expert" in the performance of a given task.

For example: In accordance with a corporate decision, cost accounting records are changed from a manual to a computer system. After awhile, it becomes clear that the new system has not lived up to expectations. The computer itself is OK; the problem is somewhere in the information flow that is input to the computer.

At this point, the manager calls in a staff computer specialist. After describing the difficulties, the manager says, "I have neither the time nor the inclination to deal with this problem. You're the expert; find out what's wrong and fix it. You have a free hand to examine the operation and do whatever analysis is necessary. Keep me posted on your findings and what you intend to do."

In this case, the computer specialist becomes, in effect, a member of the manager's staff with delegated authority to plan and implement change programs subject to the same restrictions as other members of the manager's staff.

Here is what is happening in this kind of relationship.

The manager elects to play an inactive role. He or she expects to hold the consultant responsible for results. The consultant accepts the responsibility and feels free to develop and implement action plans. The manager is expected to be responsive, to provide the assistance needed to solve the problem.

Decisions on how to proceed are made by the consultant, on the basis of his or her expert judgment. There is no need to involve the manager in technical details.

Information needed for problem analysis is gathered by the consultant. The consultant also decides what methods of data collection and analysis will be used.

Technical control rests with the consultant. Disagreement is not likely because it would be difficult for the manager to challenge "expert" reasoning. If the manager seeks to exert control over technical decisions, the consultant will see it as unjustified interference.

Collaboration is not required. Problem-solving efforts are based on specialized procedures.

Two-way communication is limited. The consultant initiates and the client responds. The consultant expects and is expected to initiate communication in a question-and-answer mode.

The consultant plans and implements the main events. Or the consultant provides detailed instructions for implementation by the manager.

The manager's role is to judge and evaluate after the fact.

The consultant's goal is to solve the immediate problem. Neither the manager nor the consultant expects the manager to develop skills to solve similar problems in the future.

Problems

Internal consultants, especially, are well aware of the problems involved in operating in the role of expert. Here are two big ones.

Consider the consultant's ability to make an accurate assessment. Given a problem of a purely technical nature, the consultant can use certain technical expertise to isolate the problem and develop a solution. But problems that are purely technical are rare. Most problems have a "people element" in them. And if the prevailing organizational climate is fear, insecurity, or mistrust, essential information on the people part of the problem may be withheld or distorted. Without valid data, accurate assessment becomes impossible. Action programs based on faulty discovery have little chance for success.

Consider the commitment of people to take the recommended actions. Studies done by "outside experts" seldom carry the kind of personal ownership and commitment needed to deal with difficult management issues.

Pair-of-Hands Role

Here the manager sees the consultant as an extra "pair-of-hands." The manager says in effect, "I have neither the time nor the inclination to deal with this problem. I have examined the deficiencies and have prepared an outline of what needs to be done. I want you to get it done as soon as possible." The manager retains full control. The consultant is expected to apply specialized knowledge to implement action plans toward the achievement of goals defined by the manager.

Here are some of the clues that the consultant is acting as a pair of hands.

The consultant takes a passive role. The order of the day is responding to the manager's requests, and the consultant does not question the manager's action plans.

Decisions on how to proceed are made by the manager. The consultant may prepare recommendations for the manager's review and approval.

The manager selects methods for data collection and analysis. The consultant may do the actual data collection in accordance with procedures outlined by the manager.

Control rests with the manager. The consultant is expected to make suggestions, but outright disagreement is avoided as this would be seen as a challenge to the manager's authority.

Collaboration is not really necessary. The manager feels that it is his or her responsibility to specify goals and procedures. The consultant can ask questions for clarification.

Two-way communication is limited. The manager initiates and the consultant responds. The manager initiates in a descriptive or evaluative mode.

The manager specifies change procedures for the consultant to implement.

The manager's role is to judge and evaluate from a close distance.

The consultant's goal is to make the system more effective by the application of specialized knowledge.

Problems

The major problem emerges in the discovery phase. In a pair-of-hands mode, the consultant is dependent on the manager's ability to understand what is happening and to develop an effective action plan. If the manager's assessment is faulty, the action plan won't work. The consultant who provided the "service" becomes a convenient scapegoat.

To avoid the big trap, the consultant may ask for time to verify the manager's assessment. And then the consultant may face other problems—managers who have a preference for consultants who take on the pair-of-hands role may interpret such requests as questioning their experience, their authority, or both.

Collaborative Role

The consultant who assumes a collaborative role enters the relationship with the notion that management issues can be dealt with effectively only by joining his or her specialized knowledge with the manager's knowledge of the organization. Problem solving becomes a joint undertaking, with equal attention to both the technical issues and the human interactions involved in dealing with the technical issues.

When consultants work through a collaborative role, they don't solve problems for the manager. They apply their special skills to help managers solve problems. The distinction is significant. The key assumption underlying the collaborative role is that the manager must be actively involved in data gathering and analysis, in setting goals and developing action plans, and, finally, in sharing responsibility for success or failure.

Here's what happens.

The consultant and the manager work to become interdependent. They share responsibility for action planning, implementation, and results.

Decision making is bilateral. It is characterized by mutual exchange and respect for the responsibilities and expertise of both parties.

Data collection and analysis are joint efforts. The selection of the kind of data to be collected and the method to be used is done by both the consultant and the manager.

Control issues become matters for discussion and negotiation. Disagreement is expected and seen as a source of new ideas.

Collaboration is considered essential. The consultant makes a special point to reach understanding and agreement on the nature and scope of mutual expectations prior to initiating problem-solving efforts.

Communication is two-way. Both the consultant and the manager take the initiative, depending on the issues. Information exchange is carried on in a problem-solving mode.

Implementation responsibilities are determined by discussion and agreement. Assignments are made to maximize use of available resources in line with responsibilities appropriate to each party.

The consultant's goal is to solve problems so they stay solved. That is, the consultant establishes a helping relationship designed to broaden the competence level of managers to develop and implement action plans that will make the system more effective. Next time the manager will have the skills to solve the problem.

Problems

There are also problems in trying to work collaboratively.

Consultants often have special skills (e.g., in budget management) that managers see as a quick answer to their problems. Managers who prefer to work with consultants in an *expert* role may interpret any attempts at collaboration as indifference or foot dragging. Managers with a preference to work with consultants in a *pair-of-hands* role may interpret moves toward collaboration as insubordination.

Collaboration and the Fear of Holding Hands

In a recent presentation on collaborative consultation, a person in the audience kept asking questions about the nature of collaboration. "Can't it be a sign of weakness? Don't you have expertise that you are denying if you operate too collaboratively? Clients want answers, not questions, don't they?" Finally, with a lot of frustration, he said, "Well, I don't want my consultants just sitting around holding hands with a client!" He was pointing to an area where there is considerable confusion about the distinction between the expert role and the collaborative role.

The core transaction of any consulting contract is the transfer of expertise from the consultant to the client. This holds whether the expertise is very tangible, such as skill in furnace design or computer programming, or whether the expertise is very intangible, such as problem-solving or team-building skill. Whatever the expertise, it is the basis for the consultant's being in business.

Part of the fear of holding hands seems to be that if you get too intertwined with the client, your expertise will somehow be diluted and blurred. So when I encourage a collaborative approach with the client, it can come across as implying that the consultant and the client have equal expertise and are partners in technical matters. This might force the consultant to unconsciously under-play his or her own expertise in order to maintain a 50/50 relationship. If this were to happen, the fear of diluting expertise would become a reality. One consultant expressed this fear and confusion by saying, "I have forgotten more about managing inventories than most of my clients will ever know. They can hardly spell the word, and I am the corporate guru! How can I be collaborative under those conditions?"

The confusion is between collaborating on the technical aspects of the problem (which I don't mean) and collaborating on how the stages of the consultation will be carried out (which I do mean). Here's an example of where you draw the line between them.

Areas of Collaboration	Areas of Expertise
Expressing the wants of the client	Furnace design
Planning how to inform the organization of the study	Training design
Deciding who is involved in data collection	Questionnaire design
Generating the right kind of data	Computer programming
Interpreting the results of discovery	Systems analysis
Deciding how to make a change	Pricing strategy

Regardless of the area of expertise, the way the consultation process itself is managed (the left side above) will greatly affect the client's utilization of even the most technical expertise. I believe the more the consultative *process* can be collaborative, the better the odds for implementation after the consultant has left.

Staging the Client's Involvement— Step by Step

We have been talking in a somewhat general way about consultant role orientation and ways to make a project more collaborative. The following sequence will make this concept very concrete. The stages leading up to implementation of a change—what are called the preliminary events—can be divided into twelve specific action steps. Each of these steps provides an opportunity for you to involve the client in the process without unnaturally downplaying your specific expertise.

Maximum client involvement and commitment will occur to the extent that you, the consultant, act at each stage in the following ways. These are steps you can take to make the 50/50 responsibility for the project a reality.

Step 1. Defining the Initial Problem

Ask the client to state what the problem is. Add to this statement what you think might be some more underlying causes of the problem.

Example

Engineer Consultant

Consultant: What do you think the problem is?

Client: The process equipment you guys designed is down half the time. I think the design may be faulty. I want you to check the monitoring devices and make sure the gauges are accurate.

Consultant: I will check the gauges and devices. Also, as a potential part of the problem, I think we should consider how well the operators understand the equipment. Plus the kind of supervision the operators receive. Especially on the night shift.

Comment: It is not just up to the client to make the initial problem statement. You should feel free to add your 50 percent, even at this early stage.

In the decision whether to proceed, you also have some choice. If the project is set up in a way that you think it won't succeed, this should be negotiated.

Example

Systems Analyst Consultant

Client: Let's go ahead with the project to have a field sales reporting system to give the figures by the fifth of the month. And let's have the system in thirty days.

Consultant: Having a system where you get your figures by the fifth of the month is a big order. To accomplish this in thirty days is almost impossible. We have a list of projects that have to be reviewed by our committee. If those expectations of yours are firm, we had better reevaluate whether we can give you what you want.

Comment: Clients usually feel that the decision to go ahead is strictly up to them. By questioning the decision, the consultant is acting as a 50/50 partner. The intent is not to say no to clients, but to make the decision to go ahead a joint decision.

**Step 3.
Selecting
Dimensions to Be
Studied**

Given your expertise in the project, you may know best what aspect of the problem should be analyzed. The client, though, has operating experience with the problem and the people, and can be asked what to look for.

Example

Engineer Consultant

Consultant: Starting next Monday I will begin studying the monitoring devices and the gauges and examine the quality of the raw material being used. I will also interview the operators and ask them several questions about certain operating procedures. It would help if you and your plant superintendent would make a list of the areas you would like investigated and also any questions you would like the operators to answer.

Comment: It only takes a simple question to involve the client in deciding what kind of data should be collected. Often the simple question is not asked. If a questionnaire is to be used, you can have the client select some of the questions.

Step 4. Deciding Who Will Be Involved in the Project

The client often expects the consultant to do the whole job. Creating a consultant-client team to do the job is a good way to build client commitment.

Example

Systems Analyst Consultant

Consultant: To make this project successful, I would like two people from your organization to work with me on the project. I will need five days of one of your regional sales manager's time and eight days of one of your home office sales staff. The three of us will be responsible for ending up with a system that will meet your sales reporting requirements. I will be in charge of the project and make the major time commitment, but two people from your group will help the project immensely.

Comment: Doing the job by yourself is always simpler and faster. Having people from the client organization takes more time and agony, yet directly encourages commitment and promotes eventual implementation of the study.

Step 5. Selecting the Method

The client has ideas about how the data should be collected. Ask.

Engineer Consultant

Consultant: I will definitely look over the operating figures, look at the equipment, and talk to the operators. Who else should I talk to? Should we meet with people in a group or individually? What other areas of the plant should we look into, and how should we approach them?

Comment: Again, simple, but important questions to ask the client. You are doing this 30 percent for the new information you might get, 70 percent to model and act out a 50/50 way of approaching this kind of project. By your behavior you are helping the client learn how to solve problems like this for themselves.

Step 6. Data Collection

Have the client do it with you.

Example   **Engineer Consultant**

Consultant: I would like one of your supervisors to work with me as I go through the plant and talk to people. Perhaps the supervisors could interview a sample of the operators to determine what they think could be done to better maintain the equipment.

Comment: There are two main risks in having the client do some of the data collection: (1) People may withhold information because they are talking to people who have some power over them, and (2) some of the data may be distorted because the line organization has a stake in making themselves look competent and guilt free.

These are risks you can be willing to take. You will get your own data, and usually you have enough experience to know rather quickly what is really going on. If need be, you can go back to the people a second time, alone. The advantage of having the line people do some of the data collection is that whatever information is shared up the line, the right people are hearing it—the people who can do something about it. It does no good if the consultant hears the "truth," but the line people don't believe it. Above all, though, the process keeps beating the 50/50 drum.

Steps 7, 8, 9. Funneling the Data, Data Summary, Data Analysis

Funneling a huge amount of data into a manageable amount of information and then summarizing and organizing it takes a lot of time. You also get a real feel for what you have by suffering this through. Urge the client to be with you at certain points in this procedure. Analyzing what the data means is more fun—involve the client in this too.

Example

Systems Analyst Consultant

Consultant: Spend three days with me organizing the data and figuring what its implications are for the reporting system we are developing.

Comment: Again the simple, assertive request, giving up some of the efficient use of your own time in trade for a client who has more invested in the outcome. On a highly technical project, the client may just not have the background to meaningfully contribute to this stage of the project. In that case, you have no choice but to do it alone. Be careful though; the client's lack of background is our favorite excuse for excluding them at various stages.

Step 10.
Feedback of
Results

More of the same. Have the client share in presenting the data analysis in the feedback meeting.

Example

Engineer Consultant

Consultant: For this meeting, I am going to report what we learned about the monitoring devices and the accuracy of the gauges. George, the plant supervisor, will report what we learned about operator skills and attitudes toward maintenance.

Comment: When line managers have the experience of reporting negative findings, their defensiveness goes down and the feedback step is less likely to become an adversary conversation.

Step 11.
Making
Recommendations

More than any other stage, developing workable recommendations requires the integration of your technical knowledge and the client's practical and organizational knowledge. Ask the client what he or she would do about the situation, having now heard the results of the inquiry.

Example

Systems Analyst Consultant

Consultant: We know that the sales reps' dislike of paperwork is a major obstacle to getting timely field sales figures. What can we recommend that would reduce our dependency on them to get us the information?

Comment: The action is simple once your strategy becomes clear. Even if clients cannot be very creative about what to recommend, it is important that they struggle with the question.

Step 12. **Decision on** **Actions**	Once the study is done and the recommendations made, the client may want to totally take over the process and dismiss the consultant from the decision-making meeting. I always resist this.

Example

Systems Analyst Consultant

Client: Thank you very much for the reporting process you have developed and the program to support it. We will think about it and let you know when we think the organization will be ready for this.

Consultant: I would like to be a part of the meeting when you discuss this. I care a lot about the project and know I could contribute to the question of timing and implementation. I realize your usual procedure is to discuss this without the consultant present, but in this case, I wonder if you could make an exception.

Comment: The danger here is that the client will take 100 percent of the action and leave you out in the cold. So you have to ask to be included. In addition to your own needs for inclusion, you are also saying to the client, by your actions, that when someone in their organization has made an important contribution to a project, the person should be included in the decision-making meeting. If they still choose to exclude you, there may be little you can do other than sulk and look hurt.

Each step leading up to the implementation of a solution can be viewed as a series of opportunities to engage the client, reduce resistance, and increase the probabilities of success. Taking advantage of these opportunities entails giving up some consultant prerogatives and freedom of action in the service of the longer range goal of having a real impact.

Checklist #1. Assessing the Balance of Responsibility

On the scales below, rate who is taking responsibility in an important project you are now engaged in. Put a mark where it currently balances out. (The points listed in the left-hand column are described at the beginning of Chapter 11.)

	Client Has Major Responsibility, I Have Little	I Have Major Responsibility, Client Has Little
		50/50	

1. Defining the Initial Problem ├─────────────┼─────────────┤

2. Deciding to Proceed with the Project ├─────────────┼─────────────┤

3. Selecting Dimensions to Be Studied ├─────────────┼─────────────┤

4. Who Is Involved in the Study ├─────────────┼─────────────┤

5. Selecting the Method ├─────────────┼─────────────┤

6. Data Collection ├─────────────┼─────────────┤

7. Funneling the Data ├─────────────┼─────────────┤

8. Data Summary ├─────────────┼─────────────┤

9. Data Analysis ├─────────────┼─────────────┤

10. Feedback of Results ├─────────────┼─────────────┤

11. Recommendations ├─────────────┼─────────────┤

12. Decision on Actions ├─────────────┼─────────────┤

13. Planning How to Involve Others in Implementation ├─────────────┼─────────────┤

14. Convening the Implementation Meetings ├─────────────┼─────────────┤

Connect the marks you made. Any place the line deviates from the center shows an opportunity for you to restructure this project, or your next one, to take full advantage of using client involvement to increase your chances of success—especially the chances that your project will still be active and used after you have left the scene.

Chapter 3
Flawless Consulting

CONSULTING HAS A WAY of seeming vague and overly complicated. It doesn't have to be. It is possible to consult without error and to do so quite simply. The way to keep it simple is to focus on only two dimensions of consulting. Ask yourself two questions whenever you are with a client.

1. Am I being authentic with this person now?

2. Am I completing the business of the consulting phase I am in?

Being Authentic

Authentic behavior with a client means you put into words what you are experiencing with the client as you work. *This is the most powerful thing you can do to have the leverage you are looking for and to build client commitment.*

There is a tendency for us to look for ways of being clever with a client. We agonize over ways of presenting our ideas, of phrasing the project so that it will appeal. Many times I have been with a client and found myself straining to figure out what will convince them that I am everything they are looking for. Projections of bottom line savings are made, solutions for sticky employee problems are suggested, confirmations that the client has been doing everything humanly possible are suggested with a nod and a smile.

It is a mistake to assume that clients make decisions to begin projects and use consultants based on purely rational reasons. More often than not, the client's primary question is: "Is this consultant someone I can trust? Is this someone I can trust not to hurt me, not to con me—someone who can both help solve the organizational or technical problems I have and, at the same time, be considerate of my position and person?" When I operate in too clever or manipulative a way, or lay it on too thick, clients pick this up. They are saying to themselves, "Wow! This guy is really laying it on thick. He is making me look like a fool if I say no." Line managers know when we are trying to maneuver them and, when it happens, they trust us a little less.

Lower trust leads to lower leverage and lower client commitment. Authentic behavior leads to higher trust, higher leverage, and higher client commitment. Authentic behavior also has the advantage of being incredibly simple. It is to literally put into words what you are experiencing.

Here are some examples.

> *Client says:* Well, this audit shouldn't take you too long. Couple of days and you will be done. I wish I had some time to spend with you, but there are some really important things I must attend to. My secretary can give you some assistance. Also, don't take too much time from any of my people. They are under a lot of pressure.

> *Consultant experiences:* Feeling unimportant, small. My work is being treated as a trivial matter. This is how I make my living, but to this character, I am an interruption.

> *Non-authentic consultant response:* This audit could have far-reaching implications. The home office is looking closely at these audits to assess our top divisions. They are also required by the company.

> *Authentic consultant response:* You are treating this audit as though it is unimportant and small. Like a trivial matter. If it is

an interruption, maybe we should reassess the timing. I would like you to treat it with more importance.

◆

Client says: I want your opinion whether my people are making mistakes and what they should do to correct them. If you decide they are incompetent to operate this piece of equipment, I want you to report directly to me at once. With names and specifics.

Consultant experiences: Feeling like a judge, like I have to police the client's employees.

Non-authentic consultant response: My report will describe how the equipment is being utilized and why there have been so many breakdowns. It will be up to you to take corrective actions.

Authentic consultant response: I feel I am being seen as a judge or police officer on this project. This is not the role I feel is most effective. I would like you to view me more as a mirror of what is happening now. You and your people can then evaluate what needs to be done and whether training is required. I am not a conscience.

◆

Client says: To really understand this problem, you have to go back thirty-five years when this operation was set up. It all started in November of 1946 on a Thursday afternoon. There were three people in this operation. At the time, their only function was to fill orders and answer the phone. George was the nephew of the sales manager and only had a high school education. Our customers were mostly on the East Coast and on and on and on and on . . .

Consultant experiences: Impatience, boredom. Spending too much time on history. Losing energy.

Non-authentic consultant response: Silence. Encourage client to go on, assuming client will get to the point or that it is therapeutically essential for the client to go through all this detail.

Authentic consultant response: You are giving me a lot of detail. I am having trouble staying with your narrative. I am eager to get to the key current issues. What is the key problem *now*?

◆

Client says: If you will just complete your report of findings, my management group and I will meet later to decide what to do and evaluate the results.

Consultant experiences: Exclusion from the real action. Postponement of dealing with the problems.

Non-authentic consultant response: There might be some information that I have not included in the report that would be relevant to your decision-making process. Or acquiescence.

Authentic consultant response: You are excluding me from the decision on what to do. I would like to be included in that meeting, even if including me means some inconvenience for you and your team.

◆

In these examples, each initial client statement acts to keep the consultant distant in some way. Each is a subtle form of resistance to the consultant's help and serves to reduce its impact. The non-authentic consultant responses deal indirectly and impersonally with the resistance. They make it easier for the client to stay distant and treat the consultant's concerns in a procedural way. The authentic responses focus on the relationship between the consultant and the client and force the client to give importance to the consultant's role and wants for the project. Simple direct statements by the consultant about the consultant-client interaction put more balance in the relationship; they work against either total client control or total consultant control. Imbalanced control in either direction acts to reduce internal commitment to the project and reduce the chance of successful implementation.

Authentic behavior by the consultant is an essential first part to operating flawlessly. Much of the rest of this book gives detailed and specific expression to what authentic behavior looks like in the context of doing consulting.

Completing the Requirements of Each Phase

In addition to being authentic, flawless consulting demands a knowledge of the task requirements of each phase of the project. These requirements are the "business" of each phase and must be completed before moving on.

Here is a very brief description of the requirements of each phase. They will be discussed in more detail in the chapters that follow.

Contracting

1. *Negotiating Wants.* Setting up a project requires the client and the consultant to exchange what they want from each other and what they have to offer each other. Too often, consultants understate their wants and clients understate their offers.

2. *Coping with Mixed Motivation.* When clients ask for help, they always do so with some ambivalence. They want you to get involved and be helpful, but at the same time wish they had never met you. One hand beckons you, the other says stop. A requirement of contracting is to get this mixed motivation expressed early in the project so it won't haunt you later.

3. *Surfacing Concerns About Exposure and Loss of Control.* Most of the real concerns clients have about pursuing a consulting project with you are expressed quite indirectly. They ask about credentials, experience, results elsewhere, cost, timing, and more. Often what they are really concerned about is: (1) Are they going to be made to look or feel foolish or incompetent? and (2) Will they lose control of either themselves, their organization, or you the consultant?

These concerns have to be addressed directly as part of the contracting phase.

4. *Triangular and Rectangular Contracting.* You have to know how many clients you have. Your client has a boss and you may have a boss. Your client's boss and your boss may have had a heavy hand in setting up this project. If so, they need to be part of the contract. At least, their roles need to be acknowledged between you and your client. If it is you, the client, and the client's boss, you have a triangular contract. Throw in your own boss and the triangle becomes a rectangle. Clarifying who is involved and getting them into the contract is a requirement of the contracting phase.

Discovery and Data Collection

1. *Layers of Analysis.* The initial problem statement in a consulting project is usually a symptom of other underlying problems. The task for the consultant is to articulate the different layers of the problem in a coherent and simple way.

2. *Political Climate.* Whether your client is a family or an organization, politics is affecting people's behavior and their ability to solve problems. Your task as consultant is to understand enough about the politics of the situation to see how it will affect your project and the implementation of your recommendations. Too often we collude with the client in pretending that organizations are not political but solely rational.

3. *Resistance to Sharing Information.* The client always has some reluctance to give us the whole story or all the data we need to understand what's happening. This resistance, which often comes out indirectly with passive or questioning behavior during the data collection, has to be identified and expressed.

4. *Interview as a Joint Learning Event.* Once we begin to collect data, we have begun to change that organization. We are

never simply neutral, objective observers. Beginning the process of our analysis portends the implementation process, and we need to see it that way. When sticky issues come up during the data collection phase, we need to pursue them and not worry about contaminating the data or biasing the study. Too often we see our role in the data collection phase as a passive one.

Feedback and the Decision to Act

1. *Funneling Data.* The purpose of data collection is to solve a problem, to get some action. It is not to do research for its own sake. This means the data needs to be reduced to a manageable number of items. Each of the final items selected for feedback to the client should be *actionable*—that is, they should be under the control of the client.

2. *Presenting Personal and Organizational Data.* As we collect data on equipment, or compensation, or information flow, we also pick up data on our client's management style. We learn about the politics of the situation, about people's attitudes about working in this place. One requirement of the feedback phase is to include this kind of information in our report. Personal and organizational data are not included to hurt anyone or to be gossipy, but as information on the context in which our recommendations might be implemented. It is also a unique kind of information that the client often cannot obtain from anyone else.

3. *Managing the Feedback Meeting.* The feedback meeting is the moment of truth. It is the moment of highest anxiety for both client and consultant. Anxiety for the consultant because of what is to be said, anxiety for the client because of what is to be heard. The consultant needs to keep control of this meeting so that the business of the meeting is covered. Presenting data to the client is only a part of the agenda: The main goal is to work on the decision about what to do. The more the feedback meeting can address what to do, the better the

chance of implementation. The feedback meeting may be your last chance to influence the decision about implementation—so take advantage of the opportunity.

4. *Focusing on the Here and Now.*   Another requirement of the feedback phase is identifying how the client is managing the feedback itself. Usually, the feedback process becomes victim to the same management problems that created the need for your services in the first place. If the organization is suffering from a lack of structure or direction, this will also affect how they handle your report. You need to be conscious of this and call it to your client's attention. If you are not meticulously aware of how your own project is being handled, you will simply become the latest casualty.

5. *Don't Take It Personally.* This is the toughest. The reaction of the client to your work is more a response to the process of dependency and receiving help than it is resistance to your own personal style. You do have your own peculiarities; so do I. If, however, you start agonizing about them, even to yourself, during the feedback process, you're in big trouble. The resistance you encounter during the process is resistance to the prospect of having to act on difficult organizational issues. Don't be seduced into taking it personally.

Engagement and Implementation

1. *Bet on Engagement Over Mandate and Persuasion.*   Even though a decision has been made, the real work lies ahead. How we involve people will determine their commitment at each stage. The instinct is to focus too much on the decision and not value the importance of how people are brought together to make it work.

2. *Design More Participation than Presentation.*   Each meeting has to be an example of the new way of working and demonstrate that employee attitude will dictate success. This demands high interaction and forms of proceeding. People will not invest in what they have been sold, even

though it seems as though they just want you to be clear about what is expected from them.

3. *Encourage Difficult Public Exchanges.* Trust is built by dealing with the difficult issues early and publicly. Create room for doubt and cynicism right in the beginning. Reservations that are postponed will come back to haunt you. The way we handle the difficult conversations will determine the credibility of the project and their view of whether the consultant is an agent of the top or in service of all parties.

4. *Put Real Choice on the Table.* Bring people into the decision about change as early as possible. Commitment comes from having choice. Resist the temptation to package the whole solution early in the name of speed. Commitment may be more important than perfection. There are always several right answers to every question.

5. *Change the Conversation to Change the Culture.* Encourage dialogue that is void of blame, history, attention to who is not in the room, and too quick to action. Structure the conversation toward personal responsibility, questions of purpose and meaning, and what will be unique and new about this round of changes.

6. *Pay Attention to Place.* The structure of the way we come together has more impact on the attitude and commitment of our clients than we realize. The room itself, how we are seated, and the way we run the meeting carry strong messages about our intentions and who is important to success. Most of the places we meet reinforce high control, mandated strategies. When we have choice about the structure of the room, take advantage of it.

It's entirely possible to move through the phases and skip some of these task requirements. In contracting, for example, most of us are pretty good at assessing client wants. But if we fail to identify consultant wants or client offers as clearly as we assess client wants, we are in trouble. Wants skipped in the beginning are much harder to recover in later phases. An example is the consultant's desire to have the client manager support the project and tell his or her people about it. If this were not negotiated in the contracting phase, you would feel undercut later when you went to collect data from people who don't really know why you were talking to them.

Another key task of contracting is to discuss the client's motivation to proceed with the project. Sometimes your desire to begin the project may lead you to minimize this discussion. You may never ask the client point blank whether they want to go ahead with the project and how much enthusiasm they have for it. If you find out later in the feedback meeting that the motivation is low, it may be too late to do anything about it.

Also, because of our desire to get a project going, most of us have a tendency to overlook and downplay the early resistance and skepticism we encounter. We delude ourselves into thinking that once clients get into the project, they will get hooked by it and learn to trust us. This can lead to our bending over more than we wish in the beginning, hoping that we will be able to stand up straight later on. This usually doesn't work. When we bend over in the beginning, we are seen by the client as someone who works in a bent-over position. When we avoid issues in the beginning, we are seen by the client as someone who avoids issues. It is difficult to change these images and expectations of us—particularly if the client wishes us to bend over and avoid.

By not confronting the tasks of each phase, we are left with accumulating unfinished business that comes back to haunt us. Unfinished business always comes out somewhere, and usually indirectly. The client who felt we were coercing in the beginning of the project, but never expressed it directly, is the client who endlessly questions our data in the feedback meeting. The endless questions are fueled by the early feeling of coercion, not by our faulty data. It will be much harder in the feedback meeting to rework those feelings of coercion than it would have been to discuss them in the contracting meeting when the project got started.

Finishing the business of each phase. Being authentic in stating what you are experiencing to the client. All you need to consult flawlessly.

But what about getting results and what about accountability?

Results

By definition, being a consultant—and not a manager—means you have direct control and responsibility only for your own time and your own staff resources. The line manager is paid to take responsibility for what the line organization implements or doesn't implement. If the client manager takes your report and chooses to do nothing about it, that is the manager's right. In the final analysis, you are not responsible for the use of your expertise and recommendations. If consultants really believe that they should be responsible for implementing their recommendations, they should immediately get jobs as line managers and stop calling themselves consultants.

This desire to take responsibility for activities that rightly belong to our clients can become, in itself, a major obstacle to our consulting effectiveness. When we take over and act as if it is *our* organization (a wish we all have at times), the line manager is let off the hook. The organization may get the immediate problem solved, but will have learned little about how to do it for themselves. When something goes wrong with our system, as it must, we are either called back in again and again or the line organization will claim that our system was faulty to begin with. Both client overdependence and client disdain are bad for the consultant. It is essential to be clear on what you, the consultant, are responsible for and what the line manager is responsible for.

Accountability

Just because we are not responsible for what the client does with our efforts does not mean we don't care what happens in the end. In fact, it is deeply important to me what impact my consulting efforts have. I want my efforts to be used. Every time. If an engineer consultant is called in to fix a furnace in a plant, the engineer will make recommendations so the furnace will be fixed and operated to run perfectly forever. The problem is that the consultant doesn't control *how* that furnace is operated.

This is the deepest frustration of doing consulting. You know your recommendations are sound and should be followed, but you are not responsible for how the furnace is operated and need to accept that fact. All you can do is to work with clients in a way that increases the probabilities that they will follow the advice and make the effort to learn how to operate the furnace.

The key to increasing the chances of success is to keep focusing on how you work with clients. All we can really control is our own way of working, our own behavior, our own strategies of involving clients and reducing their reluctance to operate the furnace differently. This is what we should be held accountable for: How we work with clients. Not what clients do in managing or mismanaging their own operations.

The downside of our need to be useful is the desire to prove that our work led to good results. Needing to claim credit for the risks and efforts made by clients is a measure of our own inflation and the anxiety that underpins it. Our clients will know, even if they cannot name it easily, what contribution we made to their effort. Our need for concrete demonstration of our results is either to reassure our doubts or to serve our needs to market our services.

A big part of how I work with clients is whether my specific expertise is well-founded and whether my recommendations are sound. But both clients and I are assuming from the beginning that I know my stuff when it comes to technical skills. That leaves my consulting skills—how I contract, conduct discovery, collect data, feed it back, deal with resistance, engage in implementation—as the major factors contributing to my effectiveness. They are what affect consulting results.

If I—

know my area of expertise (a given),

behave authentically with the client,

tend to and complete the business of each consulting phase, and

act to build capacity for the client to solve the next problem on their own—

I can legitimately say I have consulted flawlessly. Even if no action results from my efforts. Even if the project aborts in the early, contracting phase. Even if my services are terminated the day I make my recommendations. Even if all these things happen, it is possible to call it a very competent job of consultation. If these things happen, it is not a happy consultation, for we all wish for the world to transform at our touch. But it is the best we can do.

This way of viewing consulting accountability restrains us from taking over for our clients and from uselessly pressuring them to do something they won't or can't do. I believe taking over client organizations, pressuring to be heeded, complaining about the way a manager manages—all reduce my effectiveness. Focusing on my own actions, expressing my awareness of what I am experiencing with the client and how *we* are working—all increase my effectiveness.

Our own actions, our own awareness—this is what we should be held accountable for. Fire me for not contracting well. For not confronting the client's low motivation until the feedback meeting. Fire me for packaging the recommendations so completely and perfectly that the client was afraid to touch them. But reward me for contracting solidly with three managers who terminated projects when a new vice president was announced. Reward me for not beginning a project when a plant manager said it was necessary, but all signs were to the contrary.

Completing the business of each phase. Behaving authentically with the client. That's what flawless consultation, consultation without failure, requires. In thirty years of consulting, all my failures (which I remember with distressing clarity) occurred either because I was so carried away by how *I* was going to solve the client's problem that I didn't pay attention to client motivation or because I wanted that client so badly that I didn't care what the contract looked like. In each case, I ignored some step in the consulting process, did not attend to the business of a particular phase, or chose not to deal authentically with my concerns about the client. Had I focused more on exactly how I was working with each client, these failures could have been avoided.

Failures can be avoided, but this doesn't mean a consultant can expect to see meaningful improvement as a result of every single project. Internal consultants often ask, "You mean if I behave authentically and take care of the business of each phase, I will win the support of a plant manager who up to now won't talk to me?" When they ask that question, they are expressing their skepticism. It is a rightful skepticism. No action by a consultant will guarantee results with a client. There are several reasons for this.

Each of us learns and uses information in different ways. It is often difficult for managers to accept help and be publicly open to suggestions. Privately they may be strongly affected by our work, and we may never know it. Pressuring clients to feel we have immediately helped them can be a tremendous obstacle to the learning we are trying to promote. If we can stay focused simply on the way we are working with clients, we will avoid compulsively pressuring the client, and the results will take care of themselves.

A second reason consultants can't judge their work just by managers' reactions is that, like it or not, client managers have a right to fail. Managers have a right to avoid dealing with operator problems on the furnace, to keep loose controls on petty cash, to have inconsistent pay policies for the field sales force. Managers also have a right to suffer, and as consultants we are usually too much on the periphery of their lives to really change this.

A manager's right to fail is especially hard for internal consultants to accept. If we are in an organization we care about, and we see a division going down the drain, we feel obligated to the organization and ourselves to try and turn that situation around. The wish is a fine one, for it gives meaning to our work. The mistake consultants can make is to take on the rehabilitation of that division as a personal objective. The manager of that division is responsible for its rehabilitation, not the consultant. Taking over the manager's rights, including the right to fail, leads to consulting errors. It can also lead to frustration and despair, for you may be taking on a task that you are just not positioned to accomplish. Your own responsibility as a consultant is to present information as simply and directly and assertively as possible. And to complete the tasks of each phase of the consultation. That's all there is to do. And it's within each of us to do that perfectly.

Chapter 4
Contracting Overview

AT THE BEGINNING of every workshop I conduct on consulting skills, I ask people what they want to learn about consulting. The first wave of answers is very reasonable and task oriented.

How do you set up a project?

How do you measure consulting effectiveness?

Can you act as an umpire and helper at the same time?

What do you do to elicit client expectations?

How do you get in the door when you are not welcome?

How do you establish trust?

What are consulting skills anyhow?

When do we break for lunch?

. . . and on and on.

As we get into the workshop, it is easy to see the real desires that underlie these wishes. What do consultants want to learn about consulting? We want to learn how to have *power over our clients*! How do we influence them, get them to do what we want, manage in our own image? And while we are doing all of this to them, how do we keep their respect and appreciation?

The phrase "power over our clients" is a distortion of the more promising expectation to have power *with* our clients. If we want to control our clients, it puts us on a pedestal and them on the ground floor. This is a very unstable arrangement because clients soon realize we want to control them and are able to topple us with ease. Why shouldn't they be able to topple us: Managers get rewarded for keeping control and have to have political smarts or they wouldn't be managers. So the desire to have power *over* the client is a no-win position for the consultant. The realistic alternative is to have power *with* the client. To have direct and constructive impact while standing on the same level.

The point of maximum leverage for the consultant is probably during the contracting phase of the project. There are possibilities for impact that may be lost for the life of the project if they are not pursued in contracting. The contract sets the tone for the project, and it is much easier to negotiate a new, initial contract than to renegotiate an old one. Anyone who has been married more than a year understands this.

Contracting— The Concept and the Skill

The kind of contract here is really a social contract. A contract is simply an explicit agreement of what the consultant and client expect from each other and how they are going to work together. It is usually verbal, sometimes in writing. Contracts with external consultants are more often in writing because external consultants are trusted less than internal consultants, especially when it comes to money. Some internal consultants always like to have a written document describing the project they are working on. This is probably a good idea, even if it is in the form of a letter. But essentially a contract between an internal or external consultant and a line manager is a social contract. It is designed not so much for enforcement, but for clear communication about what is going to happen on a project.

The Word— **Contract**	"We are not lawyers," people say. "A contract is a legal document that is written in formal language, it is binding and in writing, and it is stiff and formal. Why not call it a working agreement?" The word *contract* is useful in two ways. Because we are not accustomed to thinking of social or work relationships in contractual terms, the word calls attention to the need for specific expectations in the consulting relationship. Also, some of the legal connotations of the word *contract* are applicable to consulting relationships.

Legal contracts contain two basic elements that apply to consulting relationships—mutual consent and valid consideration.

Mutual Consent	Both sides enter the agreement freely and by their own choosing. The concept of mutual consent directly addresses the issue of how motivated the staff person and the line manager are to engage in a project together. There are many forces in organizations that tend to coerce people into working together. For example, the fact that everybody is doing it is often a pressure on managers. They don't really want to do a survey of their employees, but that is the thing to do, and so it leads them into a conversation with a staff consultant about doing a survey. Internalized "shoulds" or the fad of the day can become powerful coercive forces. The staff person also operates under many "shoulds." "A staff person should never say no to a line manager" is a belief that can lead to beginning a project that a staff person does not believe in.

The coercion can also be very direct.

When some variation of this dialogue occurs, the client and the consultant have an agreement about work to be done, but they are not working with a solid or valid contract. The consultant is operating under coercion and has not freely entered the agreement. It is often not possible to negotiate a valid contract. That's OK. The key is that when a manager is eventually dissatisfied with the results of the new appraisal form, the problem should be defined as the imbalance of the original contract, not the elegance of the form.

Key Concept: Valid consideration must be given *both* parties for a solid contract to exist.

Valid Consideration

For our purposes, *consideration* is the exchange of something of value between the consultant and the client. Internal consultants are especially accustomed to focusing on the consideration given to the client. The initial impetus behind a discussion between a line and staff person is to discuss services to be provided to the line person. This service—or consideration—takes the form of advice, analysis, or just reflection. For a valid contract to exist, however, the staff person needs to receive something of value in return. It is this side of the equation that is often undervalued, ignored, or assumed without discussion.

Staff people will often say that all they really need is appreciation—some knowledge that they have made a contribution. On an emotional level that may be true, but there are some more tangible items that consultants need that should be a part of the original contract.

- *Operational partnership in the venture.* This means having influence on what happens, finding out about significant events, maintaining respect for the unique contribution you bring.

- *Access to people and information in the line organization.* Freedom of movement to pursue issues and data that seems relevant to you.

- *Time of people in the line organization.* The major cost to most improvement projects, even where heavy equipment is involved, is the time of people in the line organization to plan and incorporate changes into their operation. Many times the consultant is given an assignment with the proviso not to take up too much of the time of the line people because "they" don't want to interrupt production. This is a warning signal that the contract is inequitable and needs to be renegotiated.

- *Opportunity to be innovative.* Consultants generally want to try something different. You have a right to ask for this opportunity directly and not have to bootleg it.

In the next chapter we will get into consultant needs and wants much more fully. What's important to remember here is that you only undermine your leverage if you underplay your own needs and wants at the beginning. The contract needs balanced consideration to be strong.

Contracting Skills

To contract flawlessly is to

1. Behave authentically, and

2. Complete the business of the contracting phase.

The business of the contracting phase is to negotiate wants, cope with mixed motivation, surface concerns about exposure and loss of control, and clarify all parties to the contract. Before getting into the actual steps in a contracting meeting, here is a list of the consulting competencies required to complete the business of contracting.

You should be able to:

- Ask direct questions about who the client is and who the less visible parties to the contract are.

- Elicit the client's expectations of you.

- Clearly and simply state what you want from the client.

- Say no or postpone a project that in your judgment has less than a 50/50 chance of success.

- Probe directly for the client's underlying concerns about losing control.

- Probe directly for the client's underlying concerns about exposure and vulnerability.

- Give direct verbal support to the client.

- When the contracting meeting is not going well, discuss directly with the client why this contracting meeting is not going well.

More detailed competencies will surface as we work through a contracting meeting in the next chapter. The list above contains the very crucial ones, the ones that many of us have a hard time doing. The hard time we have is not really with the action itself, but with valuing the importance of these actions. Having direct discussions with the client—about control, vulnerability, your wants, the chance of success, and how the discussion is going—make the difference between an average contracting meeting and an excellent one. The problem is that it is possible to have a contracting meeting in which none of these subjects are discussed directly. When this happens, the consultant and client are actually colluding with each other in not bringing up certain touchy subjects. The rationalization we use is, "Well, I'll deal with these areas if it becomes necessary." *It is always necessary to talk about control, vulnerability, your wants, and chances of success.* If you are thinking as you read this that *you* always confront these areas with your clients, then you should feel good—you may be operating more flawlessly than you think.

Elements of a Contract

Up to this point we have focused on the process of developing a contract. This section offers some suggestions about what the content of the contract should include. But first, a word about form.

People always ask whether the contract should be in writing. If you have the energy and the time, the answer is yes. The reason for putting it in writing is for clarity, not enforcement. If it is in writing and the client changes his or her mind about the services wanted from you, you are going to have to renegotiate a new contract or stop the project. Having the original agreement in writing isn't going to change that. If you are investing out-of-pocket dollars or billable time in the project, then a written contract will help your claim to be paid for the money and time invested, should the project be terminated. For most internal consultants, the real value of a written contract is to clarify the understanding with the line manager before the project begins. It is a good test of whether you have a solid contract. Writing down the agreement forces you to be more explicit about what you are going to do.

The form of the written document should be brief, direct, and almost conversational. The purpose is to communicate, not to protect yourself in court.

The following elements should be covered in most of your contracts, especially when the contract signals the beginning of a significant project.

1. The Boundaries of Your Analysis

Begin with a statement of what problem you are going to focus on. If it was discussed in the contracting meeting, you can include a statement of what you are not going to become involved in.

Examples:

"The study will deal with the Brogan Reactor Furnace and its peripheral supporting network. We will not get into the problems existing in Power Plant B."

"We will assess the effectiveness of the current Marketing organization structure and its interface with the Sales department."

2. Objectives of the Project

This identifies the organizational improvements you expect if your consultation is successful. This is your best guess on the benefits the client can expect. Sometimes this statement is to help the client be realistic about the limitations of the project. You are not a magician and need to keep reminding the client of this.

There are three general areas where you can expect to help the client. You should be clear in the beginning which of these are part of your contract.

To Solve a Particular Technical/Business Problem The client is willing to talk to you because there is some pain somewhere in the client's organization. The immediate goal is to reduce the pain, whether the pain is from currently unsatisfactory results or from the fact that opportunities to improve a situation are not being exploited.

To Teach the Client How to Solve the Problem for Themselves Next Time It is possible for you to develop a solution and merely hand it to the client. If there is the expectation that the client can do it alone when the problem occurs again, be clear about it. This will require a lot more involvement from the client during the life of the project if the problem-solving process you are using is going to be transferred to the client.

To Improve How the Organization Manages Its Resources, Uses Its Systems, and Works Internally Every business or technical problem has a component where the problem being managed is part of the problem. This is sometimes called the "politics" of the situation. Many internal consultants are reluctant to get into this area. The more you can include this as an objective of the project, the more long-range help you are likely to be. (There is more on this in the chapters on data collection and discovery.)

Examples:
Business Objectives

"The objective of the study is to increase operating efficiencies of the furnace by 4 percent."

"Our goal is to increase the responsiveness of the Marketing department to shifting consumer demand. We particularly expect to develop ways to reduce the time it takes to introduce a new product by six weeks."

Learning Objectives

"A second objective is to teach the plant engineering group how to perform this kind of reactor analysis."

"The Marketing staff should become more effective in assessing its own market responsiveness and restructuring itself in the future."

Organizational Development Objectives

"This project will help the plant manager develop ways to better manage the interface between plant engineering and plant operations."

"A goal of the project is to increase cooperation between the market research group and the product directors."

3.
The Kind
of Information
You Seek

Access to people and information are the key wants of the consultant. The major ambivalence of the line organization is how far to let you into the bowels of their organization. They want to tell you what is really going on and at the same time are afraid of telling you what is really going on. Come close, but not too close. Despite what the line manager says to you, there is always some desire for confirmation that the organization is doing the best that can be done under the circumstances. This desire at times can be stronger than the desire to solve the problem. One way to hedge against this ambivalence is to be very explicit at the beginning about what kind of information you need.

Some of the kinds of information you may want to specify in the contract are technical data, figures, and work flow; attitudes of people toward the problem; and roles and responsibilities.

Examples: Technical Data, Figures, Work Flow

"To complete the project, we will require daily output figures for the equipment and the operating temperatures and pressures for the furnace."

"Your part in the project will require providing a list of procedures for reconciling daily ledgers and the turnover figures for the group."

"We will want to see the planned and actual schedules for the last six product-improvement introductions after we get into the project."

Attitudes of People

"We want to interview at least fifteen people to identify how they currently view the marketing function."

"We want to talk with the operators of the furnace to identify the kind of training they feel they need and to uncover their perceptions of the way the supervisory group rewards good and poor performance. We also plan to ask the same questions of the supervisors."

Roles and Responsibilities

"The marketing organization will provide a definition of who is responsible for major decisions on new products at each stage of the process."

"We will obtain information from all supervisors on their view of their jobs and the authority they have to manage their sections of the operation."

**4.
Your Role
in the Project**

This is the place to state *how you want to work* with the client. If you want a collaborative relationship, this is the place to state it. Make it a statement of intent and spirit. It doesn't pay to spell out all the ways you are going to work together. It is hard to predict at the beginning what is going to come up. You can make some statements about the desire for a 50/50 sharing of responsibility for identifying problems, interpreting the findings, and developing recommendations and action plans.

Example:

"Our primary role is to give you a clear and understandable picture of how your plant is currently operating and maintaining the reactor furnace. While we have expertise on the design of the equipment, your group has a great deal of knowledge of day-to-day operations. We would expect to present our analysis of the efficiency problems and then jointly develop recommendations with you on what changes should be made. A major part of our role is to help you solve this problem for yourself next time. This requires that the plant supervisors have some involvement at each step of the study. We are committed to both develop specific solutions to the present concerns and to play an important educational role with you and your supervisors."

**5.
The Product
You Will Deliver**

Here it is important to be very specific about what you are offering. Will your feedback be an oral or written report? How long will it be and how much detail will the client receive? Is the report likely to be five pages or fifty pages? How far into specific recommendations will you get? Will you give some general suggestions about how to improve things or will you give a list of steps that can be implemented right away? Will you present actual solutions or steps that can be taken that will eventually lead to solutions?

Of course you can't predict all of these in the beginning, but you do know from your own experience how specific you will be. This dimension of a consulting relationship—specificity and nature of recommendations—is a major cause of client disappointment in the consulting services they have received. This doesn't mean that recommendations should always be specific or should always be general; that depends on the task the consultant is engaged in. It does mean there ought to be a clear understanding with the client on what your product will look like.

Example: A Promise for Specific Recommendations

"The outcome of this project will be a detailed written description of our findings running somewhere between fifteen and forty pages. For each major finding, we will offer specific recommendations that you can act on."

Example: A Promise for General Recommendations

"The outcome of these interviews will be roughly a one-page outline of our major conclusions. These will only identify the critical areas to be considered. Actual recommendations will be developed jointly with you after the outline of issues has been discussed. These recommendations will be developed in the half-day feedback meeting we have scheduled at the end of the project."

In promising results to the client, remember that you will be turning the action over to the client at some point. It is the client who is going to actually deliver continuing results, not you. You *can* guarantee a solution to a problem, but you *can't* guarantee that the solution will be followed. To take the solution totally on your shoulders may feel comfortable to you, but it can deprive clients of responsibility for the solution that is rightfully theirs.

6.
What Support and Involvement You Need from the Client

This section is the heart of the contract for the consultant. This is where you specify what you want from the client to make this project successful. This list is what the client is offering to you. Include here particularly those wants that were the subject of some discussion in the verbal contracting meeting. Writing down your wants ensures clear communication, and if there was a sensitive point discussed, to make sure it was resolved.

Example:

"You (line manager) have agreed to communicate the existence and need for this project to your organization. We have also agreed to meet with the division vice president to get his view on the problem and to include him in the second feedback meeting. [An example of what might have been a sensitive topic of discussion.] In addition, two people from your staff will be made available to us for a maximum of seven days each to help with the data analysis and summary."

7.
Time Schedule

Include starting time, any intermediate mileposts, and completion date. If you want to give interim reports to the client before you tie the ribbon on the package, schedule them at the beginning. It is always easier to cancel a meeting than to set one up at the last minute.

Example:

"We can begin this work in six weeks and plan to complete it ten weeks from when we start."

8.
Confidentiality

Since you are almost always dealing with a political situation as well as a technical one, who gets what report is a constant concern. I tend to be quite conservative on this and prefer to give the client control on the people they want to share the findings with. This is a luxury of being an outside consultant. As an inside consultant, you may not have any choice but to send a technical study or an audit report up the line. All you can do is to acknowledge to the client who you are required to give copies of your report to. This gives clients a choice about how to protect themselves, if necessary.

Example: Easy Case

"The results of this study will be given to the director of engineering (the client). Any further reporting will be up to the director. Should the internal consultants be required to report any results to the larger organization, the director will be informed and invited to attend any meetings held on the subject."

Example: Hard Case

"The results of the audit will be reported to the Management Audit Committee. Before the report is released, the division controller (the client) will be able to review and comment on the audit findings and recommendations. The intent (and the common practice) is that the audit report goes to the committee with the support of both the division controller and the audit team. The final report also includes the list of corrective actions that the division plans to take."

9. Feedback to You Later

An optional element to the contract is to ask the client to let you know the results of your work six months after you leave. If you want to know, but usually don't find out, ask for it.

Example:

"About six months after the project is completed, the consultant will contact the client for feedback on the impact of the project. This might take the form of having people complete a questionnaire, respond over the phone, or send some recent operating data to the consultant."

Checklist #2. Analyzing One of Your Contracts

Pick a complicated contract that you have negotiated. Write up the elements of that contract using the following headings:

1. The Boundaries of Your Analysis

2. Objectives of the Project

3. The Kind of Information You Seek

4. Your Role in the Project

5. The Product You Will Deliver

6. What Support and Involvement You Need from the Client

7. Time Schedule

8. Confidentiality

9. Feedback to You Later

Ground Rules for Contracting

A model for a contracting meeting is presented in the next chapter. Underlying the model is a set of ground rules for contracting, which have come primarily from my exposure to Gestalt psychology.[4]

1. The responsibility for every relationship is 50/50. There are two sides to every story. There must be symmetry or the relationship will collapse. The contract has to be 50/50.

2. The contract should be freely entered.

---

[4]I attended a workshop run by Claire and Mike Reiker in which they presented these ground rules in such a clear and powerful way that I have used them ever since.

3. You can't get something for nothing. There must be consideration from both sides. Even in a boss-subordinate relationship.

4. All wants are legitimate. To want is a birthright. You can't say, "You shouldn't want that."

5. You can say no to what others want from you. Even clients.

6. You don't always get what you want. And you'll still keep breathing. You will still survive; you will still have more clients in the future.

7. You can contract for behavior, you can't contract for the other person to change their feelings.

8. You can't ask for something the other person doesn't have.

9. You can't promise something you don't have to deliver.

10. You can't contract with someone who's not in the room, such as clients' bosses and subordinates. You have to meet with them directly to know you have an agreement with them.

11. Write down contracts when you can. Most are broken out of neglect, not intent.

12. Social contracts are always renegotiable. If clients want to renegotiate a contract in midstream, be grateful that they are telling you and not just doing it without a word.

13. Contracts require specific time deadlines or duration.

14. Good contracts require good faith and often accidental good fortune.

Chapter 5

The Contracting Meeting

THERE IS AN OLD David Steinberg joke about the person showing up for his first meeting with his psychiatrist. He walks in the office and is faced with the choice of two chairs to sit in. He turns to the psychiatrist and says, "Which chair should I sit in?" The psychiatrist says, "Either one." The person sits in one. The psychiatrist jumps up, points an accusing finger at him and shouts, "AHA! EVERYTHING COUNTS!"

So it is with contracting. Almost every event and action carries with it a message about what this project and what this client is going to be like.

The personal interaction between the consultant and the client during the initial contracting meetings is an accurate predictor of how the project itself will proceed. If you can accept this concept, you will pay close attention to the process of those early meetings. In fact, the critical skill in contracting is being able to identify and discuss process issues between the consultant and the client as they occur.

The contracting meeting is usually set up via phone call. During this call, there are certain things to find out to help prepare for the meeting. Who requested the meeting? This will be the first indication of where the responsibility lies. If someone else suggested a meeting with a staff person to the line manager, this is a warning flag that the manager may be feeling some pressure to proceed. Find out who will be at the meeting and what their roles will be. How much time is there for the meeting? This gives an early indication of the importance of the project to the manager. You get a different message if you hear, "We have half an hour," than if you hear, "We have as much time as we need." Clarify what outcome is expected from the meeting. Is it a meeting to decide how to get started or whether to do anything at all? Is a proposal going to be required? Dealing with these issues even before the meeting gives you more data to prepare for the meeting. It also signals to the client that this is likely to be a 50/50 proposition—that you are a responsible actor in the process, and not just a servant.

All this is easier, of course, when the client is initiating the meeting with you than when you are knocking on the door. Later in this chapter we will focus on selling to clients who don't know, yet, that they need your services. However, when the client wants to meet with you, I would recommend these questions, at a minimum, over the phone.

> What do you want to discuss?
>
> Who is the client for this project?
>
> Who else will be at the meeting? What are their roles?
>
> How much time will we have?
>
> Do you know that you want to begin some project, or are we going to discuss whether we do anything at all?

Who Is the Client?

When you meet with the client to begin contracting, the key question is: Who is the client? Most projects have multiple clients. The line manager you are talking to is one client. There are others who may have a piece of the action (see Chapter 7). One of the ground rules of contracting is that you cannot contract with someone who's out of the room. If there are major actors not present as you are setting up a project, you can't assume that they support the project until you actually meet with them.

In general, the client(s) on a project are the people who:

> Attend the initial planning meeting

> Set the objectives for the project

> Approve any action to be taken

> Receive the report on the results of your work

This means the client can be a person, a top management team, a whole department that you work with through a representative planning group, or even your own boss. Try to have at least one meeting with each person who is part of initiating this project. Even if they are at a very high level of the organization. This will allow you to get your own information on what they want from you and whether what you are planning will satisfy them.

Navigating the Contracting Meeting

Reaching agreement on how you will work with a client can follow a logical sequence. Outlined in Figure 2 is a series of steps that lead to either an agreement to work together or an agreement not to work together. Using this model you will ensure that you are adequately completing the business of the contracting phase. In describing the sequence of steps below, I want to give you both a clear statement of each task to be accomplished and also what an authentic way of accomplishing the task would look like.

The objective we are focusing on here is to develop a stable, balanced, and workable contract between the consultant and the client.

Step 1. Personal Acknowledgement

No matter how motivated a line manager is to seek your assistance, it is a difficult thing in organizations to ask for help. I have been consulting for years, and yet when my own organization hires a consultant to help us with a problem, I feel some uneasiness. So the first item on the agenda of the contracting meeting is to do something that will help to increase the personal comfort level between the consultant and the client. Some people try to do this by discussing the ball scores or the weather. It would be better

Figure 2. Navigating the Contracting Meeting

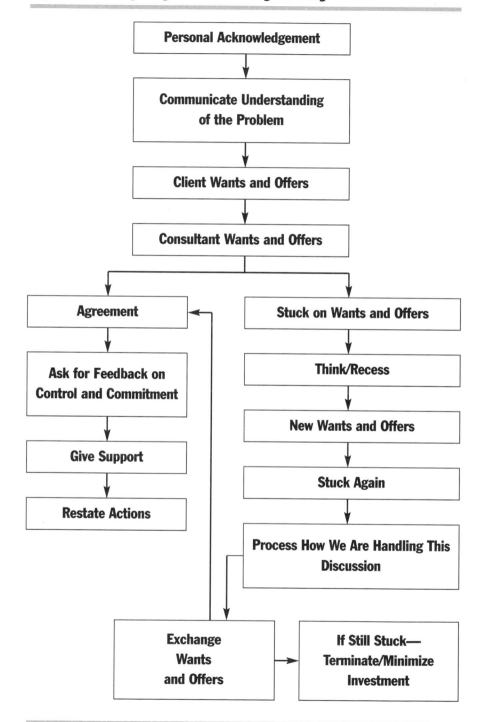

to make it a little more personal. My advice to people in consulting skills workshops is this:

> Make personal statements of your feelings about being
> in this meeting with the client today.

Some Examples:

"This is one of the few plants I have never worked with; I'm glad you called."

"I was surprised that you were interested in what we are doing. I hope we can work something out."

"It looks like things are hectic for you. I hope this is a good time for us to get together."

Step 2. Communicate Understanding of the Problem

Clients are usually eager to tell you about the problem or the general situation. Behind the eagerness is often the line manager's belief that this situation is unique in some particular aspects and this organization is really very special. Line managers can also feel that their situations are so special and unique that no one could possibly understand them without living there for a year.

The client's declaration of uniqueness, often accompanied by doubt that the consultant can understand the situation, sometimes gets expressed in very roundabout ways. Clients ask about work you are doing elsewhere in the organization, about whom you report to if they don't know, about how long you have been doing this kind of work, and whether you can be of any help anyway. Underneath all the statements and questions is the concern about whether or not the client can be helped and the problem can be solved. After all, before the consultant comes on the scene, clients have made their best efforts to solve the problem themselves. It is understandable that they are frustrated by the lack of a solution and somewhat skeptical about the consultant's possible contribution.

The following basic client concerns require a direct response early in the contracting meeting:

"My situation is exquisitely unique."

"The problem is complicated and defies an obvious solution."

"So, how could you, a consultant, an outsider, offer significant help in a short period of time?"

The consultant needs to communicate an understanding of the problem in ways that acknowledge the unique aspects of the situation, respond to the seeming complexity of the situation, and speak to the client's fear about being beyond help.

Here's how you do it.

Acknowledge the Unique Aspects of the Situation

Because each client has different people and operates in a different environment, the line manager's claim of uniqueness has some validity. From the consultant's vantage point, we tend to be more aware of what is similar between this client and other clients we have worked with. Initially, though, it is important to put into words what is different about this project.

Examples:

"There are two unique aspects to your situation, the pressure being placed on you from above and the desert climate of this location."

"Your situation has several unique things that make it both interesting and frustrating."

Restate, in Your Own Words, Your Perception of the Problem

Here you express the thought that even though the problem is indeed complicated, you can already begin to understand it. This is an act of reassurance, designed to make the client feel understood and supported. At this point you don't know what the real problem is, for the *real* problem is often quite different from the client's opening problem statement. What you are accomplishing is letting the client know that you are listening and have enough technical expertise to grasp the situation quickly.

Most line managers have been listened to so little by experts that they are surprised by my "perceptiveness." The manager says,

"The design engineering and the plant engineering groups are always blaming each other for plant failures." I respond by saying, "I bet when they get together they have trouble coming up with a single plan of action they can support." The manager says, "That's right. How did you know that? You're perceptive." It's not perceptiveness, it is just listening to and restating what the manager said.

Examples: "Even though you have covered many elements of the problem, it sounds to me like the operator's attitude toward maintenance is a primary concern."

"You have mentioned in great detail your concerns about expense vouchering, petty cash, and accounts payable, but what you really sound concerned about is the lack of specific controls in certain areas."

"I can see you are concerned about the slowdown, the wildcat strike, the suspicious explosions, the wanton destruction of property, and the fact that someone glued and soldered every moving piece of equipment over the weekend. But what I really hear you're concerned about is that people just don't seem to be happy working here."

Reassure the Manager that There Are Solutions to This Unique and Complicated Problem and that You Can Be of Help

Your reassurance has to be genuine. You are stating that you can help find a solution and not that you know the solution right now. Your expertise is really knowing the steps that have to be followed to find a solution. This is what you have to offer. The client at this stage is wondering, "Is this consultant someone I can lean on and trust to help me with this problem?" The consultant's answer is a tentative, "Yes." Your answer is tentative at this early stage because you don't know specifically what the client wants from you or what support the client is willing to offer you. Until you know the specific wants and offers from the client, you don't know whether this is a project on which you can succeed.

Examples: "Despite the frustration you are feeling, I can help you with this problem."

"This is the kind of situation that makes good use of my background. I think I can help."

"This kind of project is of a great deal of interest to me, and it's the kind of thing we have worked with a lot lately."

In communicating your understanding of the problem, it helps to use short, simple sentences. Many of us have a tendency to get a little carried away, getting too deeply into an analysis of the problem at this early stage. The task here is to respond to the underlying concerns of uniqueness, complexity, and whether the client can be helped. The task is not to analyze the nature of the problem—this comes later. Responding to the client's emotional concerns is done better with short sentences than with long sentences, short words are better than long words, direct statements are better than inferences. Make simple statements expressing understanding and support without being overly protective or falsely reassuring. The next step is to get into the specifics of what you and the client really expect from each other.

Step 3. Client Wants and Offers

After saying hello and hearing an initial statement of what the line manager is concerned about, you look the manager in the eye and say, "So . . ., what do you want from me?" The answer is the heart of the contracting process, and the question must be asked directly. It is the key qualifying question to determine whether and how you can succeed on this project.

There is a difference between what the client wants from *the project* and what the client wants from *you*. The client can be very clear about what is wanted from *the project*—better cost control, reduced overhead charges, fewer equipment failures, better morale from the troops, more skilled first-line supervisors, an improved sales reporting system—and still not express what is expected from *you, the consultant*.

Some common things clients want from their consultants are:

A study of a specific business problem

Recommendations on how to solve a problem

A training program designed and conducted

Personal advice and support

An evaluation of key line personnel

A piece of equipment fixed

A design for a cheaper process

These are generally pretty straightforward requests for your services. It becomes more complex as you begin to understand *how* they would like you to work. To understand this, you ask the client whether there are any specific notions about how you should proceed or what the constraints on this project are. Asking about constraints helps you find out early that:

You have two weeks to do a four-week job.

You shouldn't talk to any hourly people.

Nobody knows the real reasons for this study and you shouldn't tell them.

You shouldn't upset anybody or open Pandora's box.

The project has a budget of $1.85.

After this meeting the client won't have any more time to spend with you.

Constraints on how you proceed are, of course, vital for you to know now. *How you proceed* is often the most difficult part of the contract to negotiate.

The skill in surfacing constraints is to ask the client directly for:

1. Any thoughts he or she has on how you work with them, and

2. What constraints exist on the way this project is conducted. This includes the data collection method, who is involved, who hears the results, schedule, and cost.

After hearing what the client wants from you, you next want to ask what support the client can offer you on the project. If the client is going to pay directly for your services (you are not part of the client's overhead), you want to know what the budget is for this project. The other two offers the client can make to you are the time of his or her people and access to information. You will want to explore these areas in detail when you get around to expressing your wants.

Most people doing consulting are in fact quite good at this stage of the contracting process. Staff people especially seem to be oriented to client needs and are skillful in identifying what the client wants. Staff consultants have a much harder time with the next step, identifying and expressing their own wants and needs.

**Step 4.
Consultant
Wants and Offers**

One of the most critical skills in flawless consultation is to put directly into words what you, the consultant, want from the client to make a project successful.

When I tell internal consultants they should make clear what they want from the client, they often say, "We are in a service role and our job is to satisfy the line manager's needs and wants. If we do this successfully, our job is done. We are not in a position to make demands on the people whom we serve." This pure service orientation can be self-defeating. Making clear what the consultant wants from the client is in the interest of making sure the project is successful; it is not to satisfy the consultant's own personal whims and wishes.

The consultant wants we are talking about here include such things as the need for enough time to do the job right, access to the right people and information, support from the client at difficult moments, people from the client organization to work on the project, and agreements on confidentiality, follow-up to the recommendations, uninterrupted time from the line manager. *These wants have to be expressed in the contracting phase.* The risk of not expressing your wants is that the project will not succeed, and an unsuccessful project is worse than no project at all.

Some things we want from clients are more important than others. In planning a contracting meeting, it's helpful for you to break your wants into two kinds: essential wants and desirable wants.

Essential wants are the things you must have as a minimum. Some people call them *must wants.* If you do not get an essential want from a client, then you would do better not to proceed with the project. Essentials will vary from situation to situation.

Some essentials might be:

>   Access to the key people who have a part in the problem I am being asked to solve
>
>   Enough time to do the job professionally
>
>   An agreement that I will not be asked to individually evaluate the performance of people that I work with on this project
>
>   Money
>
>   Access to certain records and documents
>
>   The commitment of the top person in the organization to proceed with the project
>
>   Return my phone calls

Knowing what is essential comes with experience and from getting burned a few times. We never get all that we want on a project, so in the beginning, we tend to pressure ourselves to give in a little and get on with the project. If we give in on an essential—whether from hunger for a client or pressure from our boss to "get that client into the fold"—we will be sorry. Giving in on an essential means the project will be on shaky grounds, and we risk failure.

If you are in the middle of a contracting session and the suggestions from you and the client keep shifting around and suddenly you have to decide whether to agree to something or not, stop the process and give yourself a little recess. You can break for coffee, go to the bathroom, drop some marbles on the floor and think while you search for them, or whatever you do to give yourself space to think. During the recess, which doesn't need to be any longer than three or four minutes, ask yourself only one question: Does the suggestion on the table violate in any way what I consider essential *for me* on this project? If the answer is yes, then return to the meeting and say, "What you are suggesting makes great sense, but it does not give me what I consider to be essential for the success of this project." Then continue the search for agreement.

There is no better thing you can do for yourself when beginning a project than to realistically define what the essentials for you are on a project. If you have done this honestly—with neither greed nor self-sacrifice—then little else can happen to you during the contracting to really hurt you. A lot can happen to make you miserable, but if your essentials are met, the project can succeed. If they are not met, the project can only fail.

Desirable wants are the things you would like to have from the client but you *can* live without them. These are not casual or capricious wants: They will help make the project more effective, but you know you can succeed without them.

Some desirable wants may be:

Someone from the client organization to work with you on the project

The manager to personally meet with all the people involved in the project to explain and support it

The top management of the group to personally get deeply involved in your project

A certain time schedule

The cooperation of people at all levels of the organization without reservation

Agreement that the client will spread the word to others in the organization if I do well on the project

Sometimes internal consultants are so oriented to meeting their client's needs that they have a hard time identifying what they want in return from their clients.

Here is a list of what some internal consultants have said they wanted from their clients:

A clear definition of the job

Work the problem together

Commitment to the project

Share the blame and the glory

To be wanted and useful

No bias about the outcome

Take care of physical needs to accomplish the job (in this case—car, driver, and translator in Pakistan desert)

Openness to feedback during the project

Tell me about problems with the projects as they happen

Feedback on what happened after I left

Feedback to my boss

More time

The client to work toward becoming a better manager

The client to shoulder more responsibility

Stop giving me lip service

Understanding

Tolerance of mistakes

Accept that certain things just can't be done

Do your part

Forgiveness

Putting It into Words

Identifying what you want from the client is the first step. The next step is to act on those wants. This corresponds to the two requirements of consulting flawlessly: attending to the business of each phase and acting authentically. The business at this point is identifying what you want; acting authentically means putting those wants into words as simply and directly as possible.

Sometimes there is a tendency to complicate asking for what you want. We think we need elaborate explanations and justifications for our wants. We introduce a want with a paragraph about other experiences or the unique requirements of this organization, and we make the want rather vague and general. Sometimes we ask for what we want with a question. All this does is fog and undermine the expression.

Here's an example of two ways of expressing wants.

The Want

A manager of training is talking to a division director about sending her subordinate to a course on performance appraisal skills. The want is for the division director to become directly involved in the project by also attending the course.

Fogged Expression of Wants

Training Manager: We have found from prior experience that the learning in a training course tends to be retained longer if there is some visible evidence of positive reinforcement back on the job. This allows for better utilization of the newly acquired skills, and in your case the performance appraisal course is introducing a totally different approach to the important and productive counseling of employees. If this positive reinforcement does not take place, then you can expect a decay of the learning and the cost/benefit ratio of your investment is significantly diminished. Have you ever attended a course on performance appraisal?

Comment
The points being made here by the training manager are all true. There are good reasons for the division director to attend the course. The problem is that the want is being buried in the justification. The question at the end may eventually lead to the suggestion that the division director take the course, but this path is indirect and unnecessary.

Here is an alternative.

Authentic Expression of Wants
Training Manager: I would like for you also to attend the course on performance appraisal.

Comment
This may seem too simple. It's not. The power of the statement is primarily because it is simple and in everyday street language. The goal of flawless consulting is to maximize your leverage and impact on the client so that your expertise gets utilized. Acting authentically is the most powerful thing you can do—at every stage of the process.

When we identify what we want from the client, the want comes first, the justification afterward. We know that we want the manager to attend the course. Then we start to think of how we can justify it to the client. We start worrying about how to phrase it, how to explain it in "bottom-line" terms, to find words that the client will understand. All this effort is not only overdone, but it can act as a fog and obstacle to getting what we want.

The skill is to:

1. State the want first in simple street language.

2. Be quiet and let the client react.

3. If you get some questions from the client, give a two-sentence answer and restate the want.

4. Be quiet and listen for a yes or no.

You will not always get a yes answer. Life is like that. If you state the want simply, use silence to get the client to talk about their feelings, and make very short explanations, you have done all you can. The long paragraphs may make *you* feel better, but they get in your way. Making simple authentic statements gives you your best chance to get what you want and to know where you stand with the client on that issue.

Your Chance

Get out a pencil and a piece of paper. Divide the paper into two columns: essential wants and desirable wants. Think of a client you are concerned about, and write down your list of essential and desirable wants from that client. Don't worry about whether you would ever ask for these things from a client; just write them down in as uncensored a way as possible.

Consultant Offers (Step 4 Continued)

In addition to stating wants to the client, state what you have to offer. This requires you to be realistic about the limit of what you can promise. Most often, the consultant's promise is a clear picture of what is happening in the client organization plus recommendations on how to improve things. The consultant can promise actual improvements only if line management takes its 50 percent of the responsibility. Operating improvements can only be a joint promise between consultant and client, not a unilateral consultant promise. If I offer results as a result of simply my own efforts as a consultant, I am presenting myself as a magician. I can't offer something that I can't control. I can't control the client's behavior or actions. If I do let my enthusiasm lead me into promising specific results that are really the client's to achieve, I am colluding with the client's secret wish to sit back and watch the consultant perform miracles.

An example of the choice.

Client:	How soon can I expect results from you?
Magical Consultant Offer:	We'll have the machine back on stream in three days and you won't have any trouble with it after that.
Realistic Consultant Offer:	We'll have the machine back on stream in three days. After that, it is up to you to keep it running.

For most of us doing consulting, there are two things we need to constantly work on:

1. Stating clearly, sometimes running the risk of overstatement, what we need and want from the client to make this project work

2. Being cautious, sometimes running the risk of understatement, about the results we alone will deliver on this project

Step 5. Reaching Agreement

After exchanging wants with the client, either you reach agreement or you get stuck.[5] If, as in most cases, you can reach agreement, you should pause for a moment and just feel good about it. If you are feeling expansive, you can even say to the client, "It looks like we agree on how to proceed. I am really happy about that." It also helps to restate what the agreement is.

Consultants often act like the contracting meeting is over when agreement has been reached. It is not over. There are still three important steps before a stable, balanced contract is assured.

---

[5]What to do when you get stuck begins on page 88.

Step 6. Asking for Feedback About Control and Commitment

This is an insurance step. Most weak contracts are faulty for one of two reasons:

1. The client entered the agreement under some kind of coercion, however subtle and indirect.

2. The client agreed to the project, but increasingly felt that they did not have adequate control over what was happening.

So, at the beginning of any project, be compulsive about testing for the existence of each of these flaws.

Test No. 1

Ask the client, directly, in words, "Is this project something that you really want to see happen? Are you satisfied with the way we have agreed to set it up?"

There are many ways the line manager can feel coerced into the project. Top management may have suggested this project. It may be the latest organizational fad to begin projects like this. The manager may feel that it would be politically unwise to say no to you.

Asking the question about client commitment does not mean that you will withdraw from the project if the client is not that committed. You ask the question so that you know what you are up against from the beginning. If the client is acting out of coercion, you want to know it now. That's the way life sometimes is. It is important to be realistic about this so that you don't overinvest or pretend that the contract is strong when it is not.

Asking clients about their commitment has one additional benefit: It forces them to take responsibility for the fact that they too are beginning a project without supporting it fully. Sometimes the act of clients' acknowledging they are acting under some coercion can actually serve to increase their commitment to a project.

Having the conversation about commitment to the project near the end of the contracting meeting is important. Do it.

Test No. 2

After discussing client commitment to the project, ask the question, "Do you feel you have enough control over how this project is going to proceed?"

Line managers (as well as the rest of us) tend to value control above all else. If the client begins to feel that control of the situation is slipping away, the contract and the project will be threatened. As with your questions about commitment, you want to know now about any client uneasiness. Giving up control is a major cause of organizational uneasiness. Each time clients bring in a consultant, they give up a little bit of control, so as a consultant you should find out the extent of the uneasiness.

When I suggest to internal consultants that they ask these questions about commitment and control, they ask in return, "Yeah, but how do we know we will get an honest answer? Will the client be truthful with us?" If you ask about control and commitment in a way that shows genuine interest in the answer, the client will give you a straight answer. If you ask the questions with a persuasive or pleading tone, honest answers are less likely. The purpose of the questions is to help managers express any reservations they are having. The questions are not indirect selling techniques.

Even if you ask the questions sincerely, sometimes you won't get a direct answer. It is still worthwhile to have asked them.

**Step 7.
Give Support**

Make supportive statements to the client about his or her willingness to begin this project with you. It takes some courage to invite or allow people into your organization to make recommendations about how you should shape up. Even if the client is seven feet tall, has scales, and breathes fire, I always assume there is a wish for support and I am happy to fulfill that wish.

The support needs to be genuine and specific. Here are some examples:

"Starting a project like this takes some risk on your part and I appreciate your willingness to take that risk with me."

"You have lived with this situation for a long time. It's terrific that you are now in a position to do something about it."

"You are very perceptive about the nature of these kinds of problems. That is going to help a lot on this project."

"I know at first you were very skeptical about whether to let me in the door. I am glad we got past that."

Step 8. Restate Actions

As a final insurance step, make sure you and the client know what each of you is going to do next. Simple statements will do it.

"You are going to send a memo to your people about the project."

"I am going to show up on the 4th of March to begin interviewing people."

"Starting tomorrow, I will review the records with George. You and I will meet at 4:00 p.m. on Friday."

After agreeing on next steps, the contracting meeting is complete. No social contract will last forever; in fact, the contract usually is renegotiated often during the life of the project. If, however, you have gone through the eight steps above, you have done what you can at this stage.

Step 5–S. Getting Stuck on Wants and Offers

After Step 4, we discussed what to do when you reach agreement. So what happens if agreement is difficult? This is called Step 5-S-S for stuck. There are two phases to dealing with being stuck.

First, you have to know that you are stuck.

Second, you have to do something about it.

Knowing When You Are Stuck

It is possible to feel that you are just having a reasonable discussion with the client about the pros and cons of the project and not realize that you are at an impasse. However, there are several very clear operational signals of when you are stuck.

1. *You are stuck when you hear yourself re-explaining something for the third time.* The first time you explained why you want something, you might have used jargon or clumsy language. The second time you explained, you might have felt the client wasn't really listening. When you are struggling for the third time to express something in different, clearer words, you should admit to yourself that you are stuck.

Much organizational communication is in code.

When People Mean	They Express It by Saying
I don't like it.	I don't understand it
I don't want to do it.	Let's get more data.
	or
	I'll get back to you.
	or
	Let me talk it over with my staff.
I don't understand a word you are saying.	Nothing
Do as I say, dammit.	Why don't you think it over and get back to me?
I wouldn't let your group even get close to my organization.	We want to talk to some other people about alternative approaches to this problem and we'll let you know.
	And on and on.

You need to learn and trust this code because it is an early warning signal when you are getting stuck with your line manager.

When you are saying to yourself, "The client really doesn't understand what I am talking about," the truth is that the client really *does* understand what you are talking about and does not agree. When this happens, don't explain for the fourth and fifth time. Instead, acknowledge that you are stuck.

2. You are stuck when you notice the client diving into the third explanation of the same idea. When the client thinks that you still don't understand, the client says, "Let me see if I can put it another way." The re-explaining process assumes that lack of clarity is the problem. By the third try, it is not lack of clarity, it is lack of agreement. You are stuck. Acknowledge it.

3. Your body will give you clear messages that you are getting stuck. When you start suppressing yawns, take it as a signal that the meeting is not going your way. Boredom and fatigue are usually indirect expressions of irritation. You start to get very subtly irritated with the resistance you are getting from the client. Perhaps it is the lack of enthusiasm you are getting from the client. As you get irritated, you say to yourself that you shouldn't be irritated, so you start holding back the irritation. The strain of holding back the irritation, especially if it happens unconsciously, is tiring. Your shoulders and neck start to ache. You start to yawn and turn it into a laugh at the last minute. You start looking at your watch and think about the tennis game you played yesterday. Or you notice the client also looking very tired, turning yawns into laughs, staring out the window, or secretly napping as you talk.

All of these are signs that the conversation is stuck. If you were making progress and moving toward agreement, your energy would be increasing. If your energy is decreasing and you start feeling irritated, then it simply means that you aren't getting what you want and you are stuck.

4. Your eyes give you the best cues that the contracting process has bogged down. Trust what you see. Believe nonverbal messages.

There is a lot written about body language—how to interpret different positions and how to posture yourself to either communicate or conceal certain messages. Using body language or nonverbal behavior to either manipulate a situation or to "present" yourself in a certain way is a mistake. When you force your body into a position that hides how you are really feeling, you look to others like someone who is forcing your body into a position to hide how you are really feeling.

If you can let go of trying to "do" something with your nonverbal behavior, or being psychological about others' nonverbal behavior, it can be a valuable source of information to you.

If you are looking for nonverbal cues during the contracting process, you will notice the client moving forward into the discussion or moving backward away from the discussion. You will notice the client's hands—gestures of pushing you away, grabbing you like a fist, pointing at you like a gun, or opening wide, palms up, saying, "I am here by accident, a helpless victim of fate. What can any of us mere mortals do about this situation?"

These gestures can be accurately interpreted only at the grossest level: Are they acts of support or rejection? Does the client want into this project or out of it? Is the conversation going well or poorly?

The client's physical behavior and your own movements are only cues to help you know when you are stuck. They don't tell you why you are stuck. Resist the mind game of interpreting specific gestures. Do trust the general messages.

There is often a sharp contrast between what clients are saying and their nonverbal behavior. They are saying that they are really interested in this project, and they are also backed against the wall with their arms folded over their heads in bomb shelter fashion.

If I am forced to choose between believing the words and believing the body, I would believe the body. We all have very sophisticated verbal defenses, but nonverbal defenses are much less sophisticated. So I trust what I see. But I use it only as a signal. I don't comment directly on their behavior. I resist the temptation to say, "Each time I suggest interviewing your subordinates, you back up your chair to the wall, put your head into your arms, and hold your breath until your face turns pink. Why? Are you uncomfortable with what I am suggesting?"

The act of inferring the motives for another person's behavior is very aggressive and always leads to defensiveness on their part. Your objective is to help the client express the reservations more directly. You want to get a single message from the client so you know where things stand. When you get a double message, when the body language doesn't match the words, ask an open-ended question about how the client feels about what you are discussing.

Again, the purpose of focusing on nonverbal behavior is to set up an early warning system, to gather a more accurate set of cues, so you have a more realistic view of how the client is reacting to what you are saying.

Your own body is also an indication of how you are really feeling about the contracting meeting. If the conversation seems to be going well on the surface, and you also find yourself low on energy and slumping in the chair, you should begin to wonder whether your body isn't picking up some caution flags that your mind is choosing to ignore. If the conversation *is* going well and you are slumping in the chair, you might just be tired. And that's OK, too.

What to do when you notice you're stuck?

Step 6–S.
Think/Recess

I think the most difficult part of dealing with being stuck is just admitting to yourself that you have reached an impasse. When you acknowledge to yourself that you are stuck, the first thing to do is to mentally pull back from the conversation. Become an observer to the contracting meeting you are engaged in. You can continue talking and listening and, at the same time, be thinking whether you can change your position in some way. Are there different wants you can ask for and still meet your objectives?

Sometimes it is wise to adjourn the meeting. Make the statement, "We seem to be hung up on this point, and I would like some time to think about it some more." This gives you time to re-evaluate whether there is really an unresolvable difference between you and the client or whether the difficulty you are having is due to some misunderstanding growing from the way the meeting itself has progressed. When you mentally or physically withdraw from the firing line, you make time to identify a different way to approach the project or a different way to seal the agreement.

Step 7–S. New Wants and Offers

If you think the differences between you and the client are negotiable, present any new ideas on what you want from the client or what you have to offer. We often get stuck in the contracting meeting over schedule. The client wants the job in thirty days, and we think we need sixty days. Both of us have good reasons and so we get stuck.

You may decide after the thinking and recessing step that you could complete the project in thirty days if the client provides two people to work with you and agrees that your final report can be in outline form instead of elaborate prose.

Here's what you say.

Changing your offer: The job will be done in thirty days instead of sixty days.

Changing your wants: Give me two people to work with and accept a shorter final report.

Developing different wants and offers is always worth at least one try. Sometimes it still doesn't help.

Step 8–S. Stuck Again

If you realize that changing the wants and offers has just led to another impasse, then it is time to really shift gears. You have made two passes at reaching agreement that aren't working, so you should ask yourself whether the way you are working with the client and the relationship between you and the client might not be the real problem.

Line managers make decisions on the projects based on their feelings about the people involved. Does the manager trust this consultant or the consultant's department? Consultants make agreements with line managers based on whether they trust the manager. When consultant and client get stuck on how or whether to proceed, a different kind of discussion is needed.

**Step 9–S.
Process How
We Are Handling
This Discussion**

When you're stuck again, the conversation needs to shift to how this meeting is going. For the moment, put aside the actual project under consideration. There are many ways of processing how a discussion is being handled, and they will be covered in more detail in Chapters 8 and 9, where we talk about dealing with resistance.

Here are a couple of ways of shifting the focus of discussion to the process of the meeting.

1. Say, "I think we are stuck." This is probably the single most powerful thing you can do. A simple declarative statement of fact—the meeting isn't going anywhere. Of course you will use your own language and style, but the key is to put directly into words the fact that you have reached an impasse. If the client keeps talking about the project, restate the fact that you are stuck and encourage a discussion of why you seem to be stuck.

2. Ask an open-ended question about how the client feels the meeting is going. You don't have to be subtle. Say, "How do you feel we are doing in reaching agreement on how to proceed?" If you stick with the question, you will soon find out how the line manager is reacting to working with you. The manager may be worried about:

> Keeping control of the project
>
> How stubborn you seem to be
>
> How misunderstood they feel
>
> The reputation your group has in their organization
>
> How vague the benefits of this project seem

The jargon and motherhood statements you use

And on and on

If the line manager is concerned about these kinds of process issues, you want to know it. So simply ask the question. Most cases of stuck contracting stem from these kinds of concerns, not from the specifics of how to set up the project. They need to be talked about directly, by the client and by the consultant. When these concerns are expressed, the specifics become much easier.

Step 10–S. Rediscuss Wants and Offers

The discussion of how the meeting is going will usually unclog the impasse. You can go back to the specifics of the project and usually reach some agreement that puts you back on the original track (Step 5. Reaching Agreement) and allows you to continue on to close the meeting.

Sometimes, despite all your skills, after following all these suggestions perfectly and consulting flawlessly, you remain stuck.

Step 11–S. If Still Stuck— Terminate/ Minimize Your Investment

Despite their importance to you, all projects were not meant to be. It is vital to accept this now, early in the project, and not count on later miracles to save the day.

When you are irreparably stuck with the client, you need to say, "We are having a hard time reaching agreement; perhaps now is not a good time to do this work," or "I would suggest that we not begin this project, since we can't seem to agree on how to proceed." Using your own style and own words, end the contracting process and cut your losses.

The Problem with Saying No

Internal consultants especially feel they are taking tremendous risks if they tell line managers that they would be better off terminating the project. Despite the risk, it is in the consultant's and the client's best interests to refuse projects that do not have a reasonable chance for success. When you are stuck in contracting with a client, it is because both of you feel that if you don't get your way, the project will not succeed. If you go ahead with a project you don't believe in, you run the risk of failure. The reason to terminate projects is not because of consultant petulance, or pickiness, or the desire to engage only in exotic and professionally stimulating work. The reason to say no is simply to avoid failure and the waste of your resources.

Another reason to stay open to the possibility of saying no to a client is that you are trying to manage the relationship with the client in a way that you would wish them to manage their relationships with their own people. Saying no says that we have limits, that we have a right to declare boundaries and decide on our own what we commit to. If we cannot say no, then yes loses its meaning. And commitment also is taken off the table. We become programmed to say yes and after a while do not know when the yes is sincerely felt or simply is habit born of institutionalized habit.

If you can't usually say no to a client, what choices do you have? You can minimize your investment of time and hope and keep your potential losses down. The easiest way to do this is to postpone the project. "I am willing to go ahead with the project as you have requested, but I would suggest that we begin it in eight months." By this time, this manager may have moved on to another job or you might have moved on to better things.

If you can't postpone the project, minimize the scope of the job and the time it will require. Narrow the objectives of the project. Do what you can to reduce the visibility of the project and reduce the drain on your time and energy. The key is to be honest with yourself about the limitations of the project.

We often kid ourselves. A client comes to us and wants to use us as a pair-of-hands, wants us to work in a way that feels to us like a bent-over position. We operate under the illusion that if we work for this client now in a bent-over position, our sacrifice will build trust with the client and later on we will be able to work in a standing-tall position. Being very compliant with a client, not making our wants known, going along with something we don't have confidence in—all make us feel bent-over. So we work bent-over. The client also notices our bent-over position and, after a short while, begins to think that is the way we normally work—bent-over. As a result, when the client needs someone who works standing up straight, someone else gets called in.

So be realistic about unattractive projects. Be clear with your boss and others that the project is beginning on shaky grounds, that you would rather not proceed, but that you feel you have no choice because you can't afford to say no to this client. Then do the project in a low-key way.

The critical point to consider is whether it is really in your best interest to go ahead with a project. It may be better to live without the project, and not having "converted" that client, than to begin a project that might fail. If you pull back from one client, perhaps that client will be angry with you and feel rejected. But you only lost one client. If you proceed with a project that you think might fail and it doesn't go well, you are in bigger trouble. The client is going to tell five other managers how disappointing the project was and how it failed. Now you are in the hole with *six* managers instead of only one. So it is just not good for business to take on low-chance-of-success projects.

At this point you have all the information you need to conduct a contracting meeting flawlessly.

The sequence of steps covers the business of the contracting meeting. There are three major sections to the meeting: (1) Understanding the problem and exchanging wants, (2) closing the meeting by checking on client concerns and commitment, and (3) getting unstuck when agreement is difficult. Each step is essential and should never be skipped. If you cover the steps and still don't get the contract you wanted, you have done all you can and consulted flawlessly.

Here is a checklist to help you prepare for a contracting meeting. Answer the questions before each contracting meeting and you are ready.

Checklist #3. Planning a Contracting Meeting

1. What imbalance do you expect in the responsibility for this project? Do you think the client will want to treat you as the expert and give you 80 percent of the responsibility? Or will the client treat you as a pair-of-hands and keep 80 percent of the responsibility?

2. What do you want from the client?

   - What are your essential wants?

   - What are your desirable wants?

3. What are you offering the client?

   - Technically?

   - Personally?

4. What do you think the client might want? List all possibilities.

   - Technically?

   - Personally?

5. Are the key clients going to be in the room?

   - Who can make a decision on proceeding with this project?

   - Who will be strongly affected by this project?

   - Who is missing from the meeting?

   - What are their roles? (For example, get some action on the problem started, actually implement the outcome of your consultation; they have the best information on the problem.)

6. What resistance do you anticipate?

7. What are the conditions under which it would be best not to proceed?

Even though some of the questions in Checklist #3 may be unanswerable at this point, trying to answer them helps you focus on the essence of the meeting. If you are part of a consulting team, the checklist gives you a vehicle to get your act together. Mostly the questions keep you centered on what you need from the meeting so that you don't get swept away with overresponding to the client's view of the world.

Selling Your Services— Good Selling Is Good Contracting

When the client comes to us, it's easy. We can assume there is some real need, some motivation, some respect for our abilities. Most of us, though, also have to go out and convince the clients that they want to work with us. Internal consultants have their own departmental objectives to meet. They are told that a certain group ought to be using the department's services, and they are evaluated on whether they bring certain clients into the fold.

Basically, the skills for selling your services are the same as those described for regular contracting. But here are a couple of additional concepts about the selling situation that might be helpful.

Reverse the Expression of Wants

When the client calls you, you begin the discussion of wants by asking what the client wants from you. When you initiate the contact, you need to say straight out what you want from the client. Figure 3 shows the reversed sequence.

You must have a reason for choosing to talk to this client, and you explain that by defining the problem that you think the prospective client faces. Before going on to wants, stop and ask the client if the problem you have defined is indeed the problem. If it isn't, give it another try, then consider a quiet retreat.

After defining the need to the client, state what you want from the client. Acknowledge that you are making a sales call. Staff consultants feel successful by getting line managers to use their services. Everybody knows this, even line managers. One thing the staff consultant wants from the meeting is to have the line manager as a client—so acknowledge it. To say you only want to be helpful is just half the story.

Figure 3.   The Beginning Contracting Steps When You Are Selling

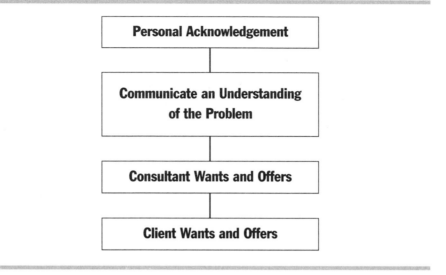

Personal Acknowledgement

Communicate an Understanding of the Problem

Consultant Wants and Offers

Client Wants and Offers

Selling Is Removing Obstacles More than Lighting Fires

We have all grown up with the image that a good salesperson is energetic, dynamic, quick with the words and phrases, and sincerely inspirational. This probably has some truth to it. Good salespeople are also people who are quiet, slow-moving, struggle to find the right words, and come across as nicely average. Both kinds are successful, but there is great overemphasis on personality as the key to selling. So people who come to my consulting workshops tend to think that good consultants have to have Charisma and Presence.

Charisma and Presence are two mythical virtues that are highly overrated. I must admit that I have a vested interest in downplaying Charisma and Presence. I am quiet, slow-moving, a struggler for words, and come across as nicely average. Workshop participants look at me and ask me if I have always been this way. I say, "What do you mean, this way?" They say, "Well, so low-keyed and half-asleep." Then they back off and think that my style is all by plan and design—that I am cooling it for the sake of their learning experience and that when I am out with clients I release the Mack truck idling underneath the surface. Of course, this is not true. We are the way we are. Their underlying concern is that there is a certain right kind of personality to do consulting, and this concern is heightened when it comes to selling. I don't believe it, and here is why.

If I have a service that responds to a real need in the client's organization, then I assume that there is a part of the client that would definitely like to say yes to my proposition. If I have assessed the need accurately and the client is denying the need or denying that my services can help the situation, then I ask, "What obstacles are in the way of the client trusting in what I offer?" If the client is saying no, I try to understand the nature of the resistance. Usually, it's:

They don't trust the competence or confidentiality of the department I represent.

They feel they will lose control if they say yes.

They feel they will become too vulnerable if they say yes.

They don't trust or respect me as a person.

They have had bad experiences in the past with something similar.

When I am selling a program and the client is resisting, the client's feelings give fire to the resistance. If I duck into a phone booth and step out magically equipped with my Charisma and Presence and really start "selling," I am just adding fuel to the fire. The client's resistance increases. My personality, high-keyed or low-keyed, is not the problem. The problem is that the client is not buying because negative feelings are saying to not trust me and what I am saying. The way out of the resistance is to help the client express directly, in words, the negative feelings. The more the client can express the feelings of distrust, the freer the client will be to really consider my offer on its merits. The more authentic I am, the more the client trusts me, the quicker the resistance disappears. So, here are some tips on what to do when you are selling your services.

Don't be any different when you are selling than when the client called you in.

Don't try to overcome the resistance with more explanations and pleas for the good of the organization.

Do help the client express the reservations about you and your product.

Do admit you are there to sell and want them to buy.

Do be authentic and follow the contracting sequence.

And, if you do all of this—and the reservations are expressed and there is trust in the relationship—and still get a no, then back off and reassess whether you have identified a real need and whether you are offering the right service. It is much better to lose the sale and maintain a solid relationship with the client than to keep pushing a sale that won't pan out.

A Comment on Time and Money

Clients often refuse a contract on the grounds that they do not have the money to go ahead with the project or the organization does not have the time to invest. Both of these are indirect reasons not to do something and I never take them at face value. These excuses are almost always a mask for the fact that the manager just doesn't want to do the project.

The problem here is one of motivation, not time or money. Managers spend their own and their organization's time on things they want to do. They spend money on things they want to do. They are managers, and they have control, and they pretty much do what they want—regardless of time and money. If they wanted to do your project, they would find a way. If you agree with them that time or money is the problem, you are just colluding with them in avoiding the real reason. Don't collude. Get to the real reason and you will have a better chance.

The Meeting As a Model of How You Work

Consulting is primarily an educational process. Line managers learn something about how to manage their organization or solve a technical problem as a result of their contact with you. Even if you are brought in on a highly technical problem, the manager can learn about approaching these kinds of problems from watching you. In fact, more is probably learned from watching consultants than from listening to them. This is why authentic behavior is an integral part of your consulting flawlessly.

You can use the contracting meeting as an example of how you work with clients. In this meeting, you are collecting data on the problem, testing out some of your own theories, and giving feedback to the manager on your reaction to it. You are also *jointly* defining the problem and making plans. When clients ask you how you would plan to work with their organizations, you can use the contracting meeting as a mini-example of your approach, pointing out that the whole project will follow these steps in a more elaborate way.

The clearer you are about your procedures, the more you help reduce client fears about loss of control and vulnerability. In cases where a manager was really having a hard time understanding how I could help—even after I've gone through the contracting meeting as an example of how I work—I have suggested that we engage in a very brief demonstration of what I do. The manager and I agree on a twenty-minute consultation, right now, during the contracting meeting. For the next twenty minutes, I will act as the manager's consultant on some problem of his or her choosing. At the end of twenty minutes, we will stop the mini-consultation and talk about the process we just went through. This method helps me explain and demonstrate how I work, and it helps the manager decide how it would feel to work with me and whether my orientation is what the manager is looking for.

Here's how a mini-consultation works.

The manager identifies a problem. I ask questions about the situation and react to the manager's way of looking at the problem and what the manager has tried to solve it. I focus on the manager's own role in the problem. Near the end of the twenty minutes, I give some feedback on his or her role in the problem, along with some recommendations based on the limited data generated in this discussion. We then stop the consultation. Before we go back to contracting, I ask the manager how the twenty-minute consultation felt. This experience gives both of us some data on what proceeding together on a project would look like.

A sample consultation like this is especially useful when the project is rather broad and ambiguous, and the manager is worried about losing control over the project. During your brief consultation, the manager has the opportunity to experience you as someone who is responsive and collaborative, yet who still has some different ways of looking at the world.

Closing the Contracting Meeting

Here are two other suggestions to keep in mind.

How to Measure Success

Ask how you and the client will know whether you are successful. It may be an unanswerable question, but at worst, it will clarify the manager's expectations. At best, it will give good guidance on how to structure the project.

Twenty Minutes Before the End of the Meeting

No contracting meeting should end without your asking for feedback about how the manager feels about the project, the meeting, and you. Ask, "How do you feel about the meeting—any reservations?" and "How do you feel about what I have said and my approach to this—any reservations, or unbridled enthusiasm?" Leave twenty minutes to discuss these questions. It may only take two minutes, but if the questions do uncover new issues, it's best to discuss them now.

After the Contracting Meeting

Checklist #2, Analyzing One of Your Contracts, gives you a way to summarize the agreements reached in a contracting meeting. Here are some questions you can ask after the meeting to get clear on how the *interaction* went with the client. The contracting meeting is a leading indicator of how the rest of the project is going to go. Examining your answers to these questions will give you an idea of what problems you are continually going to have to deal with on the project.

Checklist #4. Reviewing the Contracting Meeting

1. How would you rate?

	Client		Consultant
• Balance of participation?	100% _____	50/50 _____	100%
• Who initiated?	100% _____	50/50 _____	100%
• Who had control?	100% _____	50/50 _____	100%

2. What resistance or reservations did the client express?

   • Which did you explore directly, in words, with the client?

   • Which did you not really explore?

3. What reservations do you have about the contract?

   • Which did you put into words with the client?

   • Which did you express indirectly or not at all?

4. How did you give support to the client?

5. How were the client's concerns expressed:

   _____ Silence?

   _____ Compliance?

   _____ Attack?

   _____ Questions?

   _____ Giving answers?

   _____ Directly, in words?

6. What facial and body language did you observe?

7. How would you rate the client's motivation to proceed?

8. How would you rate your own motivation to proceed?

9. What didn't you express to the client?

10. Review "Navigating the Contracting Meeting." Did you skip any steps?

    • Which ones?

11. What would you do differently next time?

Chapter 6

The Agonies of Contracting

THERE ARE SOME particularly rough spots in contracting that are worth highlighting. The first is the difficult situation when the client is willing to go ahead with a project, but you know the client's motivation toward the project is low. Line managers take an unnatural stance when they proceed with a project that they don't really want to do. When they agree to do a project they don't want to do, it usually means that they were coerced to say yes. They may have been coerced by their boss, by their subordinates, or even by their difficulty in saying no to you, the consultant. You also may be acting out of pressure from your boss to go ahead with the project.

Dealing with Low Motivation

Figure 4 is a model to help you when you encounter low motivation.

Here is some guidance on each of the steps in dealing with low motivation.

1. If the client has low energy for the project, the first choice is to consider just not doing it.

   If you or the client feel you must go ahead with the project anyway . . .

2. Acknowledge, at least to yourself, that the project is beginning with coercion. Ask the client if he or she is feeling at all pressured to go ahead. Usually the client will own up to any feeling of pressure.

   When the client does acknowledge pressure . . .

3. Suggest that the client go back to the person exerting the pressure and renegotiate whether the project has to be done. The client may either agree to stop the project or change the form it is taking so that it feels more comfortable. If you are in an auditing or policing role and are the source of the pressure yourself, acknowledge that you realize the client has no choice but to work with you.

   If you must go ahead in the face of some pressure . . .

4. Contract with the client for a small-step project. Suggest that you and the client work together on a small piece of the total project, so that the client can get a feel for whether the process is as bad as it is feared to be. Usually if the client has some positive experience with you, concerns will go down.

   Acknowledge to the client that you are proceeding despite the low motivation, then . . .

5. Ask the client whether there is some way that you could proceed that would minimize his or her concerns. Clients' concerns are often about losing control or being vulnerable. So ask, "Is there some way we can set this up so that you don't feel you have given up too much control over the situation? Is there some way we can set it up so that your vulnerability is protected?" You can negotiate how to proceed on the project so that you still get what you need from it and the client doesn't feel like such a victim.

6. Hope for the best. These are tough contracts to manage. People in the auditing role are up against it all the time. The best thing they can do is to acknowledge the pressure and

Figure 4. Steps in Dealing with Low Motivation

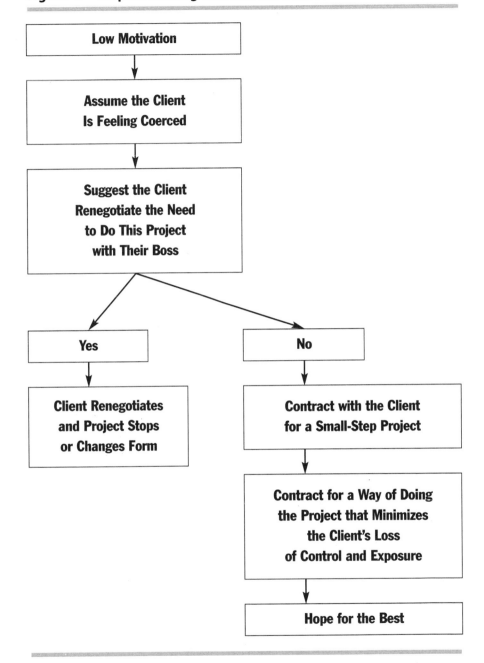

give the client support for the pickle they are in by helping the client put their feelings into words. There is not much more you can do except get on with it.

Ceaseless Negotiation— The Shifting Tide of Your Role

Consulting projects take place out in the world, in the middle of very political organizations, where the people and the pressures are constantly changing. So do some of the pieces of your consulting projects. Another thing that can change is the way you are dealt with by the client. Because the client both wants you on the project and at the same time wishes you to be more distant, your role definition with the client becomes subject to the process of ceaseless negotiation.

Sometimes a change in the project is very obvious: A new manager arrives, the budget is cut, findings in the middle of your audit indicate new problems. More often the changes are more subtle. Without your realizing it, the client has begun to treat you a little differently. You thought you were going to be invited to a meeting but weren't. The scheduling the client does for one of your meetings gets fouled up. These cues are harder to read but might indicate the need for some renegotiation.

Here's an example from my work with a large drug company. A large management development conference was planned for May. About seventy-five high level managers would attend, and the purpose was to have them do some joint problem solving on three critical new product introductions planned for the following year. It was now January and I was working with a planning committee in preparing for the May conference. The committee was made up of two line managers, Jim and Lou; a staff person, Rich; and myself, an outside consultant. Jim, Lou, and Rich were vice presidents, reporting to the president. I was primarily responsible for the detailed design and structuring of the meeting. The president had originally suggested having the May conference, so the committee knew we had his support. The committee had met several times, and I felt included in their process, really a part of the committee. The scene picks up on a bleary Tuesday morning in January.

Jim and Lou, the line executives, have been discussing how the top management group has been having a hard time getting its act together lately and that if they don't reach agreement on some things soon, they are going to look awfully foolish at the large meeting in May. Out of the discussion comes the fact that the president is part of the problem. He is very quiet, people don't know where they stand with him, and it's making everyone uncomfortable—and that discomfort is going to become obvious at the May meeting. Lou finally suggests that maybe we should postpone the May meeting until the management group is more ready. Jim says maybe it would be good for the management group to stumble in the May meeting, because then it would force them to work things out with the president. Rich, the staff person, says maybe we are making too much of a thing about the management group, the problems aren't that great and people might not notice.

Lou says stop the meeting, Jim says hold the meeting, and Rich says what's the real problem here, fellas, and our meeting goes round and round. I am strongly in favor of holding the meeting, but not with this cloud hanging over it. I finally suggest that we meet tomorrow, Wednesday, with the president, identify the problem in a general way, and suggest he deal with the problem before the May meeting. The president is quite unaware of the impact his quiet style is having on the group. I know this from other conversations I have had with him. There is a lot of discussion about my suggestion. Lou is worried he will be shot as the carrier of bad news; Jim says why not meet with him; Rich says well, if we could phrase it right and not make it too much of a problem, maybe it would be all right. Finally, after considerable pressure from me, the group agrees to meet with the president tomorrow at 4:00 to discuss the concern. I agree to present the idea and the others can chime in as they wish. As we are leaving, Lou says to me, "It's easy for you to push to confront the president because you don't work for him like the rest of us do." I agree with him, it is easier for me to do it, and that's the reason I suggested it. I left the meeting tired and with the feeling that meeting now with the president was the only rational way to resolve the question and unblock the committee so it could complete its task of planning the May meeting.

On Wednesday, I arrived early for the 4:00 meeting with the president and sat down to talk with Rich. After a little small talk, he says, "By the way, the 4 o'clock meeting was canceled." The committee had met first thing Wednesday morning and reconsidered the decision to meet with the president. Lou had thought it over and felt that it was too risky. Jim and Rich went along with him. So the committee is going to meet at 4:00 to proceed with the planning of the May conference.

Surprised, disappointed, a little angry, I meet with the committee at 4:00. I ask a lot of questions about why they canceled the meeting and what we are going to do about their original concerns for the May conference. Lou repeats his story about how risky it is to go to the president and what a vulnerable position that puts him in, reminding me once more that it was easy for me because I didn't live there—and besides the problem isn't as big as we made it out to be. There is some truth about Lou's concern about the risk. If he feels that vulnerable, he probably has reasons.

I figure I have done what I could and after letting them humor me for awhile, we finally go on to planning the May meeting. Rich makes a statement that one of these days, when the time is right, he will raise the subject of the management group's relationship with the president and see what kind of response he gets. It's a nice gesture, an offer we all silently know will never happen. The moment has passed, the meeting ended.

◆

I leave the meeting troubled about the whole thing and puzzled why I am troubled. I understand Lou's concern about the risk: I don't believe in taking blind risks. I know that the problem is not a crisis and business will go on as usual. An opportunity has been missed, but that happens every day.

After grousing around for a couple of hours, trying to pretend I'm really not upset, it starts to dawn on me what I'm really disturbed about. In the course of twenty-four hours, my role with that group has radically changed. When I left the meeting on Tuesday, I was a full-fledged member of the committee. I joined in the important decisions, and I had my share of influence, if not more than my share. I was where the action was. When I returned the next day, all that had changed. They had made a major strategy decision without me—not to meet with the president. And they had implemented that decision without me—they canceled the 4:00 meeting.

My role had changed in one day—from a person with full status as a committee member to someone who was merely informed of a decision and had to be appeased and cooled off. They hadn't called me to see whether I could make a morning meeting, they hadn't called me to discuss what to do over the phone, they hadn't called me to explain their change in strategy before they implemented it. I had turned from being a committee member to a specialist in charge of structuring the specifics of the May meeting. It happened right before my eyes, and I didn't even realize that my role had changed until three hours after the meeting. After getting clear on what happened, I met with Rich a couple of days later with the intent of renegotiating my role or contract with that group. We agreed I would be treated as a full member and it pretty much stayed that way through the rest of the project.

What is important about this incident is how quickly and subtly the consultant's contract can shift—which means that sustaining and renegotiating the agreement is a ceaseless process.

The timing of your renegotiation is also very important. It has to take place as soon as you sense the client is treating you differently, that something has changed. If you let it slide for awhile, it is much harder to sit down and discuss what happened a month ago. It was difficult to sit down with Rich and discuss what had happened three days ago. His first response was why didn't I bring it up at the meeting. It was a question I couldn't answer. I wish I *had* brought it up at the meeting, because then I could have renegotiated my role with the whole committee instead of just with Rich.

When your contract looks like it's starting to change or the client is changing some of the ground rules, your leverage on the situation is highest right at the moment of the change. The longer you wait to raise the issue of the client's wanting more or less from you, the more difficult it is to renegotiate your contract. Still, no matter how long the time lags, the discussion of a changed contract needs to take place. It helps a little when you know going into it that the contracting process takes place over and over through the life of the project. You are constantly recycling through different stages of the consultation, and negotiation really is ceaseless.

Some Other Specific Agonies

The Flirtatious Client

Sometimes you find out that you are the fourth person the manager has talked to about this project. You could respond to this by selling harder. An option is to ask the manager why a decision is so difficult. Preoccupation with the consultant selection process usually means the manager wants to start a project, but does not want anything to really happen. Otherwise, why control the process so meticulously?

Credentials? Still . . . at Your Age!

The questions come up, "What have you done elsewhere?" or "What are your credentials?" There are two responses to this kind of grilling. One is to have your favorite war story well-rehearsed and tell it. Your best hope is that it will speak to the client's situation. The second response, after the war story, is the question: "You are concerned about whether I can really help you?" If the manager owns up to being concerned, don't take it personally. Managers (no matter how burly or gruff) are likely to see themselves as beyond help. They need reassurance that improvement is possible. Give it to them. Don't get into a recital of degrees, clients, successes—defending your credentials.

Go-Betweens

Sometimes there is a go-between between the consultant and the manager, someone on the manager's staff or from another department. If the go-between is too active or protective, a screen is built up between you and the manager. It is hard to find out where things really stand through a screen. Urge for the manager's attendance at meetings with you to discuss the project.

Defining the Problem to Death— A Common Mistake

In conducting consulting skills workshops and watching hundreds of consultants try to deal with a resistant client, one mistake stands out clearly: We spend too much time in the contracting meeting trying to define the problem.

If we have a one-hour meeting, we will spend fifty minutes understanding the problem and leave only ten minutes to conduct the real business of the meeting—negotiating wants and dealing with concerns of control and exposure. This happens because during the meeting we can take on the confusion or obstinacy of the client. We aren't sure what to do next, so we keep asking questions about the problem. It provides a nice relief for us and the client.

Don't spend so much time figuring the problem out. You will have the whole consultation to do that. If you don't know what to do next, or if the meeting is going to pot:

1. Look at the client and say, "Let's stop talking about the problem for a moment. Tell me what you want from me." Or . . .

2. Look at the client and start making statements. Anything will do; it will lead you to where you ought to be going. Say,

"You seem confused about the nature of this problem," then, "Here is what I would like from you to help us take the next step." Then move into the exchange of wants.

Keep the discussion of the problem to no more than 35 percent of the total time for the meeting. If you really don't understand what the client sees as a problem, then negotiate a small contract to find out more about the problem. If you can't get clear after twenty minutes of meeting, you aren't going to get clear in the meeting no matter how many questions you ask.

The Bonner Case

Up to this point, we have covered some of the essentials of consulting skills: the phases of consulting, the steps in the contracting process and its recycling nature, plus the objective of maintaining a 50/50 balance in taking responsibility for the consulting action. What follows is a case study of a small consulting project. As you read through it, try and identify how Dave, the consultant, and Alan, the client, move through the entry, contracting, data collection, feedback, and decision-to-proceed phases of consulting. Also pay attention to the ceaseless negotiation over Dave's and Alan's roles.

THE BONNER CASE

By Mike Hill

Background Data: The Bonner case concerns a large manufacturing organization. It deals with the efforts of David Bell, an internal staff person, in responding to a request for assistance from Alan Kane, the manager of the company's engineering laboratory. Alan is one of six engineering managers who report to Tom Bonner, vice president for engineering.

The telephone rang. It was Alan Kane. The conversation went something like this.

Alan: I've got a problem, Dave. I think you can help me with this one.

Dave: What happened, Alan? Is Bonner boiling over again?

Alan: Something like that. I've just come from Bonner's staff meeting. He is very unhappy about our quarterly staff meetings.

Bonner holds weekly meetings with his staff (six unit managers who report to him). Every three months, he also holds an expanded staff meeting which is attended by all engineering management down to the first-line supervisors (about forty people). He has been using this expanded staff meeting to present general information concerning the company's financial health: the current business picture, new business plans, status of major programs, etc.

Dave: What's the matter with them?

Alan: Bonner feels they are dull and unproductive. He feels that first-line supervisors have information needs that are not being met and that the current meeting format is off target.

Dave: Do you agree?

Alan: Yes, they are on the dull side. I think what started this flap was that at the last meeting Bonner scheduled some time for a question-and-answer period. The staff has discussed a number of things that are bugging people, such as arbitrary cuts in labor estimates that cause cost overruns, differences in pay levels between this and other divisions, rumors about impending layoffs, and so on. Bonner feels they may have a lot of misinformation on these subjects, and he felt a question-and-answer period would help to straighten things out. Well, a few questions were asked—nothing of any significance—then there was an awkward silence. Bonner is unhappy about this. He wants something done.

Dave: Did he tell you what he wanted?

Alan: Not exactly. We discussed several ideas. None were acceptable. We ran out of time so it ended with my getting the job to present a proposal at the next meeting.

Dave: Why you?

Alan: Bonner knows I've been working with you to revise my staff meeting format. He questioned me about what we have done. To make a long story short, I got the job—I'm now a meeting expert.

Dave: Your staff meeting and the quarterly meeting are not the same thing at all.

Alan: Right. That's why I want to get you on this—today. Dave, I've given you all the information I have. I want you to put together a proposal on this for me. I'm really bogged down right now, but I can see you Wednesday.

Dave: Hold it, Alan. I can't write a proposal in the dark. I'll need some data. Look, I don't think we can work this on the phone. Why don't I come over and we'll talk.

Alan: Dave, I'm really tied up for time. I've told you all I know. This will be an easy one for you.

Dave: Alan, if this were easy, you wouldn't have called me. I'll be glad to help, but we need to talk.

Alan: OK. If you insist. Come over after lunch.

Dave: How about 4:30? I'll need at least an hour—maybe more—with no phone calls, side meetings, or other interruptions. OK?

Alan: OK. See you at 4:30.

Dave met with Alan as agreed. He began by summarizing their telephone conversation. Alan has a flip chart in his office, so at the end of Dave's brief summary, he walked up to the flip chart and wrote:

OBJECTIVE: Create a meeting format that will speak to the information needs of our first-line supervisors.

Dave: This is a one sentence summary of what I heard, right?

Alan: Right. That's about it.

Dave: OK. Let's brainstorm some ways to do this.

As they talked, Dave listed each item on the flip chart. They quickly came up with a dozen ideas. Then they went back over each item to test for feasibility. Time was the toughest factor to deal with. The quarterly staff meeting was two weeks off, leaving them little time for any data

gathering from the first-line supervisors. One item, however, had possibilities. Dave underlined it on the flip chart: "Ask first-line supervisors for agenda items that Bonner would speak to."

Dave: With the time constraints we have, this is the only one we can work with. Do you agree?

Alan: Yes. I think we can work with it. I like the logic. It's simple: If you want to speak to their information needs, a good place to start is to ask them what their information needs are. We learned something like this working with my staff—remember?

Dave and Alan discussed the pros and cons awhile and decided they would give this idea a try for several reasons.

1. It would ensure that they would be speaking to the information needs of the first-line supervisors (Bonner's criterion).

2. It would provide a good test for Bonner's notion that "they have information needs we are not dealing with."

3. It wouldn't eat up a lot of the supervisors' time.

4. It could be done in the time available.

Dave: OK. This is a start. But I think we should consider some of the conditions Bonner and the staff will have to accept to give this approach a chance.

Alan: Meaning what?

Dave: Meaning we better spell out some ground rules. For example, answering questions takes time. Bonner will have to agree to spend the time required.

Alan and Dave talked along these lines awhile. As they talked, Dave made notes on a flip chart. Their final list was as follows:

1. Staff must agree to spend time required.

2. There may be some tough questions. Bonner would have to agree to provide straightforward answers.

3. **There would be no screening, editing, or elimination of any question submitted.**

4. **Each manager would have to agree to gather agenda items from his or her own people and turn them into Bonner one week before the meeting. This would have to be a firm deadline.**

At this point, they had been talking for about an hour and Alan suggested they call it a day.

Alan: OK, Dave. I think we have it. There is enough here for you to write a proposal.

Dave: Alan, we have a good start, but we're not finished. We don't have time to go back and forth on this. More important, for me, is that this has to be your proposal—not mine.

Alan: Look, Dave, you can take it from here. Write it up just the way we discussed it. We don't have to go back and forth with this. You can write it up and present it to the staff.

Dave: Hold it. I thought I was working with you on this. If I present it, that puts me in the middle—it's a "can't win" position for me. I'll go to the staff meeting with you, if you like, but I think it would be a mistake for me to take the lead on this.

Alan: You're making a mountain out of a molehill.

Dave: Maybe so, but my experience with Bonner tells me to be cautious. Look, we have an outline for a proposal. Let's do it now.

Alan: We don't have a proposal. All we have is an outline.

Dave: Right. I suggest you present it just as we developed it so you get some staff involvement.

Alan: Won't that take a lot of time?

Dave: The discussion will take a little time. But if this is as important as Bonner says it is, he'll have to agree to spend some time with it. If he can't spend the time, let's put it off until he has the time.

Alan: You're playing with fire! Bonner expects a proposal—in writing.

Dave: We have a proposal. Let's write it down right now.

Alan: OK. Let's get on with it.

They wrote down their five-point proposal.

1. A general statement

2. Objectives (what they were trying to do)

3. Procedures (how they proposed to do it)

4. Ground rules (conditions that need to be understood and accepted)

5. Follow-up (how they would check on results)

They agreed that Alan would present each of the items listed. They would be presented as points of departure for staff discussion, for a decision to be made after the discussion.

Bonner's staff meeting started on schedule. After the normal staff meeting agenda was completed, Alan started his presentation.

Alan: At the last meeting, I was asked to come up with a new format for our quarterly staff meeting. I've asked Dave to help me with this and we have a proposal for your consideration. It may be best to start with a statement of the goal we used to guide our thinking.

Alan distributed the first sheet.

OBJECTIVE: Create a meeting format that will speak to the information needs of our first-line supervisors.

Alan: This is what I heard at our last meeting. We assumed that some time would be used to present general program information as in past meetings—say, forty-five minutes for this—and the remainder of the meeting—one hour or more—would be used in a question-and-answer session.

Jim: I'm not convinced we need a new format. Dave, what evidence do you have that a question-and-answer session is needed?

Dave: I have no evidence.

Jim: Then why are you proposing this?

Dave: There may be some misunderstanding about my role in this project. I was asked to help Alan develop a new meeting format using this objective as one the staff had agreed on. If this is not so, we need to find out before we go on. Jim, I don't know if you need a new format. I thought you had already decided this.

Bonner: No. That would take too long. Jim, I don't have any hard data on this. What I have is a gut feeling based on some information discussions. I want to try this as a test. I thought I heard agreement on this at our last meeting.

Several staff members nodded in agreement.

Dave: It is important, to me, that I not be seen as pushing for a change. I am not. I think it would be out of line for me to do so. I am here to answer any questions about the ideas Alan and I put together, which were based on this objective as a given. I need to hear a clear signal on this from all of you. Is this your objective?

Staff: Agreed.

Alan: OK. Using this statement as our goal, we developed a procedure to get at questions of concern to the first-line supervisors.

Alan distributed the second sheet.

PROCEDURE

1. **Inform first-line supervisors that the next meeting will be in two parts:**

   a. **General program and new business data, and**

   b. **A question-and-answer session.**

2. **Agenda for the question-and-answer session will consist of questions submitted by the first-line supervisors.**

3. **No restriction on type of question.**

4. **Questions submitted will not be edited and none deleted. They will be placed on the agenda as submitted.**

5. **Bonner will speak to all questions submitted.**

Alan: Concerning the first and second items, I think we should tell it like it is: Bonner feels they have questions that need discussion. The staff agrees. We want to provide an opportunity for two-way discussion on questions of concern to them.

Concerning the remaining items, are there any questions?

Jim: Item 4 could cause all kinds of problems. If each person asked only two questions, this could add up to a hundred questions. Dave, did you think of that?

Dave: Yes. We discussed it at length. The fact is discussion takes time. There is no way around it. We need to be clear on this. Unless the staff is prepared to spend the time needed, I would recommend against a question-and-answer format.

Jim:	Dave, how much time do you think it might take?
Dave:	I don't know.
Jim:	What would you do if the number of questions added up to a three-hour session?
Dave:	I would hand the problem back to the first-line supervisors. I would tell them, "After looking over your questions, we have estimated a three-hour session. We are prepared to stay if you are." If they agree, there is no problem. If they think this is too long, fine—I'd ask them what they want us to do. I think they should be told this is their session and that they will have to accept some responsibility for it.
Bonner:	I don't think we'll get three or four hours of questions. If we do, we can ask them to rank order the questions. We can then speak to as many as we can in an hour or so and schedule another meeting to deal with the remaining questions. Jim, I know there are some unknowns here, but I want to give this a try.
Alan:	We considered the time-consuming aspects of this. I think there will be some closely related questions and some duplications. I think the time needed will be manageable.
Jim:	I think we should screen the questions for duplications.
Alan:	We discussed screening and rejected it because of the possible bad impression. Screening will tell them, in effect, we want to answer your questions but we'll decide which questions to deal with. I don't think this is the impression we want to make.
Jim:	I agree. I didn't mean to eliminate any questions. I meant to group related questions and list them as submitted.
Alan:	Are you volunteering to do the grouping?
Jim:	I will if you will.
Alan:	OK. Jim and I will review the questions and group related questions.
Dave:	No eliminations? No rewording?
Alan:	Right. No eliminations. No changes.

Dave: Do you all agree with this?

Staff: Agreed.

Bonner: OK. Let's get on with it. I'll expect each of you to get your questions into Jane by Friday. Jane will call Jim and Alan when they are all in and they can do the grouping.

Alan: I have one more item. We discussed doing a follow-up check to get their reactions. We need to know if they see this as a useful exercise.

Bonner: Dave, what's a fast way to do this?

Dave: I can help Jim and Alan prepare a brief questionnaire they could complete at the end of the meeting.

Bonner: Do you all agree with that?

Staff: Agreed.

Bonner: OK. Do it. I'll see you on Friday.

◆

A Look into the Bonner Case

The Bonner case takes us through a brief consulting assignment. There are some important events in it that are worth highlighting as a review of the 50/50 consulting process.

Important elements of the entry phase have been taken care of before the case begins. Dave and Alan already have a good working relationship and they have recent experience working in a collaborative mode. Nevertheless, Alan has expectations that Dave does not want to fulfill, and getting clarity around Alan's expectations becomes the first order of business for Dave. Entry in this case begins with Alan's statement: "I've got a problem, Dave. I think you can help me with this one."

The first part of the dialogue is a discussion of the "presenting" problem—dull, unproductive staff meetings. In the exchange that follows, Dave tries to get at Alan's perception of the problem— Who is involved?, Who will be the client?, and What kind of help is needed. This constitutes the initial data collection. In this case, it took five minutes. In other cases, it may take six months before the consultant can get a clear picture of what's going on.

When Dave asks for a meeting with Alan, he has, in effect, made a decision to accept the task and he has identified Alan as the client. This "identifying the client" is a critical issue in the entry phase. The consultant needs to clarify and get agreement on mutual expectations before any work is done. As is almost always the case, Dave's identification of Alan as the client is tentative. This issue comes up again later in the dialogue, as we shall see.

Contracting begins when Alan says, "Dave, I've given you all the information I have. I want you to put together a proposal on this for me. I'm really bogged down right now, but I can see you Wednesday." In this statement, Alan expresses a role expectation for Dave and suggests a deadline for meeting that expectation. This is a crucial decision point for Dave. If he accepts the task defined by Alan, he has in effect agreed to act as a pair-of-hands. Once this kind of contract is made, it's almost impossible to change.

Dave responds with his own conception of his role and how he wants to work with Alan. He states, clearly, that he doesn't want to write the proposal alone, that he doesn't have enough data, that he doesn't want to work further on the telephone, and that he doesn't want to wait until Wednesday before taking the next step.

There is nothing in Dave's seemingly incessant demands that communicates he doesn't want to work on the project, that he doesn't care about Alan, or that he isn't open to influence. These are the fantasies that most of us have when we try to avoid being used as a pair-of-hands and take an assertive stance about our role. Dave gets agreement to work *with* Alan on Alan's problem. The distinction is significant. The word *contract* hasn't been used but, clearly, a contract has been made.

With the entry and contracting out of the way and initial data collection completed, they move on to the feedback stage, which in this case is expressed in one sentence: "Objective: Meeting format that will speak to the information needs of our first-line supervisors." This is a more operational statement of the presenting problem (unproductive staff meetings).

The discussion then turns to planning the main event. A key part of this planning is to spell out the minimum conditions for success, in effect, outlining the contract that must be made with Bonner and the staff.

As they move through this phase, Dave is trying to do two things: (1) help Alan solve the immediate problem, and (2) provide his help in such a way that Alan (and maybe Bonner and his staff) can learn something about how to handle problems like this in the future.

What is being taught about solving this kind of problem? First, that when trying to manage the communication process in a large organization, at least 50 percent of the action must be in the hands of the people in the lower-power positions. Second, that some kind of special structure needs to be designed so that concerns can get expressed freely. For people in lower-power positions to assert themselves, they need visible signs that their stating their needs—especially those that question management actions—will not be punished, but rather will be rewarded.

Back to the case. After they agree on an action plan, Dave and Alan once again find themselves contracting over their roles. Alan wants Dave to present the proposal to the staff. Dave objects: "If I present it, that puts me in the middle—it's a 'can't win' position for me." Dave insists that Alan is the client, that he (Dave) has no contract with Bonner or the staff.

They also disagree over the stance to be taken with Bonner. Can they collaborate with him and engage in joint planning with the staff, or do they present Bonner with "completed staff work?" The result is a compromise: Dave gets the proposal in writing and Alan agrees to present it as a point of departure for discussion and decision, not as a final proposal.

In the meeting with Bonner, the problem of "who is the client" comes up again. So, the cycle of contracting, data collection, and planning begins again. A critical incident occurs when Jim says, "I'm not convinced we need a new format. Dave, what evidence do you have that a question-and-answer session is needed?" The issue is one of getting clarity on who is taking responsibility for the change.

Instead of trying to persuade or convince the staff, Dave puts the responsibility back on Bonner, where it belongs, since he started the whole thing in the first place. "If this is not so, now is the time to find out"—Dave states his contract with Alan and asks for confirmation. With this settled (temporarily, as always), the discussion proceeds on a procedural level. When Jim agrees to participate in the grouping of the questions, this is a clear signal that the goal of collaboration has been accomplished.

It is clear that the original problem of dull staff meetings has been redefined as a problem of trust and honest dialogue between Bonner and his staff and between the managers and the supervisors. Jim's persistent questions reflect the resistance of the mangers to changing the conversation with the supervisors. Although Jim was the outspoken one, he was also expressing the doubts of the others. It is important to realize that Jim's vocal objections are condoned by the quietness of the others. This keeps us from branding Jim as the problem.

The meeting moved on as Jim yielded, but the issue is not gone. At some point Dave will have to raise the deeper question of whether Bonner and the staff want a workplace where questions and doubts are expressed. In the narrowness of the presenting problem, the larger issue can always be found. Part of the consultant's job is to understand this and to help the client see the deeper question and make a choice.

Chapter 7
The Internal Consultant

WHEN I RUN workshops on consulting skills for internal consultants, the participants sit patiently and listen to me lecture on "Saying No to a Manager," and "Confront Problems with the Manager as They Happen," and "Make Your Own Wants and Demands Clear," and "Deal Directly with the Politics of the Situation." Eventually, someone in the back of the room raises a hand and says, "That's easy for you to say. You're an outside consultant. You don't have to live inside the organization you are consulting to. We are internal staff consultants. If a line manager gets mad at us, we are in trouble. You just don't understand what it's like."

I used to resist. I would say the issues are the same. They have to do the same things I do with clients, and on and on and on. The group would then lean back, I would announce a coffee break, and they would talk excitedly to each other and ignore me. I don't resist anymore. Partly it is to avoid rejection. I also have clearer ideas about how internal and external consulting are in some ways different. Some of the noticeable differences are listed in Figure 5.

Important Differences Between Internal and External Consultants

As an internal consultant, you are at every moment embedded in some part of the hierarchy and the current politics of the organization. You have a boss you must satisfy (at least to some extent). Your own department has certain goals it must achieve. Technical departments have a new process they want to introduce to the manufacturing plants. Financial groups want new control procedures adopted.

How does having a boss and having departmental objectives affect the way internal consultants work and contract with line managers?

1. It is often not possible to respond just to the line manager's own wants and needs. You have procedures that you want the line manager to adopt that may be in conflict with what the manager's own philosophy and style are.

2. Internal consultants may get evaluated on how many managers adopt the staff group's programs. You are often asked to sell your own department's approach, and the pressure to do this can be immense.

3. Internal consultants are often expected to convert an adversary. A certain line manager may have rejected your department's services for years, but it is up to you to bring him or her into the fold.

4. Having one key manager angry at you can be a disaster. The potential number of clients is limited to the managers in one organization. If you blow one or two jobs, word can get around fast and the demand for your services can disappear quickly. If this happens, you are out of a job, even if they keep you on the payroll.

5. The internal consultant has a status and job level that is known to most people in the organization. This can limit your access to key, high-level people you should be contact-

ing directly. An external consultant's status and level are more ambiguous, so they can bounce around from level to level more easily.

6. The difficulty of being a "prophet in your own land" is overplayed and can be used as a defense, but there is some truth in it. Because you work for the same organization, line managers can see you as being captured by the same forces and madness that impinge on them. Thus, they may be a little slower to trust you and recognize that you have something special to offer them.

What this means is that internal consultants are often operating more by mandate than by choice. This makes internal contracting a higher-risk proposition. In the end all the internal consultant can do is make explicit the costs of mandated change. Just because you do not have the final say is not a reason to avoid the argument.

The external consultant faces most of these issues, but they do not have the same intensity. Being outside the organization, there is a potentially wider market for my services, and as long as my clients are happy with me, my own consulting organization is unlikely to complain.

The difference in intensity and setting for these issues makes the internal consultant's position more delicate and more vulnerable. This creates constraints on how internal consultants contract with clients and how much risk they feel willing to take in giving honest feedback. If the constraints lead to very cautious behavior in the long run, the internal consultant can come to be used only as a pair-of-hands. If they ignore the constraints altogether, internal consultants may be seen as immature and disloyal, not "sensitive to how we operate around here."

The consulting approach described in this book is a way for internal consultants to operate in the realm of higher risk/higher payoff

Figure 5.   Noticeable Differences Between Internal and External Consultants

	Internal Consultants	External Consultants
Clothing	• Blue and gray suits, skirts and jackets, occasional sport clothes depending on company, high-end country club business casual on specified days	• Sweaters, turtlenecks, slacks, pinpoint cotton shirts, sport coats, browns and greens, occasional gold bracelet or Buddhist prayer beads obtained at global spiritual retreat
Favorite Words	• Measurement • Long run • Quick • Practical • Objectives • Background • Cost	• That raises an interesting issue • Fundamental and underlying • Deal • Honor your integrity • Work through • Dilemma • Model • Implications • Reassess at some point in the process
Personal Life	• Reasonably stable, responsible, and rewarding. Only one divorce, and maintaining good relations with first spouse and kids	• Like Hiroshima right after the bomb. Has seen the world but can't remember it
Fantasy Life	• Wish for the freedom and variety of the external consultant	• Wish for the continuity and stability of the internal consultant
Underlying Anxiety	• Being ignored, rejected, and treated as unimportant	• Being ignored, rejected, and treated as unimportant

and still maintain the respect and appreciation of clients. After all, all you have to do is consult flawlessly. The rest of this chapter describes a few things to be especially careful about if you are an internal consultant.

Triangles and Rectangles

The meeting with a line manager as a client is often only the beginning of the contracting process. At a minimum the internal staff person must also contract with his or her own supervisor.

Bosses

Each staff consulting group—whether it is a technical engineering group, a financial auditing group, a personnel group, a corporate staff group—has its own priority projects it is pushing this year, and it has policies about the nature of consulting that should be done. Technical organizations have certain innovative manufacturing processes they want their technical consultants to sell to the plants. Marketing groups have certain pricing strategies to be sold to their clients. Each staff group has agreed to meet some objectives that its internal consultants will have to advocate to its client line managers. Thus, often consultants must both serve the needs of the client and fulfill a contract with their own management to implement these priorities. This forces the boss into the contracting process and means internal consultants are always in at least a triangular contract.

Figure 6.   A Triangular Contract

Consultant's Boss

Consultant   **Client**

Sometimes the contract is a rectangle or even a pentagon.

The rectangular contract can begin with a general understanding between the consultant's boss and the client's boss.

Figure 7.   A Rectangular Contract

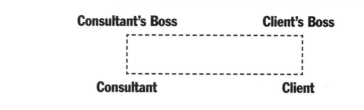

This means the consultant is showing up for work with the client in a situation in which neither of them has particularly chosen the consultation, and yet they have a given commitment to begin. The effect of this situation is to prolong the contracting phase. It is desirable for the consultant to meet with each party of the contract to clarify expectations. Sometimes this may not be possible, but at a minimum you can know what you are up against and not treat the contracting as a simple process. Each side of the rectangle or triangle needs to be explored before the data collection begins.

Your Boss's Expectations

As it turns out, when you include all parties in the contracting framework, many seeming problems between internal consultants and their clients are merely symptoms of problems between internal consultants and their own bosses. The boss can have expectations of a consultant that you cannot fulfill. You may feel that you can never say no, or that you have to convert very difficult clients.

I asked one group of engineering consultants what messages their own organization sends about how to conduct their business. Their answers form a set of norms around internal consulting.

No matter what, get the job done.

If the technical issue is that important, don't worry about the sensitivities of the client.

Don't upset or antagonize the client.

Stay long enough to do the job, but don't stay too long.

Convince the client to do what you recommend. Sell the "company way."

Every problem can be solved.

Every client can be "reached" if the consultant is really on the ball.

Be loyal to your own organization.

Don't wash dirty linen in public.

Don't evaluate people or bad-mouth anyone.

Never admit a mistake to a client.

Contracts with clients should be very, very flexible.

Don't make any commitments for future work.

Keep personalities out of it.

Always stay low-key and smooth. No emotion.

Have suitcase, will travel.

Act with dignity, tact, confidence, and decorum.

This list of expectations, of course, represents unrealistic pressures that consultants can feel: They are not all the spoken words of any one supervisor. They do represent the quandary that an internal consultant is in when the contract with his or her boss is not clear and explicit.

Contracts with Your Boss

When we talk about contracting with clients in a consulting skills workshop, it's not surprising that the participants in the workshop soon turn to a discussion of their contracts with their supervisors. The first step in contracting is to identify what you want, so we asked a group of internal consultants what they wanted from their bosses in order to deal with the pressures they were under. Here is what they said.

A clear definition of the job before I am sent out on a project

Access to the boss

Assistance on the nontechnical and political elements of the project

Don't overcommit me all the time

Freedom to negotiate contracts based on the particulars of the situation

Minimum bias on how the project should turn out, what the recommendations should look like

The same group of consultants identified what they wanted from their clients. Notice how similar the lists are.

A clear definition of the job

Access to the person who really represents the client organization, also access to data

Work the problem together—cooperation

Commitment to the project

Share the blame and glory

To be wanted. To feel useful

No bias about the outcome

Take care of physical needs to accomplish the job

Openness and feedback

Feedback on what happened after I left

The clarity of understanding and agreement with your boss greatly affects your ability to respond appropriately and flawlessly with your clients. If you are unclear about the contract with your boss, you will tend to get involved in soft contracts with clients. There will be a tendency to give in to clients too easily, to be unwilling to back away from projects that have a low chance of success. You also may find yourself pressuring for your own staff organization's priorities past the point of reasonableness, and this will distance you from your clients.

Try this exercise.

First, list the key wants you have of your boss. Then ask your boss to make a list of the key wants he or she has of you. After you have both completed your lists, exchange lists and then meet together to see whether you can agree on a contract that represents a reasonable balance between what your group or department requires to meet its commitments to the overall organization and what you need to be responsive to the needs and priorities of your clients.

If the conversation does not go well, you are ready for the next two chapters—on understanding and dealing with resistance.

Chapter 8

Understanding Resistance

THE HARDEST PART of consulting is coping successfully with resistance from the client. As we consult, it is natural for us to feel that if we can present our ideas clearly and logically, and if we have the best interests of the client at heart, our clients will accept our expertise and follow our suggestions. We soon discover that, no matter how reasonably we present data and recommendations, clients present us with resistance.

Resistance doesn't always happen, but when it does, it is puzzling and frustrating. In the face of resistance, we begin to view the client as stubborn and irrational, and we usually end up simply presenting the data and justifying the recommendations more loudly and more forcibly.

The key to understanding the nature of resistance is to realize that resistance is a reaction to an emotional process taking place within the client. It is not a reflection of the conversation we are having with the client on an objective, logical, rational level. Resistance is a predictable, natural, emotional reaction against the process of being helped and against the process of having to face up to difficult organizational problems.

Resistance is a predictable, natural, and necessary part of the learning process. When as consultants we wish resistance would never appear or would just go away, we are, by that attitude, posing an obstacle to the client's really integrating and learning from our expertise. For a client to learn something important about how to handle a difficult problem, the feelings of resistance need to be expressed directly before the client is ready to genuinely accept and use what the consultant has to offer.

The skill in dealing with resistance is to:

Be able to identify when resistance is taking place

View resistance as a natural process and a sign that you are on target

Support the client in expressing the resistance directly

Not take the expression of the resistance personally or as an attack on you or your competence.

This is hard to do and is what this chapter and the next are all about.

The Faces of Resistance

Resistance takes many forms, some of them very subtle and elusive. In the course of a single meeting, you may encounter a variety of forms. As you begin to deal with it in one form, sometimes it will fade and reappear in a different body.

For technically oriented consultants—such as engineers, accountants, computer and systems people—resistance can be very hard to identify. Our technical backgrounds so orient us to data, facts, and logic that when we are asked to perceive an emotional or interpersonal process, it is like trying to see the picture on a badly out-of-focus piece of movie film.

The following list of common forms of resistance, though incomplete, is intended to help bring the picture into focus.

Give Me More Detail

The client keeps asking for finer and finer bits of information. "What do people who work the eleven-to-seven shift think?" "When you put the numbers together, what work sheets did you use and were the numbers written in red or blue ink?" The client seems to have an insatiable appetite to know everything about what is happening. No matter how much information you give the client, it is never enough. Each conversation leaves you feeling like next time you should bring even more backup data with you. You also get the feeling that a huge amount of time is spent gathering information and too little time is spent deciding what you are going to do. Some questions from the client are reasonable; they need to know what is going on. When you start to get impatient with the questions, even though you are able to answer them, that is the moment to start suspecting the request for detail is a form of resistance and not a simple quest for information.

Flood You with Detail

A corollary to the request for detail is to be given too much detail. You ask a client how this problem got started and the response is, "Well, it all got started ten years ago on a Thursday afternoon in September. I think I was wearing a blue sweatshirt and the weather outside was overcast and threatening rain. I hope I am not boring you, but I think it is important for you to understand the background of the situation." The client keeps giving you more and more information, which you understand less and less. The moment you start to get bored or confused about what all this has to do with the problem at hand, you should begin to suspect that what you are getting is resistance and not just an effusive attempt to give you all the facts.

Time

The client says she would really like to go ahead with your project but the timing is just a little off. You are kept on the string, but the client keeps impressing you with how busy things are right now. In fact, she barely has time to meet with you. Sometimes this form of resistance gets expressed by constant interruptions during your meetings. The client starts taking phone calls or having the secretary come in. Or someone sticks his head in the office and the client turns to me and says, "Excuse me just a minute, Pete, but I have to settle this one issue with Ann." And the client starts talking to Ann while I sit there.

The message the client seems to be giving in all these examples?

> This organization is such an exciting place to work in, something is going on all the time. Aren't you impressed and don't you wish you worked here, too?

> My organization has so little time.

> I have so little time.

> I want you to think I am refusing you because of the lack of time, and not because your proposal gives me feelings of great discomfort.

The whole time issue, which we all face every day, is most often resistance against the client's having to tell you how he or she really feels about your project. When you find in December that the client would really like to do the project, but can't get started until the third quarter of next year, you should begin to suspect you are encountering resistance.

Impracticality

The client keeps reminding you that they live in the "Realworld and are facing Realworld problems." I must have heard about the Realworld a thousand times—it makes me wonder where clients think consultants live. This form of resistance from the client accuses us of being impractical and academic. As with many forms of resistance, there may be some truth in the statement, but then there is some truth in almost any statement. It is the intensity of the emphasis on "practicality" that leads you to suspect you are up against an emotional issue.

I'm Not Surprised

It is always amazing to me how important it is for people not to be surprised. It seems that whatever happens in the world is OK as long as they are not surprised. When you have completed a study, you can tell a manager that the building has collapsed, the workers have just walked out, the chief financial officer has just run off with the vice president of marketing, and the IRS is knocking on the door, and the manager's first response is, "I'm not surprised." It's like being surprised is the worst thing in the world that could happen. The manager's fear of surprise is really the desire to always be in control. When we run into it, it is kind of deflating. It can signal to us that what we have developed is really not that important or unique and downplay our contribution. See the client's desire not to be surprised for what it is—a form of resistance and not really a reflection on your work.

Attack

The most blatant form of resistance is when the client attacks us. With angry words, a red face, pounding his fist on the desk, pointing her finger in your face, punctuating the end of every sentence. It leaves the consultant feeling like a bumbling child who not only has done poor work, but has somehow violated a line of morality that should never be crossed. Our response to attack is often either to withdraw or to respond in kind. Both responses mean that we are beginning to take the attack personally and not seeing it as one other form the resistance is taking.

Confusion

Whenever a client comes to us for help, the client is experiencing some legitimate confusion. This may not be resistance, but just a desire for clarity. After things become clear to you, however, and you explain it two or three times, and the client keeps claiming to be confused or not understand, start to think that confusion may be this client's way of resisting.

Silence

This is the toughest of all. We keep making overtures to the client and get very little response in return. The client is passive. A client may say they have no particular reaction to what you are proposing. When you ask for a reaction, he says, "Keep on going, I don't have any problems with what you are saying. If I do, I'll speak up." Don't you believe it. Silence never means consent. If you are dealing with something important to the organization, it is not natural for the client to have no reaction. Silence means that the reaction is being blocked. For some people, silence or withholding reactions is really a fight style. They are saying by their actions, "I am holding on so tightly to my position and my feelings, that I won't even give you words." Beware the silent client. If you think a meeting went smoothly because the manager didn't raise any objections, don't trust it. Ask yourself whether the client gave you any real support or showed any real enthusiasm or got personally involved in the action. If there were few signs of life, begin to wonder whether silence was the form the client's resistance was taking.

Intellectualizing

When a person shifts the discussion from deciding how to proceed and starts exploring theory after theory about why things are the way they are, you are face to face with intellectualizing as resistance. The client says, "A fascinating hypothesis is implied by these results. I wonder if there is an inverse relationship between this situation and the last three times we went under. The crisis seems to have raised a number of questions."

Spending a lot of energy spinning theories is a way of taking the pain out of a situation. It is a defense most of us use when we get into a tight spot. This is not to knock the value of a good theory or the need to understand what is happening to us. It is a caution against colluding with the client in engaging in ceaseless wondering when the question is whether you and the client are going to be able to face up to a difficult situation. The time to suspect intellectualizing is when it begins at a high-tension moment or in a high-tension meeting. When this happens, your task is to bring the discussion back to actions, away from theories.

Moralizing

Moralizing resistance makes great use of certain words and phrases: "those people" and "should" and "they need to understand." When you hear them being used, you know you are about to go on a trip into a world of how things ought to be, which is simply a moralizing defense against reality. People use the phrase "those people" about anyone who's not in the room at the time. It is a phrase of superiority used in describing people who (1) are usually at a lower organizational level than the speaker, or (2) are unhappy about something the speaker has done and, therefore, "really don't understand the way things have to be."

Phrases of superiority are actually ways of putting oneself on a pedestal. Pedestal sitting is always a defense against feeling some uncomfortable feelings and taking some uncomfortable actions.

The phrase "they need to understand" means "I understand—they don't. Why don't they see things clearly and with the same broad perspective that I do? Ah, the burdens of knowing are great and unceasing!" Frequently "those people" the speaker is talking about do understand. They understand perfectly. The problem (for the speaker) is that they don't agree. So instead of confronting the conflict in views, the speaker escapes into a moralistic position.

Moralizing can be seductive to the consultant. The moralizing manager is inviting you to join him or her in a very select circle of people who know what is best for "those people" and who know what they "need to understand." This is an elite position to be in; it has the feeling of power and it is well-protected—if the rest of the organization does not appreciate what you do, this is just further indication how confused they are and how much more they need you! Resist the temptation with as much grace and persistence as possible.

Compliance

The most difficult form of resistance to see comes from the compliant manager who totally agrees with you and eagerly wants to know what to do next. It is hard to see compliance as resistance because you are getting exactly what you want—agreement and respect. If you really trust the concept that in each manager there is some ambivalence about your help, then when you get no negative reaction at all, you know something is missing.

Each client has some reservations about a given course of action. If the reservations don't get expressed to you, they will come out somewhere else, perhaps in a more destructive way. I would rather the reservations were said directly to me; then I can deal with them. You can tell when the agreeable client is resisting by compliance. You are getting this form of resistance any time there is almost total absence of any reservations and a low energy agreement. If the agreement is made with high energy, and enthusiasm and sincere understanding of what we are facing, you might simply feel lucky and not take it as resistance, even if there are few reservations expressed. But beware the client who expresses a desire to quickly get to solutions without any discussion of problems—also the client who acts very dependent on you and implies that whatever you do is fine.

Methodology

If there has been elaborate data collection in your project, the first wave of questions will be about your methods. If you administered a questionnaire, you will be asked about how many people responded, at what level of response, and whether the findings are statistically significant at the .05 level. Next will be questions about how people in the guardhouse and on the night shift responded.

Questions about method represent legitimate needs for information for the first ten minutes. Ten minutes is enough for you to establish the credibility of the project if the questions are really for information. As the questions about method go past the ten-minute mark, you should cautiously begin to view them as resistance. The purpose of the meeting is not to grill you on methods; you probably got out of school some time ago. The purpose of the meeting is to understand the problem and decide what to do about it. Repeated questions about method or suggestions of alternate methods can serve to delay the discussion of problems and actions.

Flight into Health

Undoubtedly the most subtle form of resistance occurs when, somewhere in the middle or toward the end of the project, it appears that the client no longer has the problem that you were addressing in the first place. As you get closer and closer to the time for the client to face the issue and act on the problem, you begin to hear about how much better things seem to be getting.

Here are some variations on this theme.

If profits were bad when you started the project, as soon as they start to pick up a little, the manager comes to you and says that people seem to be feeling better now that the profit picture has improved. Maybe the need for your services has diminished somewhat.

You talk to the client in May and agree to start the project on June 20. When you call on June 10 to confirm the beginning of the project, the manager says, "We can still begin the project if we want to, but for some reason, it appears the problem is not so severe." Nothing can be identified that changed the way the group does business . . . what happened was the group realized that on June 20 they were really going to have to start confronting their problems, so it seemed easier to act as if the problems weren't so important now.

I worked as a consultant to a company where the engineering and manufacturing groups were having a difficult time working together. In the study, I learned the groups had a ten-year history of conflict at all levels, the president of the company had sided with the manufacturing group and was constantly attacking the engineering group, and responsibilities and authority between the two groups were overlapping and unclear. Just before I was to feed back the results of the study, the president called me and said that the head of engineering was changing jobs. He felt now that this one person was leaving, the problems would probably go away. He was holding onto the good feeling that this person was leaving as a way of not confronting the underlying problems facing these groups for the last ten years.

The manager's process of resisting through health is similar to what happens when the fighting couple finally makes an appointment with a marriage counselor: As the session approaches, they find they are getting along better and better. By the time they get to the marriage counselor, they look at each other and say they aren't quite sure what the problems were because they have been getting along so well lately. Of course, there is nothing wrong with the situation improving for the client, but most surface symptoms have underlying problems that require attention. If all of a sudden the client is telling you that the symptoms are improving, I would be concerned that they are grasping for improvement too dearly and are smoothing over what should be the real focus of your consultation.

Pressing for Solutions

The last form of resistance is the client's desire for solutions, solutions, solutions. "Don't talk to me about problems, I want to hear solutions." Because the consultant is also eager to see the problems solved, some collusion can take place between consultant and client if the discussion of solutions is not held off a little.

The desire for solutions can prevent the client from learning anything important about the nature of the problem. It also keeps the client dependent on consultants to solve these problems. If the line manager hasn't the patience or stomach to stop and examine the problem, then the solutions are not going to be implemented very effectively. Recognize that the rush to solutions can be a defense and a particularly seductive form of resistance for the consultant who is eager to solve problems.

What Are Clients Resisting When They Are Resisting Us?

Sounds like a song title, but it's important for you to know.

The main thing to do in coping successfully with resistance is to not take it personally. When you encounter resistance, you are the one in the room. Clients look straight at *you* while they are being defensive. You are the one who has to answer the questions and weather the storm. It is natural to feel that the resistance is aimed at you. The resistance is not aimed at you. It is not you the client is defending against. Resistant clients are defending against the fact that they are going to have to make a difficult choice, take an unpopular action, confront some reality that they have emotionally been trying to avoid.

If you have been brought in to solve a problem, it means the client organization has not been able to solve it themselves. It is not that they aren't smart enough to solve it. The reason they have not been able to solve it is they have not been able to see it clearly. They are so close to the problem and have such an emotional investment in any possible solutions, that they have needed an outsider to come in and define the problem and possible solutions for them. In the problem or solution, there is some *difficult reality* that the client has had a hard time seeing and confronting.

The *difficult realities* that clients are stuck on will vary.

Someone may have to be fired or told that they are not performing adequately.

People in the group may be very dissatisfied and the manager may be reluctant to surface the dissatisfaction.

The manager may feel inadequate in some part of the job and not want to face that inadequacy.

The political situation may be very risky and the manager doesn't want to make waves.

The task at hand may require skills that do not exist in the organization now. This may mean getting rid of some people, which is always hard to do.

The manager's boss may be part of the problem, and the manager may not want to confront the boss.

The organization may be selling products or services to a declining market and this is too discouraging to deal with.

The manager knows he operates autocratically, doesn't want to change, yet sees the negative effects of it.

A developmental project in which a lot of money has been invested is turning up some negative results. This means bad news has to be sent up the line, and promises made earlier will be taken back.

All these *difficult realities* involve painful problems that seem to promise painful solutions. Most very technical or business-related problems are in some way caused or maintained by how that problem is being managed. When managers are being defensive, they are defending their own managerial adequacy—a natural thing to defend. It is even worthwhile defending. A resistant manager is much more concerned about his or her own esteem and competence than about our skills as consultants.

This is what resistance is about—defending against some *difficult realty* and how the manager has been handling it. We consultants come in and, as part of our job, start pointing to the *difficult realities.* It is important that we help the client face the difficulties. We shouldn't avoid them just because the client will become resistant.

When you encounter resistance, you are seeing the surface expression of more underlying anxieties. Two things are happening.

1. The client is feeling uncomfortable, and

2. The client is expressing the discomfort indirectly.

The reason consultants feel the victim of the resistance is that the client's discomfort is being expressed indirectly. If the client were able to be authentic and put the concern directly into words by saying, "I am concerned I am losing control of this group," or "I feel I am ill-equipped to handle this particular situation," or "People expect things from me that I just can't deliver," we consultants would not feel attacked. We would feel very supportive toward the manager.

The manager's *direct* expression of underlying concerns is not resistance. Resistance occurs only when the concerns about facing the difficult realities and the choice not to deal with them are expressed *indirectly.* They are expressed indirectly by blaming lack of detailed data, not enough time, impracticality, not enough budget, lack of understanding by "those people," and so on, as the reasons we should not proceed with a project or implement some recommendations.

Underlying Concerns

If I am facing resistance and I am trying to understand what the client is really concerned about, I would wager the client was concerned about either *control* or *vulnerability*.

If what you are suggesting does not generate *some* resistance from the client, it is probably because your proposal does not threaten the manager's control or feeling of organizational security.

Control

Maintaining control is at the center of the value system of most organizations. There is a belief in control that goes beyond effectiveness or good organizational performance. Many managers believe in maintaining control even if keeping control results in *poorer performance.* There is case after case demonstrating that more participative forms of management are more productive, yet the practice of participative management is not too common. I have seen a division of one company where the controls on the management information system were proven to be a major obstacle to improving productivity, yet the manager chose to keep the controls at the expense of better performance.

Control is the coin of the realm in organizations. The whole reward system is geared around how much control, responsibility, and authority you have. When you perform well, you don't get much more money, you get more control. At some point in history, organizations realized that you can't pay people enough money to commit themselves like they do, so instead, control is held up as the reward.

The message in all this is that control is valued very, very highly. There is nothing wrong with having control, and being out of control is a very anxious state to be in. When we get resistance, one good guess why is the manager feels he or she is going to lose control.

Vulnerability   Concern that the manager will get hurt is the second major issue that gives rise to most of the resistance that we encounter. Organizations are systems that are competitive and political. It is very important to stay ahead of your peers, stay in favor with your boss, and maintain the loyalty and support of your subordinates. To do all three of these and also get your job done is difficult. As you move up an organization and deal with people at higher and higher levels, you realize that the feeling of being judged and having to prove yourself again and again is part of *every* position in the organization, all the way up to the chief executive officer.

Politics is the exercise of power. Organizations operate like political systems, except there is no voting. The impact your consulting project has on the political situation and the power of your client is a very important consideration. When you get resistance, it may be that you are unintentionally disturbing whatever political equilibrium has been established.

An example:

> In a research and development department, the group doing exploratory research had always reigned supreme and independent. The product development groups were much more tightly controlled, held accountable for short-term results. We were asked to help in restructuring the whole R&D department because the R&D vice president had a strong feeling that inefficiencies and overlap existed and the department was not operating as one organization. During the project, most of the resistance came from the exploratory research group. They would come late to meetings and question our methods, and then be silent and say, "Whatever you think is fine with us."
>
> So, what was behind their resistance? Were our methods really faulty? Did they object to the technical basis on which our project was established? No. What they were resisting was the fact that right now they were in a

favored and powerful organizational position. They had high status, high autonomy, and a free hand at gathering resources and starting projects of their choosing. Underneath all the technical and structural questions they had, they were worried about losing status in the political system.

Their concern had some legitimacy. If an exploratory research group loses all its independence, the long-run picture for new products is dim. Yet the group's political concern—losing power in the organization—was expressed very indirectly and was therefore very hard to deal with. When they finally stated their concern directly and reduced the resistance, a compromise could be worked out with the VP and the product development group.

Summary: When you encounter resistance, try to understand it. Look for client concerns about control and vulnerability.

Sometimes It Is Not Resistance

As Freud once said when he was asked whether the cigar he was smoking was also a phallic symbol, "Sometimes a cigar is just a cigar"; sometimes client objections are not resistance. The client just doesn't want to do the project.

We can all become paranoid by interpreting every line manager's objections as resistance covering some underlying anxieties. If a manager says directly, "No, I do not choose to begin this project. I don't believe in it," that is not resistance. There is nothing in that statement that blames the consultant or presses the responsibility for the difficulties on the consultant. The manager is taking responsibility for his or her own organization and has a right to choose. If we think it is the wrong choice, well, that's life.

We are getting paid to consult, not to manage. If a manager says to me, "I am in too vulnerable a position to begin this project now," I feel appreciative of the direct expression. I know where I stand with that manager. I don't have to worry whether I should have done something differently. I also feel the manager understands the project and knows the risks, and it turned out that the risks were just too high. I may be disappointed that the project didn't go, but the process was flawless.

The Fear and the Wish

Although sometimes consultants and clients may act like adversaries, their feelings and concerns are frequently complementary. There are some common client fears that correspond to similar consultant fears. The same is true for wishes. There are three that bring you down and three that lift you up.

Client Fears	Consultant Fears
Helplessness. Futility. I have no power to change the situation. I am a victim.	I can have no impact. No reward for the effort.
Alienation from the organization and people around me. No one cares about me nor do I care about them. I don't belong here.	Distance from the client. We will remain strangers. We will never get close. I'll have to stay totally "in role."
Confusion. I have too much information. I can't sort it out or see clearly.	I have too little information. They won't or can't tell me what is really happening.

Helplessness . . . alienation . . . confusion are all underlying concerns that can cause the client to be resistant if expressed indirectly. Their indirect expression can create similar discomfort in the consultant. The way out is to help the client express them directly in words.

We can also look at the flip side of fear and resistance and identify the underlying potential for each client. Each client also has the possibility of flawlessness. As the client moves in this direction, the task of the consultant becomes easier.

Client Potential	Consultant Potential
Has choices and the power to act on the situation. Is an actor, not a victim.	High impact. Clear payoff for effort expended.
Engages the situation. Feels a part of it. Moves toward the difficult reality and tension.	Can be authentic and intimate. No "role" behavior.
Choices are clear. Mass of information is simplified.	Is included with all information. Sees situation with clarity.

Reaching this potential is one of the objectives of any consultation. The client and consultant are taking responsibility for themselves and the situation they are in. The process of dealing with resistance helps the client move from a position of helplessness, alienation, and confusion to a position of choice, engagement, and clarity. The consultant accomplishes this by internally moving from feelings of low impact, distance, and poor information to a position of high impact, authenticity, and clarity.

Being Dependent, Asking for Help

The climates of most organizations are not conducive to managers' asking for help. Organizations tend to be quite competitive, and asking for help from a staff group or other consultants can be seen as a sign of weakness. Our culture also signals early, especially in men's lives, that we should be able to solve our own problems and not have to be dependent on anyone else for anything. Being a client goes against the stream of these organizational and cultural messages. It is not easy. Resistance comes in part from the discomforts of being dependent and asking for help.

There is a closely related feeling that also makes being a client difficult—the feeling that nothing can be done to help. Before the consultant is allowed in, the manager has tried to solve the problem with limited or no success. This can lead to the unstated belief that the problem is unsolvable, that the group or manager is so set in his ways that the problem must be lived with, not resolved. The manager is feeling beyond help. When you encounter resistance, this possibility should be explored. When the manager is feeling very pessimistic that the prospect of being helped is remote, this stance itself is your immediate obstacle to solving the problem. No technical solutions will suffice if the manager has no energy to try it. The manager's feeling of being beyond help is usually not that conscious. The consultant's task is to bring it to the level of awareness. When the manager examines the feeling of futility, hope usually rises.

Wanting Confirmation, Not Change

When we ask for help, we want both a solution to the problem and confirmation that everything we have done has been perfect.

A colleague of mine, Neale Clapp, mentioned one day that people entering therapy want confirmation, not change. On the surface, it would be ridiculous for a client to bring in a consultant for help, and then tell the consultant that no change was desired and the client did not really want to learn anything. This would not be rational. But that is the point. Resistance is an emotional process, not a rational or intellectual process.

In the world of emotions, two opposite feelings can exist at the same time. And both can be genuine. Clients may sincerely want to learn and solve problems. At the same time they also want support and to be told that they are handling that problem better than anyone else in the country. Approach—avoidance. The resistance is the avoidance. Right behind the avoidance, you will find the approach. When we help the resistance get expressed, it diminishes and we are then working with a client who is ready and willing to learn and be influenced. Flawlessly dealing with resistance is understanding the two-headed nature of being in the client position—and accepting it as OK.

When a line manager has a problem and results are suffering, at least the extent of the suffering is known. The manager has a very clear idea of how bad things are and has learned to live with the difficulty. The manager may not like the difficulty, but has learned to cope with it. We as consultants come along and offer an alternative way of solving the problem. With the offer is the promise that the new situation will be better than the old situation: There will be less suffering, results will improve. This promise carries the manager into the unknown; it requires a change.

Fear of the unknown is a major cause of resistance. Simply because the unknown is uncertain, unpredictable. We all see couples who have been married for ten years and seem to be suffering every minute they are together. We wonder why they stay together. Perhaps it is because at least they know how bad things can get. They know what the downside looks like, and they know they can survive. There is comfort in knowing what to expect. To separate would be unpredictable. The fear of coping with unpredictability may be greater than the pain of staying together. Organizations also value predictability. The wish of systems to remain predictable (don't surprise me) is a defense the consultant has to deal with continually.

Not surprisingly, organizations that are in serious trouble tend to be the most difficult clients. They need to change the most and are least able to do it. For low-performing organizations, the tension of failure is so high that they are unable to take one more risk and so hold onto their unsatisfactory performance. In these extreme cases, there is probably not much consultants can do to surface the resistance to change. We may just have to accept it.

Ogres and Angels

In any organization, there are certain managers who are well-known for their disdain for staff groups and internal consultants. In workshops for people in the same organization—whether they are in personnel, auditing, or engineering—the groups can all name the one or two managers at pretty high levels who are ogres in the eyes of the staff consultants. The ogres are seen as stubborn, autocratic, insensitive to feelings—the Captain Ahabs of industry. When the subject of resistance comes up, the ogres are mentioned. We all seem to need at least one impossible client in our lives, the client who becomes the lightning rod of our frustrations in consulting. There is also a fatal attraction to the ogres—they embody some consultants' wish to be all-powerful, and successful.

Ogres don't really exist. A number of times I have heard how fire-eating and mean a certain manager is, and then actually met with the person. I approach the meeting with a lot of discomfort, not wanting to be the latest casualty. What happens is the conversation soon turns to the ogres in the ogre's life. Ogres are not really consumed with vengeance for consultants—they are worried about the people who are giving *them* a hard time. Behind the ogre's blustery facade are the same concerns all managers have—about losing control and becoming vulnerable. The more aggressive the client, the more intense are the concerns and the more the client needs support.

Angels are also one-sided images. Every group I have worked with can name a manager who is willing to do anything they ask. A progressive manager, open, trusting, risk-taking, secure, intelligent, good-looking. There are no angels either. Angels have a hard time saying no directly. There is a part of the most supportive manager that has reservations, avoids confronting real issues, and wants to maintain the status quo. We need to help that side get expressed. For the manager's sake and for our own sake.

. . . and Heroics

The need for a heroic self-image is another myth about consulting that ought to be laid to rest. We think that we should be able to overcome all obstacles. No matter how difficult the client, or how tough the problem, or how tight the time schedule—we believe it is up to us to do the best we can. This wish to be the heroic consultant more than anything else leads into taking bad contracts. Heroics often entail a hidden bargain. If we take on this bad job now, we will be rewarded later with plums. The essence of the hidden bargain is that it is assumed and never spoken. The rewards in doing consulting need to be in the present project. If it has no reward, the project should be challenged.

This heroic impulse in the consultant is the consultant's own resistance against facing the realities of a difficult project. Resist taking unstable or unrealistic contracts. If you can't say no, say later. If you can't say later, say little. Heroes have a hard life. The rewards are overrated. Most heroes, unless you are the best in the world, get paid just about what you are making right now.

Chapter 9
Dealing with Resistance

PEOPLE USE THE PHRASE "overcoming resistance" as though resistance or defensiveness were an adversary to be wrestled to the ground and subdued. "Overcoming resistance" would have you use data and logical arguments to win the point and convince the client. There is no way you can talk clients out of their resistance, because resistance is an emotional process. Behind the resistance are certain feelings. You cannot talk people out of how they are feeling.

There are specific steps a consultant can take to help a client get past the resistance and get on with solving the problem. The basic strategy is to help the resistance to blow itself out, like a storm, and not to fight the resistance head-on.

Feelings pass and change when they are expressed directly. The skill for the consultant is to ask clients to put directly into words what the client is experiencing. To ask the client to be authentic. The most effective way to encourage the client to be authentic is for the consultant to also behave authentically. That's all there is to it.

This way of dealing with resistance—by not fighting it head-on—has a Zen quality to it. If you fight the resistance and feel you have to conquer it, all you will do is intensify the resistance. If a client is objecting to your methodology (and has been doing it for more than ten minutes) and you keep defending the method, citing references, and recounting other experiences, the client is going to get even more frustrated. The client is likely to become even more committed to finding holes in your method than when the discussion started. The alternative to defending your method is to ask the client more about their concerns and try to get to why your methodology is so important. Getting the client to talk more about their concerns is helping the storm to pass. Defending methodology is keeping the storm alive.

Try this little exercise.

Put your palms together in front of your chest. Let your right arm be the client's resistance. Let your left arm be your response to that resistance. Move your right arm and palm hard to the left against your left palm. Now have the left arm and palm push at the same time, hard to the right. If you hold this position the two hands stay stuck right in the middle, the strain increases in both your arms, and you soon get tired. That is what happens when you push back against the resistance. You get stuck, the tension goes up and energy is drained.

Now put your palms together again in the same starting position. Move your right arm and palm to the left hard against your left hand. This time let your left hand give in, so the right hand keeps moving to the left. At some point your right hand will stop. It will have pushed as far as it can go. If you hold that end position, you will notice that your right hand, the resistance, gets tired and drops of its own weight. The left hand, your response to the resistance, allows the right hand resistance to move to its own ends. Contacted but unopposing, the left hand can maintain its position with no tension and little loss of energy.

This is the way to deal with resistance—to encourage full expression of the concerns so that they pass. Fighting resistance, trying to overcome it with arguments and data, doesn't work as well. Remember that resistance is the *indirect* expression of client reservations. The goal is to help the line manager begin stating the reservations directly, and stop the subterfuge. When the client's concerns are stated directly, the consultant knows what the real issues are and can respond effectively.

Three Steps

There are three specific steps for handling resistance.

Step 1:   Identify in your own mind what form the resistance is taking. The skill is to pick up the cues from the manager and then, in your head, to put some words on what you see happening.

Step 2:   State, in a neutral, nonpunishing way, the form the resistance is taking. This is called "naming the resistance." The skill is to find the neutral language.

Step 3:   Be quiet. Let the line manager respond to your statement about the resistance.

Step 1. Picking Up the Cues

People who are technically trained in such disciplines as computer science, engineering, or accounting often find it difficult to recognize the early signs of resistance. Technical training so focuses your attention on facts, figures, data, and the rational level that you are not accustomed to closely paying attention to the interpersonal, emotional level of conversations. Developing skill in dealing with resistance requires knowing what form the resistance is taking, but the first step is simply to notice what is happening.[6]

Here are some ways to pick up the cues.

Trust What You See More Than What You Hear

Pay attention to the nonverbal messages from the client. Suppose the client is:

Constantly moving away from you

Tied up in knots like a pretzel

---

[6]Gil Gordon, a friend, helped me see how the step of picking up cues from the client is separate from the step of putting the resistance into words.

Pointing a finger and clenching the other fist

Shaking his head each time you speak

Bent over toward you like a servant

Take any of these as signs that the client is feeling uneasy about this project and is most likely being resistant.

In their book *Assertiveness Training for Women*, Gloria Harris and Susan Osborne say studies show most communication takes place nonverbally:

7 percent of communication is through words.

38 percent of communication is through voice, tone, rate, inflection.

55 percent of communication is through face and body.

I believe it. Looking at nonverbal behavior is a good way to pick up the cues of resistance.

Listen to Yourself

Another way to know that you are encountering resistance is to use your own body as a thermometer. When you start feeling uneasy in a discussion with the client, it may be an early sign that resistance is on its way. Certainly when you find yourself getting bored or irritated, take it as evidence that the client is resisting. When a discussion is confronting real issues directly, it is not boring or irritating. When you notice yourself yawning or suppressing some negative feelings, take it as a cue. These reactions of yours act as red flags, attention-getting devices. They are messages that you should begin to put words on the form of resistance you are encountering.

Repetition and Telltale Phrases

A sure cue for resistance is when you hear the same idea explained to you for the third time. Or when you hear yourself answering the same question for the third time. Repetition of ideas and questions is resistance because expressing the idea or answering the questions the first time did not get the job done. There must be some underlying concern that is surfacing indirectly through repetition.

You also hear certain phrases that tell you the client is not feeling understood.

> You have to understand that . . .
>
> Let me explain something to you.
>
> I want to make sure this isn't an academic exercise.

These phrases are very aggressive in a subtle way. They express some frustration and treat the consultant as if a serious mistake is about to be made, but somehow this statement from the client is supposed to save us.

There are probably certain phrases you hear a lot that signal difficulty. Take the time to make a list of them now, and update your list as you grow more skilled in picking up the cues of resistance.

Step 2. Naming the Resistance

When you become aware of resistance, the next step is to put it into words. Name it. It is best to use neutral, everyday language. The skill is to describe the form of the resistance in a way that encourages the client to make a more direct statement of the reservation he or she is experiencing. Here are some examples of resistance and neutral language describing the form of resistance.

When the Resistance Takes this Form	Name It by Making this Statement
Client's avoiding responsibility for the problem or the solution	You don't see yourself as part of the problem.
Flooding you with detail	You are giving me more detail than I need. How would you describe it in a short statement?

When the Resistance Takes this Form	Name It by Making this Statement
One-word answers	You are giving me very short answers. Could you say more?
Changing the subject	The subject keeps shifting. Could we stay focused on one area at a time?
Compliance	You seem willing to do anything I suggest. I can't tell what your real feelings are.
Silence	You are very quiet. I don't know how to read your silence.
Press for solutions	It's too early for solutions. I'm still trying to find out . . .
Attack	You are really questioning a lot of what I do. You seem angry about something.

The easiest way is to look for everyday language to describe the resistance. Someone in a workshop once suggested that it is easier to name the resistance if you think of what you would say to a close friend or spouse, and say that to the client. The sentiment in this suggestion that is helpful is to keep the statement very simple and direct.

Here are some other forms of resistance. Try naming each resistance in a neutral, nonaggressive way.

Questions of methodology

Intellectualizing and spinning great theories

Confusion and vagueness

Low energy, inattention

How did you do? Here are some examples of naming statements you might make to these forms of resistance.

Methodology: You are asking a lot of questions about my methods. Do you have any doubts about the credibility of the results?

Intellectualizing: Each time we get close to deciding what to do, you go back to developing theories to understand what is happening.

Confusion: You seem very confused about what we are discussing. Are you confused about the problem or just not sure what to do about it?

Low energy, inattention: You look like you have other things on your mind and have low energy for this project.

In a high percentage of cases, clients will respond with a more direct statement of what they are feeling about a project. Sometimes naming the resistance won't work. It may be that there is nothing you can do about it.

A Hint for Finding the Right Words

If naming the resistance isn't helping, an option is to put into words how *you* are feeling about the discussion. When you meet resistance, it is uncomfortable, frustrating. Sometimes it makes you feel stupid, irrelevant, or unimportant. Try stating this to the client with statements like these.

> I feel very frustrated by this discussion.

> It seems my comments are treated as though they are irrelevant or unimportant.

Sometimes the client will stop short and ask you why you feel that way, and this might get you to a direct discussion of the problem. Expressing your feelings can be riskier at times than just naming the client's resistance. The client may not care how you are feeling, and say, "So, you are feeling uncomfortable. What has that got to do with getting this equipment working?" But stating your own feelings is being authentic and acts to encourage a like response from the client, which is what you are after.

**Step 3.
Being Quiet,
Letting the Client
Respond**

After naming the resistance, there is a tendency for the consultant to keep talking.

> To an unmotivated client:
>
> You seem to have very little motivation to go ahead with this project. Let me tell you four reasons why I think this project is important and you should feel differently . . .

The first sentence is good—a neutral naming of the concern. By continuing to talk, though, the consultant is taking the client off the hook and making it easy for the client to *not* take responsibility for his or her actions.

We keep talking to reduce the tension we feel when we confront the client. Don't keep talking. Live with the tension. Make the statement about resistance and remain silent.

**Don't Take
It Personally**

A client's behavior is not a reflection on you.

Many of us have a habit of analyzing what we did wrong. In a recent workshop, I asked a group of engineers to make a list of what they did well as consultants and what they did poorly as consultants. They were able to quickly list eight to ten things they did poorly or had problems with.

The lists of positive qualities averaged two items, and took twice as long to make! This passion for self-criticism is very common and gets in the way of keeping the resistance focused on the client where it belongs.

If you must take the client's reactions personally, the rule is to do it after six o'clock in the evening—on your own time. Spend the whole night at it and involve your friends. But don't take resistance personally when you are with the client. If you have, in fact, done a poor job, and the client tells you, you have to own up to it and shape up your act. This doesn't happen often—and it's not resistance from the client, it is a mistake by the consultant.

Remember that client defenses are not to be denied. In fact, they need clear expression. If suppressed, they just pop up later and more dangerously. The key is how you respond to the defenses.

A couple of points to summarize.

> *Don't take it personally.* Despite the words used, the resistance is not designed to discredit your competence.
>
> *Defenses and resistance are a sign that you have touched something important and valuable.* That fact is now simply coming out in a difficult form.
>
> *Most questions are statements in disguise.* Try to get behind the question, to get the statement articulated. This takes the burden off you to answer a phantom question.

Dealing with resistance is harder than actually doing data collection and much harder than coming up with good ideas for implementation. The meat of the consultation is dealing with resistance.

Good Faith Responses

The majority of questions you get about methodology and the project are just expressions of the discomfort and defensiveness the client is feeling. It is important, however, to respond to the substance of the questions as best you can.

One ground rule is to give *two good faith responses* to every question you are asked. If you are asked about methodology and your summary, or how you designed the questionnaire, answer each question twice. The third time the same question is asked, interpret it as a form of resistance and do not respond to the content of the question. Instead, realize that clients who ask the same question over and over are in effect expressing their caution about committing to the process and owning up to their own problems. The third time the same question is asked, the only rational response is to make the statement that perhaps what the client is feeling is some reluctance to commit to the problem or the process.

After two good faith responses, deal with the problems of commitment and taking responsibility—don't deal with resistance as though it were merely a problem of procedure or method. Make the two good faith responses, then treat the questions as resistance.

Consulting with a Stone

Every once in a while you meet your match. Your consultation is flawless, yet your progress with the client is in a nose dive.

Some of the consulting workshops I run have the participants actually engage in a consulting project with a real client as part of the learning experience. One consulting team returned from their contracting meeting with the client with very long faces. The client was resistant, withholding, uncommunicative, and even told the group in the contracting meeting that he thought they were doing a lousy job.

As a way of coping with our despair and frustration, we made a list of different ways of consulting with a stone.

1. Don't look for approval, emotional support, or affection.

2. Don't expect the responsibility to be shared 50/50. Stones dump it all on you.

3. Expect argument and criticism.

4. Don't ask for the client's feelings or express your own feelings.

5. Do ask the client for understanding. Don't ask for agreement.

6. Let the client have a lot of control over the procedure used in the project.

7. Minimize elaborating or explaining the data. Justification just makes it worse.

8. Give the client support.

9. Don't take the response you are getting personally.

10. Don't get hooked; avoid details.

11. Hope that the client may learn from this project later, after you are gone. You are not going to get closure from the project now.

12. Show confidence.

13. Look for comic relief.

14. Remember, the stone's anxiety is over losing control.

15. Keep moving.

16. Avoid stones whenever possible.

There aren't many real stones out there. If the surface of the client is that hard, the stuff inside must be equally soft. Often, clear support to the stone will be softening. If the stone client stays a stone client, minimize your investment in the project; don't pressure yourself to be heroic. If the stone turns out to be someone you work with constantly or is your boss, either plan your escape or start putting your energy into activities outside the job.

Chapter 10

From Diagnosis to Discovery

WHEN THE CONTRACT is clear, the work of understanding the problem and the current reality begins. Our focus here, as throughout the book, is on the relationship aspect of consulting. Your particular area of consulting expertise will determine what kind of specific data you will collect. Systems people will look at information requirements, engineers and scientists will look at the technical questions, financial experts look at money and economics, and so it goes.

As each of us developed our expertise, we were trained in handling data and information. The intent here is to identify some particular skills in this phase that have not received much attention but are also important. This chapter does not begin to cover all the methods that can be applied to understanding what is happening. It does look at the way the consultant works with the client in what was traditionally called the *diagnosis* phase but is more accurately called *discovery*.

There is in this phase a tension between what the client may want and expect and what is most likely to be helpful. The fundamental service we offer clients is to help them see how they can make changes in the future without having to stay dependent on our expertise. While clients may agree with this concept in theory, it is not what they want in practice. In practice clients want a turnkey solution.

It is similar to when we are not feeling well. We want to go to a doctor, get a prescription, swallow a pill, and get on with our work. Better living through chemistry. When line managers decide their organization is not functioning well, they want someone to come in, take a good look with fresh eyes, and suggest a solution that will be quick, cheap, and painless. That is why the first questions from the client are, "How long will it take?," "How much will it cost?," and "Give us a solution that will cause the least disruption." If we give the clients precisely what they ask for, we run the risk of not having served them well.

If, however, we tell the client that the solution will take awhile, will cost more than they imagined, and more time and involvement will be required of them than they want to give, we run the risk of alienating them. Some of this will have been dealt with in the contracting phase, but this tension exists at every step of the way. What is hard to realize as a client is that the long-term solution to the problem will require some rethinking on their part and some rearranging of the way they work together. This relearning is what takes the time and effort. You can outsource or contract to an outsider the research and technical problem solving, but implementing and sustaining a solution you always have to do yourself.

We serve the client best by breaking out of the medical model we have come to expect. We are not an organization doctor who describes their symptoms, who looks them over, prescribes a solution, and sends them on their way. Better to define our task as a process of discovery and dialogue more than as an act of diagnosis and prescription. The term *diagnosis* implies that a third party, the consultant, can analyze the situation, come up with an accurate picture of what is wrong, and deliver a recommendation for corrective action. And that this will be useful. This frame of diagnosis and action is a comforting problem-solving model, but it is based on the belief that organizational improvement can be engineered. Most of the time this is not realistic.

For strictly technical problems, such as a furnace that doesn't work or software that has crashed, this might seem reasonable. Especially if we were dealing with exclusively technical problems. It is rare, however, that problems originally defined as technical are amenable to strictly technical solutions. We cannot ignore that we are dealing with human systems, and human systems are not amenable to technical solutions. Human systems are complex and require more than mechanical, cause-and-effect solutions. Furnaces and software most often break down because *people* run them, *people* maintain them, and *people* ask them to do things they were not designed to do. The resolution of the problem most often requires a change in thinking and action on the part of the client, and this is the challenge.

When we accept the term *"diagnosis"* as a description of this phase, we reinforce the belief that a prescriptive, engineering strategy can improve a living system. This rational stance undervalues the emotional and affective requirements of real improvements.

The stance we want to take is that we can be a *guide through a process of discovery, engagement, and dialogue,* in which our clients will find an answer to their question and launch an implementation that will be enduring and productive. It may seem like playing with words, but it makes a difference in what we do and what we leave behind.

This chapter details the kind of discovery, engagement, and dialogue that gives us our best shot at building client capacity and solving problems so they stay solved.

The Call to Action

The concern of the consultant is how to help the client to be open to the discovery process. This is much more important than for us to be right in our analysis. This means giving more attention to dealing with resistance. It also demands work on building the client's internal commitment to the process at each step of the way. To wait until the feedback meeting to worry about client acceptance of recommendations is too late. The consultant is also concerned about how to handle the politics and personalities surrounding data collection. Even the most technical problem is managed by human beings, working in politically minded organizations. Navigating through our clients' management styles and organizational politics and helping them to look objectively at the data are vital tasks. The skill for the consultant is to address the organizational element of each problem as rationally as we address the technical part of each problem.

If the client problem were purely technical, then client commitment would not be a concern. But there are no purely technical problems. As consultants, we always have a perspective on how the technology is being utilized or managed. Even if we hire a contractor to install an electricity generator to power our house in event of a power outage, there are still questions of what size generator, where it should be placed, which technology is best for our lifestyle and budget, and who will run and maintain it. A good contractor will ask questions about client expectations, who in the household will be operating the generator, how much protection the household needs, how important having instant power is to the family, and most difficult of all, is there agreement in the family about the answers to these questions.

These are questions about how the "problem" is being managed, what it means to the "client," what attitudes surround the seemingly simple step of purchasing some technology. A good contractor will treat these questions as being as important as the knowledge of how to purchase and install an alternative power source. If you talk to architects and contractors, the hardest part of their job is dealing with client doubts and family dynamics. Designing and building a house they know how to do. Navigating their way through the politics of the family is where the challenge lies.

If this is true for a family, it is magnified when dealing with an organization. The politics of an organization is reality, always present and powerful, and this is the challenge of discovery and action.

The purpose, then, of discovery is to mobilize action on a problem. Action that will improve the organization's functioning. The purpose is not research. Research is aimed at simply understanding something and treats the understanding itself as enough. In most cases, internal consultants are evaluated on how well their expertise is utilized by the line organization. External consultants, as well as seeing clients, evaluate them this way more and more.

This emphasis on action and utilization has strong implications for how you approach discovery.

Research Approach	Action Approach
Interested in all factors that impact the problem at hand	Interested in factors that are under the control of the client and affect the problem
Being comprehensive and complete in the discovery phase is essential	Completeness and comprehensiveness are not necessary. They can be overwhelming at the point of deciding what to do
You can do research on your own. The organization doesn't have to be involved as part of the research team	The client's involvement in the study is important at each stage
You try to eliminate bias and intuition of the researcher. Heavy emphasis on objectivity and hard data	Consultants are getting paid for their own bias and intuition—it is called judgment. You use all the feelings and perceptions you have in addition to hard data
Essentially neutral toward whether the organization approves of the outcomes of the study	Deeply concerned about the attitude of the client toward the outcome of the study

These distinctions in approach may be overly polarized, but you must know that your objective is action, not understanding. When your objective is action, you need to concentrate on four things beyond the technical considerations.

1. Keep simplifying and narrowing and reducing your study so it focuses more and more on the next steps the client can take.

2. Use everyday language. The words you use should help the transfer of information, not hinder it.

3. Give a great deal of attention to your relationship with the client. Include the client at every opportunity in deciding how to proceed. Deal with resistance as it arises, even if it doesn't have impact on your results.

4. Treat data on how the client organization is functioning as valid and relevant information. Also assess how the problem you are studying is being managed.

These four competencies affect how your expertise gets utilized. They take your technical skill and problem-analyzing, problem-solving abilities as givens. This action orientation makes the assumption that *client readiness to accept your input* is as important to discovery as the technical analysis of the problem to be solved.

Figure 8 shows the basic sequence for the discovery phase.

Figure 8.   The Discovery Model

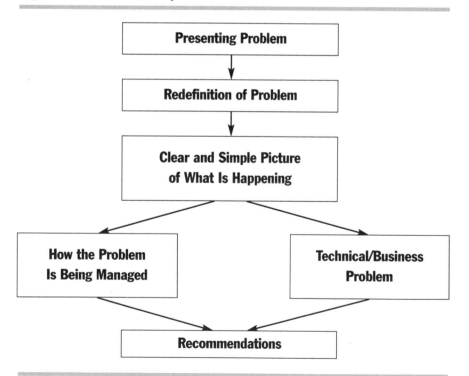

The client gives you a . . . . .Presenting problem

You begin to . . . . .Redefine the problem
or the cause of the problem

Your goal is to develop . . . . .A clear and simple picture
of what is causing and main-
taining the problem

Included in this clear and simple
picture is a description of . . . . . . .The technical or business
problem the client has asked
for help on

And also a description of . . . . . . .How that problem is being
managed—the attitudes of
people, the manager's style, and
the politics of the situation that
affect the technical/business
problem

Both of these descriptions
lead to . . . . .Recommendations on the technical solution and on the man-
agerial solution.

Juggling the Presenting Problem

Often the consultant's most important contribution to a client is a redefinition of the problem. The line manager begins by experiencing some pain. People are restless. Equipment isn't working. Output is down. Bills are being paid twice.

Consulting projects get started because managers feel pain. It would be nice if projects got started because of a desire for further success or for preventive measures, but most often there is some pain in the picture. When the organization feels the pain, managers start to describe for themselves why the pain exists. When their explanation of what is causing the pain is accurate, their attempts to solve the problem are usually successful. When consultants are called in, it is because the line manager's attempts at solving the problem have not been that successful. Or maybe the manager has no idea at all how to solve the problem. When a manager's attempts to solve the problem have not succeeded, it is probably because the manager's attempts to describe the cause of the pain have been inaccurate.

The client's initial attempt to describe to us the cause of the difficulties is called the *presenting problem.* As a consultant, I never accept the presenting problem as the real problem without doing my own data collection and analysis. The presenting problem and the real (or underlying) problem are usually different. Because the line manager started from an incomplete definition of the problem, his attempts at solution have not entirely worked out. An important contribution for the consultant is to redefine that initial problem statement for the client.

Here's an example of how presenting problems get redefined.

A large technical organization was having difficulty retaining new employees more than two to three years. The people would come to work, get training, work on the job for awhile, and then leave just when they were becoming valuable employees. The managers asked the first-line supervisors why the younger people were leaving. The supervisors said there were two reasons.

1. Salaries weren't high enough to match the cost of living in the area.

2. Housing was very hard to find. Apartments were scarce and those houses for sale were so expensive that an employee had to save for ten years to have enough for the down payment.

Top management accepted these two reasons as valid. They conducted a salary survey and made some adjustments in the compensation practices for short-service employees. They also created a housing section in the personnel department to help people find apartments and to work with realtors to identify moderately priced housing in the area. Both of these solutions responded well to the presenting problem of poor housing and unjust compensation. Unfortunately, a year and a half later, the turnover rate for the organization was not reduced, and in some sections it was higher.

Top management brought in the training group in the company as internal consultants and asked them for help on the problem. The training people first interviewed first-line supervisors and short-service employees. From these interviews came a different explanation of why people were leaving.

The employees said:

1. When they arrived they were handed a stack of company manuals and were told to read them during the next few weeks.

2. They didn't get a real assignment until they had been there for almost a year.

3. They never got any accurate feedback from their supervisors about how they were doing. This made it hard for them to know what to work on for their own development. It also left them in limbo about their prospects with this company.

4. The first-line supervisors were under so much pressure to get the work done and to do it perfectly, they just didn't have the time to spend with new hires.

The interviews revealed a very different cause of the pain the company was experiencing in losing so many people. The original, presenting problem was that people were leaving, and they were supposed to be leaving because of low salaries and a tight housing market. This initial problem statement led to solutions in the form of compensation and housing aid. The consultants developed a different explanation for the pain and essentially redefined the cause of the problem—new hires were not given enough support, attention, meaningful tasks, and feedback.

Once management had this redefinition of the problem, they could start to solve it, which they did. They began a series of programs to have supervisors and new hires contract with each other for how much time they would spend together, the tasks they would be assigned, and when they would get feedback from the supervisor. Management also supported the supervisors in devoting more time to new employees. Over the next year, the turnover rate leveled off and in the second year began to go down. The contribution of the consultants was to redefine the presenting problem and to present to the client a clear picture of what was causing the difficulty.

How the Problem Is Being Managed

This is a critical area of inquiry in action-oriented data collection— *how the technical or business problem is being managed.*

Consultants are usually aware of the client's management style and the politics of the situation, but we tend to shy away from dealing with them as part of our consultations. We feel that we have been asked to solve a business problem, not to comment on the organization. As a result, we tend to exclude organizational problems from our field of inquiry. We don't ignore the "human" problems entirely, though, for these are the things we talk about most with our colleagues and friends. The way the problem is being managed usually gets discussed in the rest room, between meetings, after work when we are eating or drinking, or during breaks during the day.

Sometimes the management issues are even more interesting than the technical issues. But there is a part of us (with support from the client) that does not want to get into the "personalities" or "politics" or "relationships." It is a mistake to avoid these areas. The way the problem is managed has a powerful effect on the way our expertise will be used. We can't really avoid it entirely, even when the client agrees that we are only technical consultants. Technical/business problems almost always have accompanying management problems that affect how the technical/business problem gets resolved.

Figure 9 shows examples of typical "management problems" that could occur along with technical/business problems in selected disciplines and functions.

Figure 9. **The Difference Between the Technical/Business Problem and How the Problem Is Being Managed**

	Technical/Business Problems	*How the Problem Is Being Managed*
Finance Systems	• Inadequate control procedures and practices	• Defensive, cover-your-tracks environment
	• Too many reports	• Withhold information and figures
	• Too few reports	• Little verbal communication between groups
Engineering	*Technical/Business Problems*	*How the Problem Is Being Managed*
	• Cost-reduction project	• Operators have negative attitude toward company and supervisors. New procedures are resisted
	• Develop new process or equipment	
	• Construction of new facility	• Supervisors too inexperienced. Passing through the job, don't deal with longer-run issues
	• Equipment failure	
		• Management pressure for product so great that operations will not give engineering any time on the floor to test new equipment or process
		• Engineers so busy with crisis after crisis that new developments get low priority
		• Vice president is so involved in each detail decision of the new building that project is lagging behind schedule

Figure 9. Continued

Scientists	Technical/Business Problems	How the Problem Is Being Managed
	• Understand the basic nature of some material or reaction • Identify products for commercialization • Transfer their technology to the marketing or business groups	• It is easy to hire a new chemist, but there are tight budget controls on adding lab technicians, equipment, or adequate space • Research, under pressure for results, over-promises, builds expectations, and then disappoints • Scientists are under such tight influence from business, no long-range viewpoint is possible • Such strong pride of authorship that it creates resistance in other groups in organization • Cultural gap between science and operations people. Have different values, speak different language
Corporate Planners	Technical/Business Problems	How the Problem Is Being Managed
	• Do longer-range planning for the organization • Obtain figures and projections from line managers	• Managers view five-year plan as just an exercise • No personal commitment from top management • Strained relationship and distrust between corporate and field organizations
Personnel	Technical/Business Problems	How the Problem Is Being Managed
	• Improve policies and practices in areas of compensation, benefits, recruiting, training • Improve general organization and management development	• Every manager is an expert on personnel • Personnel function is a low-status group and is treated accordingly • Personnel specialists used as a pair-of-hands • Managers fear personnel will be involved in their performance evaluation, so they are reluctant to trust and include personnel

Figure 9. Continued

Marketing Research, Product Management	*Technical/Business Problems*	*How the Problem Is Being Managed*
	• Policies on pricing, promotion, and packaging • Information on customer preferences and market characteristics	• Distrust and distance between marketing and the sales force • Struggle for control • Market research operates as a black box. Rest of organization operates on their private opinions, doesn't believe the black box
Management and Organization Development Consultants	*Technical/Business Problems*	*How the Problem Is Being Managed*
	• How to improve attitudes and productivity of an organization • New organization structure • New roles and responsibilities	• Certain individuals and groups have a lot of power under the current system. Changing the structure will change the power balance among groups • A new structure signals who is on the way up and whose star is fading • A very authoritarian manager may not care about how people feel
Purchasing	*Technical/Business Problems*	*How the Problem Is Being Managed*
	• Maintain good relationship with vendor, get best price and quality, assure at least two vendors for each raw material	• Material requirements are always changing. Purchasing is the last to know • Management allows line organization to contact vendors directly without including purchasing

Each discipline or function is faced with both technical and organizational problems. The presenting problem is almost always about the technical/business problem. Organizational problems include how the technical/business problem *is being managed*. The choice is whether you want to address how the problem is being managed directly or indirectly. To address the organizational side is riskier for the internal consultant. You might hear clients say that they didn't invite you in to comment on their own personal style or the politics of the situation. To not address the organizational side is to see your technical recommendations distorted and only partially implemented because of the difficulty the organization has in communicating, trusting, and managing itself.

A Reminder

To consult flawlessly you need to begin to address the organizational side of the problem as a regular part of your consultation. At a minimum, each assessment you do should have one section devoted to how the problem is being managed. This section needs only to present a clear and simple picture; it doesn't need to include specific recommendations.

The fear of confronting the client on how the client is managing the problem is a feat that resides within the consultant. Line managers usually want feedback on how they are doing, and they have a hard time getting it. Their own subordinates are reluctant to give them feedback. You, the consultant, are in a special position to provide it. The only caution is to do it in a supportive and nonpunishing manner. (There is guidance on appropriate feedback language in Chapter 13.)

Withholding data on the interpersonal or process dimensions of a problem is to collude with the organization in not dealing with them. Part of the reason they can't manage their business as well as they would like to is because they can't articulate how to handle conflict and authority and communication. If you are also unwilling to put those dimensions into words, you're colluding with them in a way that's going to keep them from solving their underlying problems.

To summarize, remember to do these things in discovery.

Ask questions about the client's own personal role in causing or maintaining the presenting or target problem.

Ask questions about what others in the organization are doing to cause or maintain the presenting or target problem.

Plan the data collection jointly with the client.

Involve your client in interpreting the data collected.

Recognize the similarity between how the client managed *you* and how they manage their own organization.

Condense the data into a limited number of issues.

Use language that is understandable to people outside your area of expertise.

Distinguish between the presenting problem and the underlying problem.

Elicit and describe both the technical problem and how it is being managed.

Chapter 11

Getting the Data

WHEN YOU FINALLY have a contract and you have entered the discovery phase, you are ready to collect some information and develop your own assessment of what is happening to create problems for the client. The business of this phase is:

1. Collecting information at three different layers of analysis, to understand both the presenting problem and the underlying problems

2. Assessing the organizational and managerial climate in which your recommendations will be received

3. Dealing with resistance of the client in sharing information with you

4. Viewing the interviews you do as an active force in beginning to solve the problem: The act of interviewing itself changes an organization

5. Reducing the data to a manageable number of issues

6. Collecting and analyzing data accurately and objectively

The Steps in Getting Data

No matter what kind of information you seek—whether you look at information flow, equipment design, people's attitudes—or what dimensions you analyze, there are some general ways to describe the steps involved in data collection that might be helpful. Each time you collect data, whether it is a six-month or six-minute project, you make these choices.

1. *Identifying the Presenting Problem.* Any discovery begins with a conversation about a concern that line managers have about their organization. The manager's first description of the problem is called the *presenting problem.* The presenting problem is usually only a symptom of the real problem, and the purpose of the data collection is to elaborate and broaden the manager's initial statement. Identifying the presenting problem is the first step in the data collection.

2. *Deciding to Proceed.* The consultant and the client together make a decision to do the data collection. Often this involves several people who work for the manager who can confirm that there is an incentive to do a study. The motivation to proceed should be based on the desire to make improvements in the organization, not just on the desire to do research.

3. *Selecting Dimensions.* A limited number of questions needs to be selected. These questions will be within the technical realm or discipline of the consultant. A financial person will select questions about financial information and control; a personnel person will ask questions about compensation, attitudes, and climate. The dimensions should be limited—under twenty. Too much data from the discovery will be overwhelming.

4. *Deciding Who Will Be Involved.* Decide what levels of the organization will be included in the discovery. How many from each level? Remember that asking people questions creates expectations that they will get feedback on the results.

5. *Selecting the Data Collection Method.* The method depends on the scope of your inquiry. Select a method that fits with the time available, the motivation of management, and the severity of the problems. Don't overinvest.

There are only a few ways to collect data.

- *Interview.* Do it individually or use a group interview. Use either a structured or unstructured interview.

- *Paper-and-pencil questionnaire.* Takes more time to prepare. Good for large numbers of people, but numerical results can be hard to interpret.

- *Document analysis.* Look at the numbers, results, written communication. Useful because it takes up your time only. Also gives the aura of objectivity.

- *Direct observation.* Sit in on critical meetings and watch what happens. Look at the equipment. It may be the only first-person data you have. This can be the best source of data if you can trust your own perceptions.

- *Your own experience.* Know that you are being managed by the client organization the same as everyone else is managed. Pay attention to how they treat you. On this project, how much information, influence, access, pressure do you have? This is valuable data on the client's management style, and it is valid data.

- *Self-discovery.* Bring those who have a stake in the problem and who will have to act on the problem together to discuss the dimensions of the problem. Here you are more a facilitator than an interviewer. Chapter 12 elaborates on this choice.

6. *Collecting Data.* Do it. Distribute questionnaires, do interviews, sit in on meetings, study reports, bring people together. Collect information until it starts to get repetitive. You will recognize this when you start getting bored.

   After data collection, you go through the remaining steps in the process.

7. *Funneling the Data.* Somehow the information needs to be reduced to manageable proportions. The purpose of your analysis is to focus energy, not describe the universe.

8. *Summarizing Data.* You need to find a format that will summarize the data for those not familiar with it. Concentrate on the visual impact of your format and how easy it is to understand.

9. *Analyzing Data.* What does the information mean? What is important? And why?

10. *Giving Feedback.* Report the data analysis to the organization. Who should be at the original feedback meeting? How are those who were involved in the study going to find out the results? Be sure you have allowed enough time in the feedback meeting to really deal with the resistance you will get. Structure the meeting so the majority of time is for discussion, not presentation.

11. *Giving Recommendations.* Sometimes this will come before the feedback meeting. They should be within the control of the group who requested the study.

12. *Making a Decision.* The process is not complete until a decision has been made to do something.

13. *Implementation*. The payoff. Stay around for this phase, even if it's on your own time. After discovery, you may have the best feel for the problems. Your information can be useful in interpreting the hills and valleys of implementation. You also offer ways of involving people in the implementation that will increase the chances that the decision will be translated into effective change.

The first six steps above are the sequence any of us go through in consulting, regardless of our technical disciplines or particular fields of expertise. You know what technical data you want, ways to get it, and what to do with it when you have it . . . so the rest of this chapter concentrates on data collection in dimensions you may not be used to, paying special attention to your face-to-face encounters with the client as you collect your data.

A Word About Bias

Having an impact as a consultant is to a large extent independent of your methodology or field of expertise. Any number of consultants will come up with different dimensions, different analyses, and different suggestions on the same problem. But the pursuit of *any* dimension will lead to core issues around the management of the organization. It is important, then, to pick dimensions that you are comfortable with and go with them in your discovery, rather than worry about whether you've selected the right or wrong one.

In selecting the dimensions of your discovery, you predefine the problem somewhat, but there is no reason to feel anxiety about biasing the data. If you decide you are going to look at how conflict is handled, or how much people level with each other, or how they plan, you may already have some idea of what is wrong with the organization, particularly if you are an internal consultant. Do not treat this as bias, treat it as insight—your predefinition of the problem is valuable and gives you good clues on how to spend your data collection time. Trust this. You do need to keep listening as you're collecting data to see whether there are other issues that you don't know about. If there are, you need to pursue them. The point is to not treat the insight of your own feeling about being part of the organization as bias, but treat it as useful guidelines.

Assessing How the Problem Is Being Managed

If you want to develop your skills in collecting information directly about how the problem is being managed, there are more than a dozen aspects of organizational life that you can explore. Your goal is to understand something about how this organization functions so that you will understand how they will manage the implementation of your recommendations. Getting data on these dimensions will give you a good picture of the organization. These are also areas that people being interviewed love to talk about, so you will have fun with it.

Ask questions about these areas.

1. *Objectives.*   What are the goals of the group and the person you are talking to? You want to see how much goal clarity and goal agreement there is.

2. *Subgroups.*   What is the relationship between groups that have to work together on this problem? Which groups are supportive? Which groups are in conflict? Are there groups or individuals who tend to be excluded from the action? Why?

3. *Support.*   How does support get expressed in this group? In many groups, support is expressed by silence. "If I like what you are doing, I will leave you alone." Who gets support and from whom?

4. *Evaluation.*   Do people know where they stand? How do they find out? What are the norms about asking where you stand . . . and getting an answer?

5. *Sex Roles.*   What roles do men and women in the organization play? What form does any discrimination take and what impact does it have on this problem?

6. *Status Differences.* Which are the high-status and low-status groups? How are the differences expressed and what impact does this have on the problem and people's attitudes toward a particular solution?

7. *Authority and Power.* Who has high and low power in this situation? How do people working the problem deal with the power differences? Openly, cautiously? What are people's attitudes about authority—do they openly resist it, overly give in to it, put up with it, or just don't care?

8. *Decision Making.* How does the group make decisions? What role does the boss play? How do people get their viewpoints considered in a decision?

9. *Norms for Individual Behavior.* What are the norms on taking the initiative, making demands, expressing disagreement, aggressiveness, asking for help, use of questions to make statements, dealing with boredom, risk taking in expressing doubts or uncertainty, openly confronting differences?

10. *Management Information.* How are resources identified, progress monitored, movement evaluated, problems identified?

11. *Leadership Style.* What are the styles of formal and informal leaders? What is their impact on this problem?

12. *Conflict.* How is it managed, confronted, smoothed over, compromised, forced, ignored, suppressed?

13. *Domination.* Is the situation dominated by one or more persons? What is their impact? Are they part of the group trying to work the problem, or are they so high up in the organization that they are unreachable?

14. *Attitudes About This Project and Your Involvement.* To understand people's attitudes about the problem and what they think of your being involved in trying to solve the problem, try some of these questions.

- How do you feel about my being brought in to help with the problem?

- Why do you think the organization needs the help of someone like me? Do you think my help is needed?

- What kind of questions do you think I should ask people to get a feel for what is going on around here?

- What ideas have been supported by people but have not gotten enough support?

- What would you recommend if you were in my position?

- How hopeful are you about making real progress on this problem? What obstacles do you see to my suggestions being accepted?

Of course, you wouldn't use all of these questions. For any one situation, you can scan the dimensions and the ones that are relevant will stand out to you. Asking any two or three of the questions will give you data on a lot of the rest. You can also assume that how the organization manages its current situation will be identical to how you and your suggestions will be managed. If you use these kinds of questions, you will know what you are getting into, and some of the answers should be part of the clear picture that you are going to report on at the feedback meeting.

Use this kind of data as part of your analysis—even if the client didn't ask for it. It is one of the unique contributions you can make to the client. If you want to be of unique value to your client, then you have to take the risk of offering unique information. Accurate information about how the organization is functioning is not available to most managers. The people they work with have such a vested interest in the organization that no one is trusted to be objective. You have less of a vested interest and are in the best position to deal with sensitive issues.

The Data Collection Interview

The interview is a method of data collection that is common to all disciplines and is often tricky to handle. Though there is much written about interviewing methods, it receives special attention here because of its interpersonal nature and the effect it has on the client organization.

The Interview As a Joint Learning Event

By the time you are starting to do something with your data, you have already had a large impact on the line organization. The mere act of asking questions can stimulate people to rethink what they are doing. Your questions express to them without ambiguity what you think is important to focus on in solving the problem you are working on. Clients can learn a lot from your choice of what to investigate.

If you encounter resistance in an interview, deal with the resistance the same way you deal with resistance at any other stage of the process. Pick up the cue, name the resistance, and wait for the person to respond. If you are in an interview and it is giving you nothing, deal with it as authentically as you can. Tell the person that you are not getting what you need. If that doesn't help, at some point terminate the discussion. You will build more trust with that person if you stop the interview than if you go ahead mechanically through your questions, while both of you know that nothing productive is taking place.

Levels of Analysis

Every problem facing persons or organizations has layers, like an onion. Each statement of a problem or situation is an approximation. As you go to deeper layers, you get closer to causes and to actionable statements of the problem.

The initial statement of a problem, the presenting problem, is almost always made in a way that inspires futility—futility on the part of the client and the consultant. If the presenting problem did not inspire futility, it would already have been solved and you would not be talking about it. To accept the presenting problem at face value is to get stuck. Your task is to work with the line manager—or group or organization—to shed light on the layers underneath the presenting problem. By position alone, you are situated advantageously to see the complexity of the layers underneath.

In working with individuals, the layers generally stack up in a pattern like this.

Top Layer   The presenting problem comes most often in the form of a concern expressed in organizational or business terms. "We aren't getting our product." "My group isn't going well." "The system isn't working."

Second Layer   The person's perceptions about how others are contributing to the problem is the next level. "People are more interested in the stock market than in work." "Two members of the group do all the talking." "The people don't understand the system."

Third Layer   This is a statement of how a person sees his or her own way of contributing to the problem. The person may be contributing by certain conscious actions or by simply not giving the problem attention.

This statement is vital because it brings the responsibility closer to the line manager. Instead of expressing the situation in terms of forces outside the person that are creating the problems, the focus is moved a little more internally.

The questions you ask to get information on each layer are very straightforward.

Top Layer   What is the technical or business problem that you are experiencing?

Second Layer   What are other individuals or groups in the organization doing to either cause or maintain this problem at its current level of severity?

Third Layer What is your role in the problem? What is there in your approach or way of managing the situation that might be contributing to the problem or getting in the way of its resolution?

Note on the third layer: The person you are talking to might answer, "I don't know of anything I am doing that is a problem. That is your job to find out." If you get this response, be a little skeptical. People usually have some idea of how they are contributing to a problem, they are just reluctant to mention it. When someone says to you that they don't know what their role in the problem is, there is a rather clever question you can ask: "Suppose you did know what your role was, what would it be?" Sometimes this jogs them enough to answer your third layer question. If people really do not see themselves as part of the problem, this, in itself, is important. Why do they not see themselves as players? Their stance of spectator, or more harshly, as victims, may be part of a pattern that speaks to the way the group is managed. Include this in your understanding of how the problem is being managed. This sense of helplessness, or being an outsider, will make a difference in the energy available to act on what you recommend.

These layers can form the basis for questions used in the data collection process. The objective of the discovery (especially with an individual) is to discover a statement of the problem that is enlightening and "actionable"—something someone can do something about. The objective is generally not to advance knowledge or generate wisdom about organizations—that is called research. Rather, the consultant's energy is directed toward continually uncovering issues for which people can take responsibility. The root issue is almost always the responsibility a person feels for the problem—how much are people in the stance of a victim versus in a position with some power to act. Uncovering deeper layers of a problem is really the search for unused resources the line manager has to solve the problem.

TOP LAYER SECOND LAYER THIRD LAYER

Try This Exercise

Experiment with the layers-of-analysis approach by interviewing another person. See whether you can identify layers of a problem that were not clear initially.

As you do this, remember:

> The resource the consultant has to offer is to clarify issues—layers of the problem—not to offer solutions. If statements of solutions were going to be helpful at this stage, the line manager probably would have already thought of them. Even if the solutions are indeed novel, the chance of their acceptance now is slim.

Try to keep moving closer to the center of the issues, not farther away. If you listen carefully, you'll notice side trips (usually about people who aren't in the room). Allow the side trips, but don't take the journeys yourself.

Some Responses to Use in the Interview

You have several options in responding to a person in a discovery interview. Try these responses.

1. *Restatement.* Put what is said into other words that communicate and check understanding.

2. *Statement of Your Experience.* Give support through identifying with the dilemma. Keep it short.

3. *Open-Ended Question.* Ask a question in a way that does not program a certain answer or allow a yes or no answer.

4. *Hypothesis About the Next Layer.* Make tentative guesses about how the person is feeling about others involved in the drama, or how the person feels about his or her own role. "You must feel frustrated." "You must feel angry with them." "You must have wondered why they didn't tell you directly."

A Final Comment on What to Look For

Small groups are the vehicle for integrating activity in organizations. Two people can be a small group—or maybe forty. Small group discovery is one step more complex than individual discovery, for it encompasses the interaction among people. It is understanding this interaction that is the core task of small group discovery. Even if the task of the small group is very technical—for example, planning a new product introduction, the interaction of people and viewpoints has to be part of the data collection.

There are two ways of understanding small groups. One is to ask them (either through interviews or questionnaires) what is happening. The second is to observe, firsthand, what is happening.

Norms in Groups— Avoiding the Leadership Love Trap

The complexity of small group functioning can be understood most easily through the concept of group norms.[7] Group norms are statements of common and acceptable ways of behaving in the group. Acceptable ways of dealing with the issues all groups have to deal with—power, conflict, support, risk taking, leveling, problem definition, problem exploration, solution finding, decision making. Each group, whether consciously or not, develops certain ways of dealing with these issues from the instant of its inception. Norms

---

[7]There are a lot of books and articles on group and organizational norms. One of the best is by Neale Clapp, listed in the bibliography.

can be identified via interview, questionnaire, or observation. They are nonjudgmental statements of behavior. "Support in this group is expressed by silence." "Until Alice agrees, the group does not move on." "The group starts its meeting with a discussion of solutions, almost before the problem is defined."

The reason for focusing on group norms is to try and balance the overwhelming emphasis organizations and consultants alike give to "leadership style." There is a great tendency to give the leader total credit or blame for how well a group is performing. People think that the solution to most organizational problems is to get a new leader. It's a sports mentality. Fire the manager.

It takes two to tango, and if a group is having trouble solving a problem, the members of that group have a part in the problem and should be a part of the solution. Pinning too much responsibility on the leader can be a defense for the rest of the group and for the consultant. The group says, "If it weren't for that manager, we could get the job done." Well, the group always has a part in the melodrama. They must be colluding in some ways to keep the situation from improving. They might be a part of the problem by remaining silent, or their sin may be one of resisting everything the manager suggests. If group members can support one another and confront the difficulty they are having with the manager, the situation usually improves. When a manager is blamed and changed, it just means that everyone has to wait around for six months or more until the new person "gets up to speed and gets a feel for the situation."

Resist putting the problems at the door of the manager only. View the group as a self-maintaining system, sharing the blame and the credit. I believe it is important to view all problems as organizational problems. And what you're really trying to do is change the norms and methods the organization uses to do business.

Your Experience As Data

A last comment on data collection. The client manages you, the consultant, the same way the client manages other resources and people. If you want to understand the client's management style, you simply have to observe how you are treated. Are you feeling controlled, listened to, supported, treated with respect or disdain? Are decisions with the client collaborative or one-way? Is the client open to options or forever on one track? Your observations and experience about the client are valid data. Paying close attention to how you are managed by the client early in the project gives you more guidance on what to explore in determining how the technical/business problem is being managed.

Checklist #5. Planning a Data Collection Meeting

To prepare for a data collection meeting, here are some guidelines to consider. They both cover the business of the data collection and also help you prepare for any resistance you might get.

1. Asking questions is an active occasion for learning. Use the meeting as an opportunity to deal with resistance and generate interest and commitment.

2. The response you get provides valuable data on the ultimate implementation of your expertise.

Notice how the client manages the discussion with you:

- How much interest and energy is there on this project?

- On which points is the client uneasy or defensive?

- On which points is the client open to learning and change?

- Where is the client unrealistic in estimating the ease or difficulty of some action?

5. What is your understanding of the presenting problem?

Now, based on your experience, what do you think your layers of analysis will yield?

- Layer 1—What technical/business problems is the client likely experiencing?

- Layer 2—What are others in the client's organization likely contributing to the problem? Who are the other likely actors in the problem?

- Layer 3—What is the client doing that is helping create the problem or preventing it (unknowingly) from being solved?

4. What organizational folklore, history, and culture surrounds this project? Who are the ogres and angels in the client's setting? Acceptance of the folklore as truth is part of what blocks resolution. Identify areas of potential blind spots.

5. You can support and confront during the meeting.

   - What support can you give the client at this point? (For example: tentative recommendations, personal encouragement and assurance, acknowledging difficulties, other similar situations you have known, appreciation for being candid with you?)

   - How might you confront the client in this meeting? (For example: about not getting good data, client over-answering questions and controlling discussion too much, client omitting key areas to discuss, answering questions with one word answers, constant interruptions in the meetings, client skipping around too much, client doesn't believe in project, playing down seriousness or implications of the problem, negative attitudes about consultants in general?)

8. What nonverbal data can you look for? What in the setting of the meeting carries a message on client commitment and involvement in your project?

9. What data do you want to collect about how the organization is functioning?

Your notes contain the content of the data collection meeting. Here are some questions to answer afterward about the process of the meeting. It also is a review of the data collection concepts.

1. How did the client manage the discussion?

   Client Control   Consultant Control
   100 percent   100 percent

   |—————————————————————————————————|

   No client energy   Very high
   for the project   client energy

   |—————————————————————————————————|

2. What is the technical problem?

3. What others are contributing to the problem?

4. What is the client doing to create the problem or to prevent its resolution?

5. What folklore, history, ogres, and angels can you identify on this project? Any blind spots client is missing?

6. What support statements did you make?

7. What confronting statements did you make?

8. What nonverbal data did you notice?

Chapter 12

Whole-System Discovery

MOST OF THE SECTION on discovery has been written from the perspective of a third-party approach, the third party being the consultant who is doing the data collection, analysis, and feedback. While this is the most typical expectation clients have of us, and also the way we have traditionally seen the consultant role, there is an alternative.

The option is to involve the whole client system much more directly in redefining the problem, naming a desired future, outlining alternative actions, and deciding how to proceed. This is a first-party or whole-system strategy, and the methodology has come a long way in the last ten years. Many consultants have adopted the whole-system approach and redefined their role to be one of convening people to collectively develop a change strategy. What is significant about this is that the people doing the discovery and making the recommendations are the same people who will implement the change. In other words, people from the whole system are involved early in the process and are active at every step.

The name, "whole system," though, is a little misleading because the whole system is not literally involved. You can have representatives from all parts of a system in the room, but not really everyone. It means that at least a large sample of those who will be acting on the recommendations is going to play a major part in creating them.

It makes the change effort more self-managing than a third-party approach.

What also is important about a whole-system approach is that it looks at the entire system, not its parts. It can involve a cross section of people that approximates a whole system much more directly and earlier than a third-party approach. A first-party or whole-system strategy engages entire units to self-assess their current reality and plan how to improve it.

Each strategy—third party or whole system—has its advantages and limitations, and I want to outline them briefly. As you read, remember that your goal in each consultation is to catalyze action, not just to have an accurate assessment.

Third-Party Consulting

The most traditional third-party process involves the lone consultant, who studies the situation and makes recommendations for improvement. The consultant may come from inside the organization or be an outsider. Sometimes the third party is a team of people from inside the organization that is given the charge of coming up with recommendations. Often called *design teams*, these groups may number ten to fifty people, and they have six months (or whatever) to work on the project, after which they are expected to return with recommended actions that management can endorse and implement. Even though the design team involves more people than the traditional, lone consultant arrangement, and members are taken from the organization itself, it still represents a third-party strategy: Whenever some individual or group develops a solution for another, it is taking a third-party stance.

The rationale for employing a third-party approach is that consultants, and design teams, have special expertise and are positioned outside the specific system in question, even if only temporarily. This is supposed to lead to a certain objectivity and a willingness to confront difficult issues that people inside the system may be unable or unwilling to face. In addition, third parties may be aware of possibilities that people closer to the problem may miss. The idea of combining a design team with an outside consultant has the added advantage of applying local, intimate knowledge of the problem. The belief is that, given adequate time for analysis and reflection, the partnership of consultant and design team, which is composed of organization members who know the work well, can make more practical and actionable recommendations than a consultant alone might offer.

The strength of any third-party strategy is objectivity. Third parties offer an independent point of view, an outlook that is not colored by being so part of a culture that they cannot see it in a new way. When we can so easily see in others those things that we are blind to in ourselves, why not use a third party to help us see ourselves? The third-party path also has the power of management sponsorship and the unique energy and impetus for improvement it may provide. We believe that if management supports the change, maybe even models it themselves, we are well down the road to making the change happen.

The limitation of third-party help comes from the separation between the discovery and the doing. Third-party recommendations have to be sold to management, and then management has to either mandate or sell the ideas to the employees. The very process of selling is based on flawed premises: It pretends that there is a right answer to the problem, that the consultant or design team knows the right answer, and that, in good engineering fashion, the line organization can (and should) be persuaded to accept the answer and act on it.

In some cases, especially when the problem is strictly technical in nature, there may be a right answer, and it may be accepted and implemented on its own merits. In most cases, however, this thinking is naïve. Whenever there are questions of management or employee commitment or issues of developing new skills or new organizational relationships, the prescriptive engineering or medical model ends in modest change at best. At worst, even if the third party's answer is right, it still may not be acted on, even with unqualified management sponsorship.

Taking a Whole-System Approach

There are times when the people affected by the change can join you in the process of discovery, recommendation, decision, and implementation. This is the whole-system approach, whereby the parties to the change work through the process on their own behalf.

The essence of whole-system discovery is to get everyone in the room at the same time. This deepens an organization's sense of community and allows people to operate with the same information, a common database. All hear what is said, and you avoid the limitations of having a few people planning what is best for a large group.

The main advantage is that there is no need to sell a set of actions to anyone, especially to people at lower levels of the system. When the goal is to build internal commitment to a set of changes, selling is the worst way to do it. People will resist change being inflicted on them, no matter how compelling the case.

The power of the whole-system approach lies not so much in management sponsorship, but in the high engagement and involvement of the entire organization. The whole-system process doesn't proceed without sponsorship, for management will be in the room, but it doesn't bet on sponsorship so heavily. It is a bet on collective knowledge, collective purpose, and the commitment that grows out of deciding for oneself.

"Whole system" means you want representatives from all parts of a system in the room, but not literally everyone in the client organization. This way, at least a large sample of those who will be acting on the recommendations is going to play a major part in creating them. It makes the change effort more self-managing than a third-party approach.

On the other hand, if the whole system can literally be in one room together and the work of the organization allows it, go with everybody in the room. Then you don't have to struggle with building a bridge between the sample of people in the room and those who were absent.

Your Choice

The value of the whole-system approach is that it engages entire units to self-assess their current reality and plan how to improve it. Making a choice about a consulting strategy, then, means deciding whether to give priority to the special expertise and neutrality of the consultant, which leads to a third-party approach, or to give priority to people's commitment to implementation, which might tilt the scales toward a whole-system approach.

Here are some considerations:

Third Party

Neutral observer. No stake in the answer

Broader view. Has seen many organizations and ways to approach the problem

Has specialized expertise that does not reside in the unit

Simple decision-making process. More manager control of decision

Has outsider credibility

Whole System

Decision-making process creates higher commitment to implement

People deciding are the ones who have to make it work

Greater local knowledge. People are intimate with the situation

More realism. People know what is doable and what will work

The learning stays with the organization

Putting Whole-System Discovery to Work

The actual technique of bringing a large number of people together to assess the situation, define a future, and talk about action goes by many different names. Because it can work with several hundred people in the room, it is often called "large-group methodology." Other proponents focus on the involvement it provides and call it a "high-interaction" approach. Because it tries to embrace all the players at once it also can be called "large scale" method. The name isn't important, really, as long as it gives a feel for the intent of whole-system methods.

Whole System

The number of people is limited mostly by the size of the room. The sessions usually last for two or three consecutive days. A design team, usually guided by a consultant, typically plans the large-group event, but they focus only on the process and do not get into statements of the problem or solutions. They deal with questions of whom to invite, what is the right focus for the meeting(s), and how to manage the logistics and stage the activities. For specifics on how to do it, there are some good books by Kathie Dannemiller, Marvin Weisbord, Sandra Janoff, Billie Alban, Barbara Bunker, Dick Axelrod, Emily Axelrod, and others listed in the bibliography.

What is special about whole-system discovery methods is the faith they express in people's capacity to name their own problems and find ways to address them. A whole-system process says that we do not need an outsider, or a special team of insiders, to tell us who we are and what we are up against. If we can create enough trust and are willing to be honest with each other, every unit has within itself the capacity to make changes that are needed.

Having the Right Stuff

To make this approach work, consultant and client have to give up some control and start down a quite unpredictable path, one quite different from the way the organization usually operates and probably not destined for comfort. Here are the conditions that have to be present:

- *There has to be complete transparency.* Management has to be willing to state to the group all they know about the current reality. This includes financial information, progress on important goals, any failures occurring, and how the organization is doing in meeting its key promises to its constituents. If management is contemplating any changes in structure or functions, these need to be on the table, regardless of the anxiety it might create.

- *Management joins the proceedings as full participants.* The session is led by the design team or planners and consultant. Each manager is one among many. Management's ideas are no better than anyone else's. While management may decide to retain some veto power, it will be hard to use without creating cries of manipulation. This is a good model when management is willing to be vulnerable to the same thing they have prescribed for others.

- *The groups must be a full cross section of the whole system.* This means that support people and every level of management and worker, even those from other units that have an important tie to the system, are involved.

- *Differences in status, power, title, and function disappear during the process.* There is a level playing field, and all enter the work as equals. Each working team in the session will have several levels and functions represented. Participants must be willing to cross social and organizational barriers.

- *Employees have to come ready to speak up.* We ask that they suspend their caution and cynicism for a couple of days.

They don't have to forsake caution and cynicism forever, but the meeting is not designed as a forum for complaint and response; it is a co-created event where all have answers and all have questions.

- *If employees choose not to participate, they surrender their right to complain or be heard.* No claiming later that they were not part of the decision. Rights of citizenship are earned by the choice to participate.

- *There is an emphasis on the future and what the group wants to create together.* There is some discussion of obstacles and the current reality, but the strategy is to talk more about what we want to create tomorrow than how to fix what we've got today.

- *The session ends with agreements on next steps and who is going to work on them.* Management and employees have to be willing to allow next steps to emerge out of this session. Everyone gives up some control.

- *Consultants give up the expert role.* We no longer analyze the data, make recommendations, and follow up. Our role is to conduct people through a highly participatory series of steps. We become less central, less visible, and less able to be an advocate for a certain answer.

Each of these conditions moves the organization in an egalitarian, self-governing direction. That is the power of the strategy, but also its limitation. Managers cannot start this process of sharing power and then pull back at moments of doubt and nervousness.

The Payoff

My intent in introducing you to whole-system discovery is simply to explain why this method is important and show how it changes the role of the consultant. But I must also admit a certain inclination toward using a whole-system strategy whenever possible.

If the conditions are right, it has a real advantage over a third-party stance in the way it builds the capacity of the organization to manage itself in the future. It also keeps the consultant in an educational role. It demands that we develop our ability to design learning experiences for others. And it requires that we expand our skills in how to convene and bring people together, how to encourage them to question their current reality and envision their future, and how to confront them with their freedom and responsibility through interactive activities, as opposed to confronting these issues in a more traditional, face-to-face way.

Chapter 13
Preparing for Feedback

A Clear Picture May Be Enough

Let's return here to the third-party role of the consultant, as this is the situation still most common. Every line manager wants to know what to do about a problem and so wants recommendations. Resist being carried away by the struggle to develop perfect recommendations. If you have presented a clear and simple picture of why the problem exists, the client will have as many ideas for recommendations as you do. The reason the manager has run out of recommendations to believe in is because of the inadequate picture of the problem the manager is now working with. The consultant's primary task is to present the picture—this is 70 percent of the contribution you have to make. Trust it.

What you do with your discovery is to focus attention on areas that your expertise tells you are the likely causes of the problem. What to focus on is under your control, regardless of the assignment. Trusting yourself to focus on what you feel is important may be the most valuable thing you have to offer the client. Treat the choice of what to examine as a very important choice and yours to influence.

Condensing the Data

You always collect more data that you could ever use. A high anxiety point in any consulting project of any length is when you have finished asking your questions, have all the information you are going to get, and now have to make sense out of it.

You may have devised a rational, logical process to sort out and categorize the data, but the selection of what is important is essentially a judgment on your part. This is what they are paying you for. Trust your intuition; don't treat it as bias. If you are an internal consultant, you are often familiar with all the organization, the people, and how they operate. Use this information in condensing the data.

When I am struggling to decide what is important in a pile of notes, I will sometimes read through all the notes once, then put them away. On a blank sheet of paper I will then list what I think is important in the data—usually about four or five items. I let that be my guide on what to report and how to organize the report. I have faith that what I can remember is what is really important. Since a person can only absorb a limited amount of data, what stands out to me is what I want to stand out to the client. Let the information that stays in the background become part of an appendix, but don't clutter the feedback meeting with a complete list of everything you found out.

As guidelines for selecting what to highlight to the client, I would prefer items that:

1. The client has control over changing

2. Are clearly important to the organization

3. There is some commitment somewhere in the client organization to work on

Some Do's and Don'ts

As you get close to planning the feedback meeting, you start making decisions about what to include and how to say it.

Don't Collude

Don't give the client support for a stance that reduces the organization's ability to solve the problem. If there are certain sensitive subjects that the client avoids and is uncomfortable with, don't collude with the client by also avoiding those subjects.

There are two things consultants typically do to collude with clients, thereby undermining themselves. The first is to develop explanations for problems that leave the solution outside the client's control. We blame higher management, we blame the general economic condition, we blame other groups in the organization. Each of these explanations has the benefit of reducing the immediate pain of the client's own responsibility, but carries the price of feeling helpless about improving the situation. Don't collude with the client in avoiding responsibility. You can acknowledge the role others play in the problem and at the same time keep the feedback focused on the client's role.

The second way we tend to collude with clients is to play down the impact difficult relationships have on the problem. The client may be having trouble with a subordinate or a boss and yet barely mention this as part of the problem. If you get wind of this kind of difficulty, mention it in your report. If the written report is slated for wide circulation, you may want to mention it only verbally. Don't avoid dealing with it. Helping the manager face up to the connection difficult relationships have to the problem may be the most important contribution you can make.

Don't Project

Projecting is placing your own feeling onto another person. If you are feeling anxious about part of the data, you assume the client will also feel anxious. If you would not like someone to tell you that your subordinates feel you are too autocratic, you assume the client also would not like to hear that feedback. The client has a right to all the information that you have collected. Let the client have it. Stay aware of your own feelings, but keep testing the limits of what the line manager can accept. If you feed back data that causes a minor uproar, stay with it. You and the client will both survive. Don't project your feelings onto the client. Make statements to the client and then ask how the client feels about the statements.

Do Confirm Their Expectations

Clients (and consultants) need support. If you have data that is confirming to the client—that reinforces the reasonableness of what the client is doing—include it in your report. If the client has a perception of the problem, and you see it the same way, say so.

I recently had a client who felt everyone in the organization was avoiding responsibility for the fact a certain test procedure wasn't working. The failure of the test procedure resulted in poor raw material being delivered to the customer. The customer unknowingly used the raw material in their finished product. They got serious customer complaints and eventually had to recall the product. This became a huge crisis that returned to my client's door. He had been trying to work the problem with the test, but to no avail. When we interviewed others in the organization about the problem, it was clear that *no one felt responsible for solving it,* although everyone felt it should be handled by a specific research group. When we reported this to the client, he was very relieved and reassured that we shared his perception of the problem. He had begun to think maybe he was crazy, and everyone else knew what they were doing.

This was a confirming and valuable experience for the client. If you have confirming data, report it to the client. Even though many clients say they only want to hear about the problem, don't you believe it. Give support even if it is not requested.

Do Confront

Your data will also indicate areas in which the client should improve. You can identify things the client is doing that are self-defeating, areas in which the client is vulnerable. Report them, even if they are painful. The hardest data to report may be about the client's own personal style: Just confront the client with this information in as straight and supportive a way as possible. If the consultant avoids information that creates tension, then why does the client need the consultant? The client already knows how to avoid tension. Your role is to help the client move toward the tension and face the difficult reality that has been skirted.

Language in Giving Feedback

The most useful guideline for giving feedback effectively—either written or spoken—is to behave assertively. There are many frameworks for looking at personal behavior and personal effectiveness. I think this one is the clearest and most practical.

Assertive

Every person has rights. Clients and consultants too. Assertive behavior is stating directly what you want and how you see things without putting down or infringing on the rights of others. Assertive feedback is stating to the client how you see the problem without implying that the client is a bad manager.

Aggressive

Aggressive behavior is expressing your own wants and views, but doing it in a way that puts down or negates the other person. Aggressive feedback is stating the problem in a way that implies the manager is incompetent, immoral, unfeeling, uncaring, or stupid. The operational test for aggressive statements is whether you can add the phrase "you dummy" to the end of the sentence. If "you dummy" fits nicely at the end, it was an aggressive statement.

Nonassertive

Nonassertive behavior is when you hold back your feelings and views and don't state them at all. Nonassertive feedback, in the name of protecting the manager or yourself, occurs when you don't present the client information on how the problem is being managed, or how the management style of the manager is affecting the problem. Nonassertion also occurs when you ignore the politics of the situation or avoid sensitive issues.

Authentic behavior and assertive behavior are very close together. It is good to be assertive with a client. Aggressive behavior creates resistance unnecessarily. Nonassertive behavior does both yourself and the client a disservice.

In wording feedback, then, the goal is to *describe* what you have found and not to evaluate it. Your task is to present a clear and simple picture of the problem. The more the feedback is evaluative, the greater the resistance. The choice is to make the feedback as descriptive as possible.

For example, it is one thing to say that when the group sits down to do work, the boss does about 80 percent of the talking—that's a descriptive statement. Another way to put it would be that the boss totally dominates and overruns this group and doesn't do a good job of running meetings. The second way would be the evaluative way.

The more evaluative the statement, the more defensive people get. Words such as *weak, strong, incompetent, indecisive, dictatorial* are very evaluative and should not be used. Avoid "judging" words.

Also avoid vague stereotypes. The more specific you are about what's going on in the organization, the better it is. A general statement like "We have a problem in decision making" is so vague that people can't really identify the problem being presented.

Long explanations and justifications should also be avoided in presenting your feedback. Most questions about method and recommendations can be answered in a paragraph or less. If the questions persist, give your two good faith answers, and then acknowledge that it is resistance that confronts you. Deal with the resistance by naming it and waiting for a response. Resist the temptation to explain the unexplainable.

The feedback is a statement of what is, not a statement of what ought to be. To discuss what ought to be is to moralize and sound like a judge or seer. The only time to talk about what ought to be is when your contract with the client is to predict or prescribe the future. Otherwise, make neutral, descriptive statements of what is currently causing the problem.

Use Language That Is	Avoid Language That Is
Descriptive	Judgmental
Focused	Global
Specific	Stereotyped
Brief	Lengthy
Simple	Complicated

A Preview of the Feedback Meeting . . . As Courtroom Drama

If you can view a consulting project as a process in search of the best decision, you can view the consultant and client as taking different roles commonly found in a courtroom. Most of these roles are negative examples of what *not* to do. I apologize for this. But you see these roles played out so often in offices, conference rooms, and production areas that they are worth mentioning. None but the last role really serves the consultant well, though I admit some do have a certain appeal.

Consultant As Judge

You are there to interpret the law. To interpret corporate policy. To tell the client when he is out of line. When a client makes a mistake, the Consultant Judge decides what the penalty should be by influencing that manager's performance appraisal next time around. Because judges sit higher than the rest of us, people fear them and don't come to see them voluntarily. The only ones really comfortable with judges are other judges (sometimes called top management).

| **Consultant As Jury** | Juries determine guilt and innocence. Consultant Juries feel responsible for ultimately deciding on their own whether the client was wrong or right. It is a very remote and very judgmental stance. |

| **Consultant As Prosecutor** | The prosecutor is there to present evidence to the jury. Some consultants conduct a feedback meeting as if they were really going for a conviction. They develop data and statistics that are irrefutable. The whole presentation is fool-proof packaged and totally buttoned up. This creates distance from the client and carries the message that the project is really up to the consultant, rather than a joint effort. |

| **Consultant As Defendant** | Sometimes we go into a feedback meeting feeling like we are the one on trial. We have all our just-in-case files with us. We have rehearsed our presentation three times, and we even have an extra set of viewgraphs in case of an accident. When we get questioned by the client, we overexplain and make promises to get more data, even when we know inside it is a waste of time. The consultant is not a defendant. If the client is treating you like you are a defendant, it is just resistance and the client's own anxiety about the project. |

| **Consultant As Witness** | This is the preferred role for a consultant. The witness is there to present accurate information. The witness has no direct vested interest in the outcome of the deliberations. Witnesses give a clear, specific picture of what they observed. The data presentation part of the feedback meeting is designed to do just that. So view yourself as a fair witness. |

> **A note:** It is a great luxury to be able to be just a fair witness for a client and to not also have the responsibility for guarding the corporate interest. Many internal consultants have to be part-time police officers and part-time judges. When this happens, these roles greatly interfere with developing the kind of trust with clients

that we would all wish. There is no real way out of this bind. The best you can do is be clear with the client when you are in uniform and when you can be just a friendly, down-home consultant. If, however, as an internal consultant you have a choice whether to take on some policing responsibilities, think twice. The attraction is that it gives you instant access and instant power over some people in the organization. The price for that power is high, and in my opinion it is usually not worth the distrust that you create in your potential clients by taking on the robes of judgment. Most internal consultants disagree with me on this, so there you have it.

Support and Confrontation

In giving any kind of feedback, you're doing two things. On the one hand, you're giving support to the organization; on the other hand, you're confronting it. Viewing the feedback process as only confrontation increases the tension and decreases the chance of getting action. It is important to express the support you feel for that organization as well as to call attention to the problem. People need support in order to have the strength to take responsibility for problems.

Support and confrontation are not mutually exclusive. The feedback meeting is a difficult time for clients, even though they asked for it. They ask for the confrontation when they commission for a discovery, but they also need support. Often, the more resistant the group, the more support they need (and the harder it is to give it to them). An example is in coping with very high control, authoritarian style managers. On the surface, they may appear very controlling and look like they don't care about you as a person or care about people in the organization. They may act in a way that says they don't have any problems, or that their problems can be solved by mechanistic solutions.

A very authoritarian style on the surface may really be an expression of the manager's own anxiety about losing control in one of two ways. One way is that the managers would lose control of themselves or would find themselves in a situation in which they would be saying things that would be regretted later. The second anxiety is about losing control of the organization if they really owned up to problems, faced them, and dealt with them. Managers fear they might end up supporting a more democratic or anarchic organization than they want. To the extent that it's accurate that underneath the resistance is an anxiety about control, one good way to respond is to give *support* to the manager.

If people are anxious, they need support, not confrontation. Even if they are being controlling and indifferent on the surface, give them support and let them know that they will be in control of the process, that they won't be in a position of doing anything they don't want to do. They won't lose control of the organization or lose the power that they think they need to manage it.

Supporting and confronting can almost come in the same sentence. The support statement often is a simple acknowledgment that you hear what the client is saying. To give the client support does not commit you to agree. It means you have listened. The confront statement then identifies the difference between how you see a situation and how the client sees the situation. Both kinds of statements should be part of your feedback.

Chapter 14

Managing the Feedback Meeting

Feedback Concepts and Skills

The feedback meeting is when you present a clear and simple picture of the current situation and present your recommendations. It is the moment of truth and high anxiety for the client and the consultant. It is also exciting and fun. Next to that moment in the beginning of the project when the client says yes, the feedback is the part of consulting that I enjoy most.

The excitement of the feedback meeting is that it holds the promise of someone's *deciding* something. Some action's taking place. Some hope that the energy the client and I have invested in this process will pay off. This is the major agenda of a feedback meeting—the commitment to action steps. Even if most of the meeting is spent in understanding the problem, the heart of the meeting is the discussion of what to do about it. This is the way to approach the meeting—as an opportunity to get action, not just an opportunity to present data. In this sense, the feedback meeting is a beginning, not an ending. It is the beginning of the main event—the implementation phase that will solve a problem or change the status quo. This chapter is about how to structure and manage a feedback meeting to make the meeting the beginning of some action.

To flawlessly manage a feedback meeting, you need to attend to the business of this stage.

227

1. *Funnel the Data.* Select what data to report. Use language that is accurate, confronting, and nonpunishing.

2. *Present Personal and Organizational Data.* Include in your data summary information on how the problem is being managed.

3. *Manage the Feedback Meeting.* Maintain control of it and structure it. Focus on what will be done about the problem.

4. *Focus on the Here and Now of the Meeting.* To have maximum leverage and get your expertise utilized, you need to watch the process of the meeting and deal directly with the resistance as it occurs. If you don't deal with the resistance in the feedback meeting, you may never get another chance.

5. *Don't Take It Personally.* A special reminder here, because this is the phase of consulting where you are likely to get the most resistance. Remember the rule—after 6:00 p.m. you can take anything personally, but during the day, no matter how many guns are aimed at you, your task is to stay focused on the client's internal struggle to confront the reality that is being resisted.

The other half of flawless feedback is to behave authentically—to state to the client what you are experiencing as the feedback meeting progresses.

How to Present Data

The data should focus on a few central aspects of the problem. The mistake with most presentations is that they are too long and too intricate. When we have spent all that time analyzing data, we fall in love with it. We find interesting discrepancies that defy explanation; we notice historical trends and comparisons. We discover curves and graphs with shapes, heights, and textures that are each worth an hour's discussion. Go ahead and fall in love with your data—but don't tell everyone about it. Keep it short and simple. The longer and more complex you make it, the more you are open for endless questions on methodology and interpretation.

To structure the presentation, there are only three general categories of data:

Analysis of the technical/business problem

Analysis of how the problem is being managed

Recommendations

You probably already have your own way of structuring a presentation. Here is one structure that I like that Harold Goldstein taught me:

Problem statement

Why the problem exists

What happens if the problem is not fixed

- in the short term

- in the long term

Recommended solutions

Expected benefits

In deciding how to present data, remember:

> The purpose of discovery is to *focus* awareness on a manageable number of dimensions. Most feedback overloads the organization. Keep the feedback down to under ten, or even fewer, issues.

> The feedback does not have to have all the answers, does not have to be complete. It is often useful to devise a format that offers a role whereby the manager or group can participate in the analysis.

> The end result with a group, as with an individual, is to have it take responsibility for its own situation.

The report should be worded in a way that expresses the group's own role. Don't collude by blaming other groups or the weather.

Structuring the Meeting

The purpose of the meeting is more than the presentation of your data. You want to get the client's reaction to the data and recommendations, and you want to get the client to do something as a result of your study.

Here is how to get what you want from the meeting.

1. It is up to the consultant to control the flow of the meeting. You are in the best position to do this—the client is going to be busy working through resistance and, for the meeting, is in a pretty dependent position. If you control the meeting, it serves as a model for the client to learn how to manage meetings like this.

2. The agenda should follow the sequence shown in Figure 10. Keep the steps in that order and don't skip any steps.

The Feedback Meeting— Step by Step

Here is a detailed breakdown for the steps. The right-hand columns suggest how to allocate time to each sequence of steps. Beginning and ending times for each sequence in a sixty-minute meeting are shown. The percentage of meeting time that should be devoted to each step or group of steps is also listed. That way if you have planned a four-hour feedback meeting, you know to ask the client how the meeting is going (Step 7) at the end of two hours.

Steps	Percent of Total Meeting	Time for a 60–Minute Meeting
1. Restate the original contract.	5 percent	Begin: The beginning
2. State the structure of the meeting.		End: 3rd minute

freedom, or will they abuse the privilege and go off in separate directions? Should we always tell the truth, or do we acknowledge the political nature of organizations? Will more technology and better information help, or is it a problem of motivation and lack of training?

Every consultation involves these kinds of questions. Even in very technical consulting, questions like these are embedded in the architecture of our solutions. We make a serious mistake if we choose one or the other, or even try to find a middle ground. We lose the benefit of the unique ideas at the two poles when we compromise for middle ground. The best outcomes emerge in the effort to understand the truth in both sides. The consultant's task is to evoke an exploration of the polarity, to postpone the quick answers, and to make sure that the complexity of the question is acknowledged before action is chosen. It is in the struggle to transcend both sides that a resolution is found.

For example, we need control, and we also need local choice. People need more freedom, and they will at times abuse it. More technology is vital, and motivation and skill are everything. It is the tension in these polarities that informs action that is based in reality and stays alive. If we can accept that this sort of tension is always present, then the action we take at a particular moment will in some ways not matter: Whatever we choose, we will pay a price for it. So why not acknowledge this, see the struggle as the path, and resist the temptation of certainty and speed?

The Question Is More Important Than the Answer

What this means is that we have to learn to trust the questions. And to recognize that the way we ask the question drives the kind of answer we develop.

We get stuck by asking the wrong question. The most common wrong question is that of the engineer who wants to know "how" we get something done. This question quickly takes us down the path of methodology and technique. It assumes the problem is one of what to do, rather than why to do it. Or whether it is worth doing.

The "how" question has several variations. Take them as warning signs.

- *How long will it take?*   We want to make good time regardless of where we are going.

- *How do we get them to change?*   If only they would change, we would be better off. The top thinks the bottom is the problem, the bottom thinks the top is the problem, and when they get together, they both agree the middle is the problem.

- *What are the steps needed for . . . ?*   Life can be reduced to a step-by-step plan. A Day-Timer notebook is the icon, lists with milestones are the drug, and more discipline is the prescription that never cures.

- *How do we measure the effect?*   There is no value in the invisible world. It is the measure of reality that becomes the point. Alan Watts once said that we have reached the point at which we go to a restaurant and eat the menu. We have become more interested in the definition and measurement of life than in living it.

- *How do we communicate this?*   The problem is they do not understand us. "A problem in communication" is the ultimate empty diagnosis. It denies real conflict and raises spin to the level of purpose. Our finest example of this is Washington, D.C., where their only work is to manage image and the news. Questions of communication are most often the easy way out of questions of will, courage, and commitment.

- *What are other organizations doing or where has this worked?*   We want to lead and wish to go second at the same time. There is some value in discovering what others are doing: It gives us hope. More often, though, the question is a wish for safety, for when we hear where it has worked, we then talk of how unique our situation is.

These questions are so appealing because they demand so little. They promise a world that is logical and predictable. They also externalize the problem and are focused on change from people who are not in the room. What's more, they shrink the problem to manageable size by treating it as a matter of skills, rather than questions of purpose and the use of power.

Beyond How

"How" questions will take us no farther than our starting place. They result in trying harder at what we were already doing. The questions that heal us and offer hope for authentic change are the ones we cannot easily answer. Living systems are not controllable, despite the fact that they evolve toward order and some cohesion. To move a living system, we need to question what we are doing and why. We need to choose depth over speed, consciousness over action. At least for a little while.

The questions that lead to a change in thinking are more about "why" and "where" than about "how." Some examples:

- *What is the point of what we are doing?* We live in a world measured by wealth and scale. Are we here to make money, to meet budgets, to grow the operation? Is this enough? And who is the beneficiary of this? Who are we here to serve, and what price are we willing to pay to stay true to our answer?

- *What has to die before we can move to something new?* We want change but do not want to pay for it. We are always required to put aside what got us here to really move on. Where do we find the courage to do this?

- *What is the real value of our product and service?* And in whose eyes? How valid is our promise and what are the side effects of our delivery? Are our advertising and the way we present ourselves a picture we even believe is true?

- *What personal meaning do people find in what we are doing?* What intrinsic rewards exist for us? Do we show up voluntarily, or have we indentured ourselves simply to sustain our life out-side of work? Many people think work is just that, work, and to expect more is to be a fool.

- *What would happen if we did nothing?* When is change for its own sake? Maybe we should just get better at what we do now.

- *What are the capacities and strengths that we are not using fully?* Give up on fixing weaknesses; find out what more is possible. Sometimes we do not even know our strengths, as individuals and as institutions. What strengths do others see in us? Years ago in our consulting firm, we asked clients why they hired us. They said that what they found attractive was our seeming disinterest and reluctance in working with them. We were shocked. We thought that if we seemed aloof, it was because we were disorganized and sloppy; they saw it as a sign of integrity.

- *And what are we leaving for the next generation?* This question is for the second half of life, but it is still a useful focusing exercise. Our materialistic culture consumes its resources and bets on science or miracles to cope with what we leave for those after us. What will our legacy be?

These are difficult questions, ones that require faith and patience. They do not substitute for action, and at some point we do have to ask "How?" But the "why's" are questions designed for learning and change, and in that way they are very practical indeed. It is in the dialogue about these questions that change occurs. They are questions for the client to engage in at the top and bottom, and in-between; they are not questions for the consultant to answer.

It is hard for some to engage in this level of abstract dialogue, even though these are the questions we each privately ask ourselves. No matter how difficult, our clients must deal with these questions publicly, because the route to genuine change is less obvious than a list and some milestones; without some depth to our inquiry, our thinking will never change and we destine ourselves to the pursuit

Figure 10.   Steps in Managing the Feedback Meeting

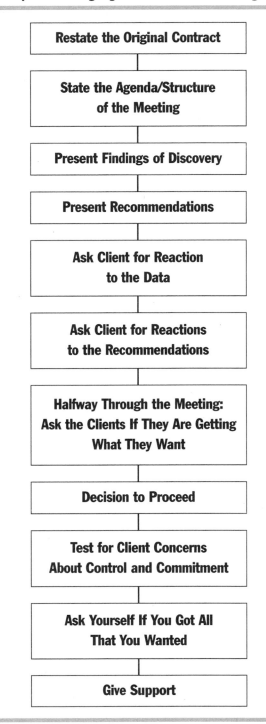

Restate the Original Contract

State the Agenda/Structure
of the Meeting

Present Findings of Discovery

Present Recommendations

Ask Client for Reaction
to the Data

Ask Client for Reactions
to the Recommendations

Halfway Through the Meeting:
Ask the Clients If They Are Getting
What They Want

Decision to Proceed

Test for Client Concerns
About Control and Commitment

Ask Yourself If You Got All
That You Wanted

Give Support

| **State the Structure of the Meeting** | State what the client wanted from you and what you promised to deliver. For example, "You asked us to investigate why the Brogan Plant Reactor broke down. We agreed to do that and come back with recommendations. We did not look into the auxiliary equipment that supports the reactor." This restates the presenting problem and reminds the client of the essentials of the contract. Sometimes consultants like to give a little history of the project. I would rather not. I only devote 5 percent of the meeting for Steps 1 and 2. |

After restating the contract, state how you want the meeting structured. Remember, you want to control the flow of the meeting. You don't have to announce that you are in charge; you just have to act that way. One way to act that way is to announce right at the beginning, "Here is how I would like to structure this meeting. I would like to present our findings and recommendations. Then I would like you (the client) to react to both our picture of how things are and to our recommendations. About halfway through the meeting, I would like to stop to see if you are getting what you want from the meeting. The last 40 percent of the meeting I would like to devote to a discussion of what action you might take to deal with the problem. The meeting is planned to adjourn at. . . . ."

Steps	**Percent of Total Meeting**	**Time for a 60–Minute Meeting**
3. Present findings.	15 percent	Begin: 4th minute
4. Present recommendations.		End: 12th minute

| **Present Findings and Recommendations** | These two steps get intermingled. Some people like to start with the headlines and list recommendations after each point of the findings. Other people present the whole thing and then move into recommendations. It helps to structure this part of the presentation so the client's reaction to the data will be separate from the client's reaction |

to the recommendations. You want to protect the recommendations from any expression of resistance. If the manager is taking your feedback hard and asking you question after question, you would rather have your analysis be the victim of the barrage of resistance than sacrifice your recommendations. If the client is eager to get to the recommendations and skip over the data, slow the process down: Say you will get to the recommendations in a minute, but first you want to get reactions to your assessment of the situation. Each organization has different norms about how to format this part of the meeting. Some are very formal; others are informal.

My preference is to avoid a lot of formality. A formal presentation, especially with slides or transparencies, puts too much distance between the client and the information. When you look at a slide, the screen is far away, and if the printing on the slide or transparency is done perfectly, it looks like it's cast in concrete. These media work against the primary objective. I know this is a blow to PowerPoint users, but after all, the point here is not to hold the power. Presenting a perfect package at the feedback meeting is a mistake. If it is too perfect, it's like the Christmas present you get from your great Aunt Alice: You know she spent six hours wrapping this one package. You really hate to open it, it looks so orderly and you know how much Aunt Alice has invested in its appearance. The same with a "perfect presentation." I prefer to use handouts and a flip chart. Both can be amended easily by me and the client as we go along.

Remember that you have to be finished with data and recommendations after only 20 percent of the meeting is gone. In a one-hour meeting, this is the twelfth minute. Figuring it took you three minutes to introduce the meeting, you have nine minutes left. This time constraint forces you to really get to the point, and to get to recommendations quickly.

The major mistake people make in the feedback meeting is to use the whole meeting for reporting data. When you are presenting the results of discovery, you are discussing a subject of great fascination to both you and the client. If you let yourselves get carried away with this fascination, the meeting will slip by and neither the consultant nor the client will know what is going to happen after they leave. This leaves you—and the client—hanging.

You also need enough time to deal with the client's resistance. *How the client reacts to the data is more important to implementation than the data itself.* If the analysis is brilliant but the client is indifferent to it, nothing is going to happen. If the analysis is noticeably mediocre and the client is really turned on by it (despite its mediocrity), some action is going to take place. So keep the presentation time down; give the major portion of the meeting to the client's reactions.

Step	**Percent of Total Meeting**	**Time for a 60–Minute Meeting**
5. Ask for client reactions.	30 percent	Begin: 13th minute End: 30th minute

Ask for Client Rections

This is the heart of the meeting. The client's reaction will determine the amount of internal commitment that exists when you leave. The client's reactions will determine whether your expertise gets used or not.

This is the point at which you want the client's reservations expressed. If the manager holds back reservations about the data or the methodology in the middle of the meeting, those reservations will come out later, at a much less desirable time—either at the moment of decision or after you have left the scene.

Sometimes you need to ask direct, specific questions to get the client's reactions. Clients will often give their reactions with no prompting at all. If you get a silent or very quiet response, you need to say to the client, "What is your reaction to the information I am reporting?" or "What concerns do you have about the data or the analysis?" There may be a portion of the data that you know touches a very sensitive issue. I would ask about this directly: "Part of our report is on how you have been managing the problem and your boss's role in this problem. How do you feel about the way we have summarized the situation?"

The goal here is to move toward any tension in the situation and to elicit any unexpressed resistance.

A certain amount of tension is useful in any feedback meeting. If there is no tension, then it is likely that the data and recommendations are ones that nobody really cares about, which means there also won't be any energy to implement. If the tension is too high, the client and the consultant can be so threatened as to be unable to take responsibility and plan for any realistic, useful next steps. What you want is a moderate level of tension.

You have 30 percent of the meeting to devote to client reactions. This is the time to ask the client to express his or her feelings, so don't get defensive when you hear them. The client's reactions are not against you: They are against having to face the pain in acting on and confronting the data you present. If you find yourself being defensive, you are in danger of being captured by part of the same anxiety that has infected the client. Be aware of when you are getting defensive and, if you notice it, you should stop it.

It is also important to stick to your assessment of the situation and your belief in your recommendations. There must have been a good reason why it made sense to you. Don't cave in when you meet resistance. You trust what you are suggesting and, while you don't need to defend it, don't give it up too easily.

Steps	Percent of Total Meeting	Time for a 60–Minute Meeting
6. Halfway through the meeting, ask the client, "Are you getting what you want?"	10 percent	Begin: 31st minute End: 36th minute

"Are You Getting What You Want?"

The single most powerful thing you can do is to ask clients, at the halfway point in feedback meetings, whether they are getting what they want from the meeting. This is an insurance question. I used to ask the manager about the meeting just before the meeting was about to end. Say with about five to ten minutes left. This was too late. A few times when the manager was in fact disappointed by the meeting, I had no time to recover. If the manager wanted more specific recommendations, or had concerns that he or she was feeling but not expressing, there was no time left to respond. If half the meeting is left, there is a good chance I can come up with what the manager might want, or can help the manager surface the reservations fully enough to get past them.

Despite the emphasis I give to this step in training other consultants, they rarely are able to ask for feedback halfway through the meeting. The consultant and the client are so immersed in the task that the time slips by. The consultant can also be reluctant to ask how the meeting is going for fear there will be no way to respond to the client's disappointment. It is better to at least make the recovery attempt than to find out after the meeting what went wrong. (Things to do when the meeting is not going well are covered later in this chapter.)

Step	**Percent of Total Meeting**	**Time for a 60–Minute Meeting**
7. Decision to proceed.	30 percent	Begin: 37th minute End: 54th minute

Decision to Proceed

The purpose of the feedback meeting is to see some action take place. The question of what to do next should be asked early enough in the meeting so the consultant can participate in the decision.

If you wait until near the end of the meeting, the real discussion of how to proceed might take place at a time and place that will exclude you. If the client makes a decision when you are not present, the chances are somewhat less that the decision will really deal with the *difficult realities* your study has surfaced. This is particularly true if your study has at all focused on the way the problem is being managed and the management style of the client. It is hard for clients to see their own roles in maintaining or creating a problem, and your presence makes it easier.

When you participate in the discussion of what to do about the problem, there are some key tasks for you to concentrate on.

1. Keep the discussion centered on things that are under the control of the client.

2. Keep raising the parts of the problem or recommendations that you think are *essential* to resolving the immediate and the longer-term problem. The essentials are often the more sensitive parts of the situation—a difficult relationship, a poor performer, or some political consideration. As a consultant, you can focus on the sensitive issues without vested interest and perform a service by doing this.

3. Keep balance in the discussion by surfacing the viewpoints of people who aren't in the room. You usually have a clear picture of how different people in the organization see a situation. As the client is considering what to do, you can make sure the different viewpoints are considered in the decision.

4. Support the right of the responsible manager to make the choice with minimal coercion from others, including the consultant.

At times, the client will want to exclude the consultant from the decision-making meeting. I always ask to be present. To be present at the decision-making point is something to ask for in your initial contract. The reason the client would want to exclude the consultant from the decision is to maintain control. To keep the consultant from the decision is really another form of resistance.

Steps	Percent of Total Meeting	Time for a 60–Minute Meeting
8. Test for concerns of control and commitment.	10 percent	Begin: 55th minute
9. Ask yourself if you got what you wanted.		
10. Give support.		End: 60th minute

Closing the feedback meeting is very similar to closing the contracting meeting. You want to ensure that the decisions made have the commitment of the client. You can also view the feedback meeting as the entry stage of the next contract you might have with this client. The closing should be as direct and complete as possible.

Here are the steps.

Test for Client Concerns About Control and Commitment

Ask the client, "How do you feel about the control you will have if we go ahead with the solution?" If the client is uneasy, you may want to discuss ways the uneasiness can be managed.

Ask Yourself Whether There Is More You Want from the Meeting

Ask the client, "Is the solution we discussed something that really makes sense to you?" If the client's commitment seems low, you may want to pursue it further in the meeting or raise the matter at a later time.

You may want some continuing involvement. You may want feedback later on the effect of your consultation. You may want feedback now from the client on whether you were helpful on this project and how you might have been more effective. You may want the client to informally tell your boss that you did good work. You may want another contract with the client, either to implement this project or to begin a different one. If there are things you want, now is the time to ask for them.

Give Support	Implementation is a time when the heaviest burden is on the client. Give support for this responsibility.		
A Recap	Here's a recap of the steps in managing the feedback meeting.		

Steps	Percent of Total Meeting	Time for a 60-Minute Meeting	
		Begin	**End**
1. Restate the original contract.	5 percent	The beginning	
2. State the structure of the meeting			3rd minute
3. Present diagnosis.	15 percent	4th minute	
4. Present recommendations.			12th minute
5. Ask for client reactions.	30 percent	13th minute	30th minute
6. Halfway through the meeting, ask the client, "Are you getting what you want?"	10 percent	31st minute	36th minute
7. Decision to proceed		37th minute	54th minute
8. Test for concerns of control and commitment.		55th minute	
9. Ask yourself if you got what you wanted.	10 percent		
10. Give support.			60th minute

Following this meeting structure ensures that you have attended to the business of the feedback phase. This is half the way to consulting flawlessly. The other half is behaving authentically at each stage of the meeting. The greatest strain in doing this is dealing with the resistance that is sure to arise in the meeting. Here are some reminders to help overcome these hurdles.

Resistance in the Feedback Meeting

The feedback meeting itself is part of the client's data collection and learning process. The crucial skill in conducting the feedback meeting is to stay focused on the here-and-now process. This is more important than even the content of the findings being discussed. Many of the issues explored in the discovery phase that deal with dysfunctional ways of operating will be acted out in this meeting. Being conscious of this will help you resist getting stuck in the meeting.

Getting stuck in the feedback meeting takes many forms:

Having to rigorously defend the data against people who are supposed to learn from it

Finding yourself providing the energy for the next steps for an organization or group that you are not really a member of

Being expected to have all the answers

Being in the position of providing solutions to very complex problems in less than three minutes

The way out of most stuck places is to put what is happening into words as it is happening: "I find myself having to defend data against people who are supposed to be learning from it," or "I keep hearing myself come up with next steps for *your* organization, and I am not even going to be around!" or "One of the norms I mentioned is that people express support with silence—is that happening right now?—help!"

The resistance you get to suggestions for next steps is valuable because it means you are on target. You shouldn't view it as a rejection or disinterest on the part of the client. It means that you're dealing with something that's important to the client, so you should move toward the resistance rather than away from it.

The response that you get to feedback will re-enact in the actual feedback meeting all the problems that the organization has in solving other issues and managing its other business. The response to feedback may be a retreat into detail, or a postponement of a decision to act, or a denial of problems. Whatever the response, you can interpret it as being the characteristic way the organization handles its decisions. It is important to interpret the response in this fashion, and to give support to an organization in seeing what it is doing.

Also, as in all the other phases of consulting, you have to trust your own feelings in talking about implementation or planning. If you are feeling uneasy about something—confused or frustrated or not listened to—or if you are feeling excited and positive and supportive, you should put your feelings into words as part of the model and methodology you offer the client.

As in contracting, giving feedback involves an affective dimension—feelings about the interaction itself. There's a process going on between you, the consultant giving the feedback, and clients hearing a statement of their problems. For example, suppose a consultant giving feedback was feeling confused and uncertain and didn't know where to go next. There are two ways to deal with this—one is to try to speak with more certainty, more clarity. The second way would be to simply say, "You know, as we're talking here, I feel confused and uncertain where to go next." You're much more likely to get to the heart of the problems around responsibility and commitment and owning up to problems if you react and present your own feelings as the feedback is going on.

Checklist #7. Planning a Feedback Meeting

Here are some guidelines you can use before a feedback meeting to help you prepare.

1. What do you want from the meeting? Understanding? Agreement? Action? Further work?

2. Structure the meeting so you have at least as much time for discussion as for presentation of results.

3. Review wording of feedback to make it as nonevaluative and descriptive as possible.

4. Which elements of your message are likely to generate defensiveness by the client?

5. What form is the defensiveness or resistance likely to take?

6. What questions can you ask to get the resistance expressed in the meeting?

7. Who might be missing from the feedback meeting who has a high stake in the outcome?

8. How can you ask for feedback on how this consultation is going?

Conducting a Group Feedback Meeting

When you are reporting your findings and recommendations to a group of people, your task takes on an added dimension. If the group is not used to working together, or works together poorly, their difficulties with each other can be taken out on the consultant. You become an easy target when they cannot confront each other directly. The skill is to not let the meeting be set up as the client versus the consultant. There are some things you can do to counter that.

Treat the group as a collection of individuals. Don't assume that they are all in agreement, that they all support each other, that they feel

or think alike. Ask each person what he or she wants from the meeting. This will surface differences and force the group to take responsibility for some of the difficulties that may arise. If they are not listening to each other, ask them, by name, to react to what another is saying. This takes some of the focus off you and puts it on the group where it belongs. Give support at all times. When people are under stress and things are not going well for them, they need support, not more confrontation.

There is always going to be some segment of the group that is going to feel tremendous anxiety and resist. They will express this in the form of aggressive questions about the change or about your data or about the program. The ground rule is not to overinvest in the resistant people. Again, the questions deserve two good faith responses, but you have to have some political sensitivity about where the power really is in the group and whose opinion is really going to sway the group. Invest your energy in those people, rather than in the most verbal or vocal people who are raising questions. You might say at some point, "Well, we've heard several questions from Bob and John. I don't know how the rest of you are feeling. Jean (if Jean is the boss), what do you feel about this?"

On the other hand, if your client gives you quick compliance to a suggestion—beware. Many styles of handling conflict are to deal with it in either a passive or compliant way, and I would be very suspicious of that.

Checklist #8. Reviewing the Feedback Meeting	Here are some questions to ask yourself after a feedback meeting. Answering these questions should help you to assess your own learning from each feedback meeting you conduct and to prepare for the next one.

1. What was the outcome?

2. What was the final understanding of the problem or solutions? Was this different from your initial statement of results or recommendations?

3. What form did the resistance take?

4. How did you respond to the resistance?

   • Take it personally?

Understanding that the client criticism and resistance are not directed at you personally

Being present at the meeting where the action steps are determined

Structuring and controlling the feedback meeting to elicit client reaction and choice of next steps

In your work with managers, you need to model the same kind of authentic behavior that you're suggesting they engage in when dealing with their subordinates. You're always acting as a model for a style of working problems and, in fact, the most meaningful vehicle for managers' learning about problem solving is to have them experience how you handle problems. That may mean much more than anything you say verbally or any kind of process you would have them engage in with their subordinates.

- Give more explanation and data?

- Seek underlying concerns about control an

8. Did you get stuck at any point?

9. What nonverbal messages did you notice?

10. What connections can you make between the
    back meeting was managed and the way the
    ness problem is being managed?

11. What effect on your relationship with the
    meeting have?

12. What would you do differently next time?

Feedback Skills Summary

The competencies for managing a feedback meetin

Confronting the client with all relevant data coll
wasn't part of your original assignment

Giving descriptive rather than evaluative feedb;

Feeding data back to the client about personal b
dling the target problem

Managing the Feedba

Chapter 15
Implementation

WHEN I WROTE the first edition of this book I devoted exactly two pages to implementation. I can't remember whether I was just rushing to finish the book or had little to say about it. Over the years, though, I have become increasingly aware of how many consulting efforts have been aimed at doing the right thing but have resulted in little change. It is frustrating to say the least to contract well, develop an accurate picture of the current reality, give feedback, and make a good decision, and yet see few concrete results from the effort.

Implementation is, in theory, the point of the consultation. The fruit of our labor. Unfortunately, knowing what to do (the product of the discovery phase) and finding the right way to do it (the focus of implementation) are two different worlds. Consultants have traditionally given too much attention to analysis and recommendations and too little attention to the complexity of translating those answers into action.

Our mistake is treating implementation as a fundamentally rational process. We believe that logical, step-by-step problem solving can bring the fulfillment of our plans. Our love of a Day-Timer™ or Palm Pilot™ is an example of this: If we can keep a list of what we need to do in one place, these things will get done. While it is hard to argue against being organized, we tend to oversimplify what it takes to act on what we know to be true. At a personal level, it is the gap between having a vision and living it out. The more serious we are about being true to a vision, the more we realize it is our life work.

Choosing Engagement over Installation

For an organization, shifting a way of thinking and a way of operating is even more difficult. Part of what makes implementation difficult is that we often treat change as if it can be installed, managed, and engineered. Installation plans rely heavily on having clear goals, a defined set of steps, and carefully specified objectives and measures—as if a blueprint can be developed for others to follow. This is the engineering mind at work, which works well for solving mechanical problems but is incomplete in trying to impact living systems. Change, unfortunately, cannot be installed and engineered, and so it always takes longer and is more difficult than we ever imagined.

The engineer in us needs to be enhanced with the thinking of the social architect and the skills of a community organizer. Any implementation requires not only a shift in what is tangible, such as methods or structure, but also a shift in what is intangible, such as relationships and personal faith and commitment. This chapter and the next two are about ways to approach the intangibles. They focus on an essential aspect of implementation–bringing people together to create and plan how to make something work.

The art of bringing people together is termed *engagement*. The ideas here are really about the means of engagement as an alternative or enhancement to strategies of installation. The steps offered are the elements of engagement. What I am proposing is that we become engaged. If you can find a better offer, take it.

There are two aspects of implementation for the consultant. One is the technical work using the expertise you have spent years developing. If you are a financial analyst, you begin introducing a system of controls. If you are an engineer, you redesign the input valves for the furnace. If you are a training manager, you start the training program.

The second aspect of implementation is how to build support for the business or technical change you are planning. This is no easy task. Implementation does not actually begin until the people who do the work decide whether they are going to make real changes or simply go through the motions. Real changes require real commitment, and part of your role is to help fire that spark. To get serious about building internal commitment among those who have to live in the system where you are simply a guest, we first need to dispel some conventional beliefs that actually get in the way.

Deciding Doesn't Get It Done

Too many consulting projects result in cosmetic change. Cosmetic change is where the thinking and rhetoric about the change is perfect, but the experience of people does not match the promise. Much of the cynicism about consultants is because we collude with strategies that begin with great fanfare and end with a world where the promises of change have made no difference to people's day-to-day work lives. Much of our collusion with cosmetic change is our belief that new behavior can be defined, induced, driven, purchased, and measured into existence. Many of the ways consultants try to change institutions actually serve as a defense against change.

One of the obstacles to change (I use "change" and "implementation" to mean essentially the same thing) is rooted in our belief in executive decisiveness. In our adoration of leaders and stubborn belief in individualism, we think that when the boss's mind is made up, action will follow. This is rarely the case. No single person runs a business, no one person makes or delivers a product, no one general ever fought a war.

It is interesting that managers understand their limitations better than consultants do. Managers know that the fact that they have made up their minds does not mean that decisions will be acted on. They are faced every day with the reality that many of their best intentions have little impact on the way that work gets done. It is consultants who have a hard time accepting this. Any gathering of consultants will at some point complain that managers lack the courage, willfulness, or persistence to follow through on their decisions and make sure that our recommendations get implemented.

We hold on to the magical belief that leadership and decisiveness is the point and what we need is more of it. Change in human systems has much more to do with the consent of the governed than the will and ability of those who govern. Even in a monarchy.

The Case Against Installation

The blueprint for traditional, installation-style implementation is to

- Articulate a vision

- Set standards for what is expected

- Put rewards on the new behavior

- Train in new skills

- Measure the change

Kept in perspective, all of these are legitimate elements of day-to-day life in every workplace. What interferes with implementation is that we misuse these tools. And when we do, they become subtle forms of coercion rather than neutral ways of managing and defining a future. We think we have to sell and induce support for a new way of operating. When consultants and managers apply centrally created vision, standards, rewards, skills, and measures as primary tools to maintain control and make the world predictable, they interfere with the implementation effort.

What could be an opportunity for people to choose accountability by designing their own answers to these questions is lost. Instead of confronting people with their freedom, we invite their compliance. It is the mandated institutionalization of useful practices that takes the life out of most implementation efforts. Here are some major ways efforts at implementation stumble over themselves.

Leadership by Lamination

We interfere with real change and service when we think that progress grows out of the vision of the leader, regardless of whether the leader is "us," as consultant or trainer, or "them," as managers. The myth is that if we can just get the message sufficiently clear and compelling, if we can describe the burning platform with enough urgency and a bright tomorrow with enough zeal, change will occur. This leads to a great emphasis on communicating the vision and the business case for change.

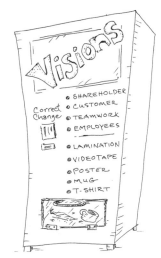

I contributed to the problem when I wrote a chapter on vision in my book *The Empowered Manager.* It was about the power of vision and how transformation begins with imagining a different future. This became the most popular chapter in the book. I received hundreds of vision statements in the mail or in my travels. Most were compelling, and most were *laminated* in wallet-sized versions so we could always have them with us. Many vision statements hung on office walls and reception rooms, many signed by the management team. All had a common theme: Building a lasting organization required the top to have a vision.

The problem here was two-fold. First, we affirmed, at the moment of lamination, that top management's vision was the one that counted. We all wanted to know what top management was seeking. Once we knew this, we could all align ourselves and proceed to live it out. This gave rise to a cottage industry in vision articulation. We consultants began each project helping the top define and express their vision. This could take days or months. Most often it was actually a staff person or consultant who wrote the vision and brought it back to management for their approval. But the product reflected management's thoughts and they gave it their stamp. This was fine for the managers who created the vision. Fine, that is, if they had created it primarily for themselves and sought guidance for their own actions through it.

Unfortunately, the visions were usually designed for others. We believed that the top should decide the culture that the middle and bottom would live by. This is the mind-set that takes the power out of vision, even though the middle and the bottom want to hear what the top has in mind. The fact that everyone wants to know the vision of the top does not make it meaningful.

Most frequently, when the organization hears the vision of the top, they are vaguely disappointed. The large meeting designed to mobilize energy actually drains it. It became clear to me after I started to read the four hundred or so vision statements I received. They all read the same. Every organization cares about customers, values teamwork, exists for shareholders or the community, believes in excellence in all they do. If we all threw our vision statements in a hat and then drew one out, we would think it was ours regardless of where it came from. I finally realized that it was the act of creating a vision that matters, not so much the content of what it was.

The second consequence of lamination was that management's vision could now withstand the ravages of wind, and rain, and dark of night. That is why we laminated it. So it would last forever. Management's vision should be permanent and enduring—that is the fallacy. Management vision is not only not the point, but it is not immortal. Everyone needs to struggle with the question of what kind of future we want to create, and that vision is something that is alive and open to change. Vision is more a dialogue than a declaration. It is an important conversation, a significant stretch of the imagination, and it needs to emerge as a collective work-in-progress from each unit. Once a vision is laminated, it loses its life.

In practical terms, if a group needs a clearer vision for themselves, by all means help them create one. But don't make any videos of leaders calling for transformation. Don't hold some large meeting for the purpose of clarifying the vision of top management. If implementation requires that people know the state of the union and where we are headed, don't have those in charge declare it. Bring people together to define the state of their own union and pool their knowledge of what the future might bring. But we are getting ahead of the story.

We Need Higher Standards, and This Time We Mean Business

There is a widespread belief that we have not set the standards high enough. This is most visible in education, where every state legislature thinks that it can improve public education by being tougher on performance standards, students, and teachers. They have been doing this for years, continue to be disappointed with its results, and keep on doing it.

Of course the belief that low standards are the problem is not confined to education. It invades all of our institutions. It is born of the belief that people will not set high standards for themselves. That they need an outside agency to motivate and inspire them. At heart it is a fear-based strategy, where those who set the standards are the subject and those who must meet them are the object.

There is some validity to the idea that standards and performance are related. We do know that people will be responsive to the expectations others have for them. If a boss expects the team to perform well, it is more likely to happen. If a boss expects failure, that may happen also. There is a difference, though, between expectations between boss and subordinate or teacher and student, and standard setting.

To have high expectations of others is to have faith in them. It is an expression of optimism and hope in the capacities of another. It is an expression of the connection between people and is experienced as support. Standard setting, as it is most commonly used to trigger change, is not born of support, but born of disappointment and demand.

To judge others to be performing poorly because of low standards is to hold them in contempt. It is a belief that they need our standard-setting intervention to wake them up and motivate them. It is an institutional act that depends on coercion. If we don't raise the bar, they will not jump higher. There is little care or connection in the strategy, and it therefore builds as much resistance as it was designed to overcome.

The myth is that setting standards will increase accountability. What it most often creates is compliance. People may be forced to find a way to meet those standards, but the institution suffers in other, less measurable ways. Instead of a more accountable culture, we find more bureaucracy, more people working to rule, more caution, less flexibility.

Bosses, of course, have a legitimate role in defining a playing field, and in defining what outcomes the institution requires of a unit. But defining outcomes is different from standard setting as a tactic in initiating change or implementing some recommendation. What corrupts the process is the belief that one group knows what is best for another. And that is why these engineering and installation strategies fall short. The focus on standards is also very seductive for the consultant. After we have been through a contracting and discovery effort with a client manager, we want to be on their side and too easily align with their traditional ways of making things happen.

We need to avoid planning something in a huddle with our client manager that is supposed to change the behavior of others outside our circle. Our task is to stay focused on what the people in the room can do about their own actions. If managers believe in higher standards, let them set them for themselves and live according to them for a while.

This keeps legitimacy in the consulting effort and in our relationship with the client manager. When we join with bosses to plan for the changes in their subordinates, we have been co-opted into the belief that the employees need to change and the managers are just fine. We then miss the opportunity to shift in a more fundamental way the beliefs about how change happens and how accountability is created. Change and accountability occur when we live them, not preach them. The common instinct to begin implementation with clearer and higher standards is most often a trap.

Matching the Reward System to the Desired Behaviors Won't Help

There is no subject that brings more energy to a discussion than rewards. You can list ten problems or recommendations, with rewards at the bottom of the list, and it will always be the topic people will begin with. I don't know why this has so much power. Sometimes I think it is the materialism that so invades our society and institutions. Other times it seems that none of us ever feels we have gotten what we deserved. We were robbed at the moment of birth and no amount of goods can make up for it.

Using rewards as a major component of change reinforces the economist mind-set that has helped create the institutions we have inherited. In its simplest terms it implies that behavior can be purchased. If we can just define the behavior that we want and place a price tag on it, the buyer (management) and the seller (employee) will be satisfied.

The emphasis on rewards assumes that institutions are primarily economic entities. I don't want to deny the economic element of our organizations; it is just that the obsession with rewards so oversimplifies the complexity of human systems that it does them damage. When we make rewards a cornerstone of our strategies, we exaggerate the instrumental aspects of our relationships to the detriment of all else that they are.

Changes in human systems are not very amenable to precise definition, barter, and purchase. When we try to define the desired behaviors, they become so general and subjective that the definition generates more questions than clarity. Plus, who is to say that consultants and managers have a corner on the wisdom of what behaviors in others will really make a difference? *Father Knows Best* played well on television forty years ago, but the script calls for compliant, well-behaved children to complete the deal. When we are seeking to create accountability among capable adults, in a marketplace that is much less predictable than we would like it to be, using an allowance to get the behaviors we want is betting on a world long past.

If Only We Had a Common Language and Common Training

Once we specify the behaviors we want, we often adopt the mindset that the behavior needs clarification and people need to be trained in that direction. In the years when I was talking about empowerment, someone in every group would make two claims: (1) that we needed a common definition of empowerment, and (2) that employees needed training in empowerment skills. While the claims have some truth, the implication is that defining empowerment and developing the skills require expert knowledge and intervention.

This instinct gave rise to an empowerment industry. Companies went to great lengths to define empowerment. In one case, Scott Adams, who has chronicled our helplessness and futility through his Dilbert cartoons, was hired to create a Dilbert series to define empowerment for a large part of a major corporation. The customized series was distributed to all employees. A well-intended effort, but the implicit message was that people needed to be told the do's and don'ts of claiming their freedom and exercising choice in serving the business.

What was most interesting was that Scott Adams now was participating in creating the very kind of organization that he once had so much disdain for. Who will draw the cartoon of employees receiving instructions from Dilbert on empowerment, empowerment boundaries, under what conditions we should make up our own mind, and when we should seek supervisory instruction? What chance do we have when Dilbert has become part of the management team and a willing instrument of bureaucracy?

In the act of so carefully defining empowerment, we take back the very offer of choice and autonomy that we intended to make. If empowerment needs to be defined, asking people to struggle with their own definition is the only way that our intention becomes authentic.

This holds for most other implementation efforts. There are major parts of any change that require definition and clarity. Ultimately this definition will have to be done locally to fit each unit. Why not have our change strategy recognize this and make the demand that if people need a better understanding of something new, they'd best get to work figuring it out?

The desire for a common language is a mask for the wish that everyone think and act similarly. It is a stab in the heart of diversity. We can pursue common goals and act in concert and still find our own forms of language and expression and give our own meanings to complex ideas. Otherwise we will use the definition of terms, and one cartoon to cover it all, to create monocultures that will be unable to adapt and compete.

The mind-set that designs a common training experience is a corollary to the instinct toward common definition. This is not an argument against training; it just questions the value of mandating training that is designed by consultants and essentially required for large numbers of people. The training may be excellent, but when it is demanded for all, the demand itself becomes another means of reinforcing patriarchy. Common training carries the message that the top, with the help of the consultants, has an answer that all should hear.

The major beneficiary of common training programs, of course, are those who provide them. Myself included. I would proceed with great care in making training a key element of any implementation strategy. If employees have learning needs, let them struggle with defining them and providing for them. When we, as consultants, find ourselves selling our answer, we have to ask for whose sake this is being done.

If We Can't Measure It, It Doesn't Matter

One more way we interfere with implementation is through our attitude about measurement. We have turned it into a god. The question here is similar to the questions above. No argument with the need for measurement; it's just a question of how central it should become and who should provide it. When we impose measurements system-wide, we have to be very careful that we really need and can make use of the measures that are collected.

Measuring the quantitative elements of work has definite value. The simplest example of the legitimate need for common measures is common accounting practices. The economics of each unit in the organization need to be folded together to meet regulatory requirements and so we know our economic viability. There is the need for common measures of product quality and customer service, and for many more measures that assess the success of the institution. We move on to soft ground, though, when we invite the economist in to develop common measures for how we are working together, what processes will create quality, and, in general, anything in the realm of how human systems operate. Every measurement of the human or qualitative dimension of work leaves more untested than it covers.

The belief that if we cannot measure something, it does not exist treats the human system as if it were a mechanical one. The belief that people will only do what they are measured against is a cynical view of the human condition, and while it may be true of certain sales situations or certain classroom dynamics, we have taken the value of measurement to places it does not belong. When we attribute to measurement the capacity to create the behavior we want, we have moved into a simple cause-and-effect relationship and hold onto the belief that implementation and change can be engineered. With a human system, that is more fancy than fact.

Each of us wants feedback on how we are doing. But the feedback does not create the doing. Imposed measures on the qualitative aspect of work may actually get in the way of the doing.

We particularly dilute the value of measurement when we separate the people who evaluate from the people who do the work. Quality control used to be separated from those who did the work. It was a judging function and created alienation between the doing and the quality assessment. This has changed in the last ten years, for the betterment of both the quality of the product and the quality of the relationships that surround the workplace.

We can learn from the quality movement that, while there are useful tools for measuring, they need to be under the control of those doing the work and need to be kept in perspective as simply one part of making change. Much of what matters cannot be measured, and our consulting needs to reflect that.

Betting on Engagement

None of this is an argument against vision, standards, rewards, training, or measurement. They are important elements of organizing people's efforts. It is just that we have over-invested in them and abused them by making them imposed instruments of control. And then we compound the error: When they do not result in genuine change, we try harder to make them work, instead of betting on other strategies. Trying harder, pressuring, and persuading have limited impact on changing a social system. And when they do help, they soon develop their own immune system.

A social system is a living system and not that amenable to linear or mechanical beliefs about organizations. Whenever management or consultants bet on definitions, inducements, measures, and standards, they unintentionally reinforce the bureaucratic mind-set that we are trying to reduce. They are the engineer's and economist's tools. Engineering and economic strategies do not build commitment and accountability, despite their appealing face value.

What we have undervalued is the power of engagement and dialogue. The recent movements toward the learning organization, total quality, and teamwork are in the direction of engagement, but with a few exceptions, they are rarely given the importance that they deserve. The next two chapters explore engagement in the implementation process and offer some concrete techniques and tools for involving people in a way that increases the likelihood of real, lasting change.

A Reminder

Before moving on, a brief recap and reminder: The most powerful leverage you have under your control is your own behavior. If people are going to learn from you or be influenced by you, they have to trust you. Authentic behavior builds trust and eases implementation.

Being clever, invoking the president's support for the project, downplaying the risks inherent in the project—all reduce trust and inhibit implementation. Our clients learn from our behavior, they learn little from our words.

Resistance doesn't die when the decision to proceed is made. We hope that if we have consulted flawlessly during the preliminary events, the resistance during implementation will be diminished. Resistance will still be there, however, especially in those people who were not involved in the early stages of the project. Keep in mind that the resistance you get during implementation is born out of the identical concerns underlying the earlier phases—loss of control and vulnerability. Deal with it the same way you did in contracting, data collection, and feedback.

Give two good faith answers.

Notice that resistance is occurring.

Identify the form it is taking.

Name it.

Be quiet.

Maintaining the relationship is the point, even during implementation. Each new person brought into the project needs to begin with a contracting discussion. Also, you need to be alert to changes in the expectations of people who have been involved in the project from the outset. Each time the client's expectations change, you need to go back and renegotiate what you want from each other . . . now.

Remember the secondary goal of consulting: to teach clients how to solve the problem themselves next time. In facing the time pressure and intensity of implementing a program, it is always quicker for you to do something yourself. Resist this temptation and stay with the process of 50/50 responsibility. If you take over the implementation, you are no longer consulting—you are acting as surrogate manager. When you do this, you support the client in

sacrificing certain learning objectives in favor of short-term res When you agree to be a surrogate manager on a project,) behavior is also communicating to the organization that you willing to take control away from the line organization. The ri that you give substance to their already intense fears about lc control.

For the internal consultant, this balance between taking contro keeping the responsibility 50/50 is especially delicate. You pl work with this client long after the immediate project is comp How you function now will teach them what to expect from y the future. Hold out for 50/50 sharing of responsibility.

Chapter 16
Strategies for Engagement

Feelings Are Facts

People choose to commit to a decision based on emotion, feelings, intuition, trust, hope. These become the playing field for change. Even the most concrete changes—such as restructuring, using a new information system, cutting costs—happen when individuals decide to support the recommendations and decisions and make the adjustments that are required at every step along the way. The decision to support change is not just based on logic and reason; we need to help our clients deal with attitudes and feelings as well.[8]

A core strategy for building emotional commitment to implementation is to design new ways for people to engage each other. This may be more critical than the clarity or rightness of a decision. Results are achieved when members of a system collectively choose to move in a certain direction. It is this act of choice that is critical. Leadership behavior is not as vital as membership behavior. It is difficult for a patriarchal society such as ours to accept this reality. We tenaciously hold on to the belief that leaders can induce

---

[8]I want to acknowledge how much I have learned about engagement from colleagues who have been part of the School for Managing and Leading Change. In particular, Dick Axelrod and Kathie Dannemiller understood engagement long before I took it seriously. They have been part of inventing the whole world of large-group methodology. Dick created The Conference Model™ with Emily Axelrod, and Kathie has been a mentor for all in the realm of real-time, high-interaction strategic change. They have offered their insights generously, and I am indebted to them.

others to act. Leaders can no more induce action on the part of their followers than consultants can induce action on the part of their clients.

Supporting the Emotional Side

Consultants can help leaders engage others in implementing decisions by following the same principles for building commitment that we explored in the process of contracting and discovery.

The contracting phase was based on

- A deep understanding of the problem

- The clear expression of wants

- An exploration of concerns about control and vulnerability

- Giving support

The discovery phase emphasized

- Treating each interaction as a learning event

- Persistently asking what the client was doing to contribute to the problem

- Seeking language that gave clarity to reality without judging it

I now want to offer some ways to sustain that same spirit when you are dealing with groups at the moment of implementation and action.

The implementation phase centers around

- High intensity participation

- Placing choice on the table

- Changing the conversation

- Transparency and the public expression of doubt

- Co-creating structures to fit purpose

The greatest service of the consultant may be to raise the consciousness of the client about the value of engagement in the implementation process. Engagement has power regardless of the content of the recommendations. The most technical content will not be acted on without a different interaction within the client system. If the quality of the interaction does not change, no amount of rewards, standards, and measurement will have an impact.

The Meeting Is the Message

Implementation of any change boils down to whether people at several levels are going to take responsibility for the success of the change and the institution. This is it. Period.

We can broadcast our intent to give people at the bottom more choice and involvement, but if the meeting that broadcasts this intent is not, itself, an example of the content of the broadcast, the promise has little legitimacy. The nature, tone, and structure of how we come together is the sampling device people use to determine the credibility of the strategy.

It always surprises me how unconscious we are about the importance of the message communicated in how we come together, how we meet with each other. If the message was ever in the medium, this is it. There are libraries of books written about group process, but I want to focus on five aspects of how we engage each other. They are pretty straightforward and get to the heart of the matter. They also do not require a heavy investment of group process expertise. They are more about how to structure the meeting, rather than how to handle a difficult moment.

Innovative Engagement in Five Easy Pieces

The elements of innovative engagement look simple enough, but they are easier to list and to talk about than to practice. Successful engagement takes place when we have meetings in which we have:

- Balance between presentation and participation
- Full disclosure and the public expression of doubt
- Real choice on the table

- New conversations

- A physical structure of the room that supports community

The Presentation-Participation Balance

It amazes me how many new programs have begun their implementation with a management/consultant lecture/presentation about goals, strategy, methods, and measures. I have watched a manager or consultant stand in front of the room for long periods of time—sometimes hours—stating vision, defining terms, giving the whole picture of what is to come. The structure of a meeting is social technology, and we keep operating out of habit rather than changing the technology to better meet our purpose. We base our meetings on the thought that when someone is confused by what you say, repeat it again louder, as if turning up the volume will solve the confusion.

Sometimes there is not even room for questions or any contact with the audience. I have often seen top executives come in, give a prepared speech, and leave. In each case, the purpose of the meeting was to build commitment and give people a sense of the whole. This will never happen from a speech, especially since most of us in consulting or management are not that charismatic. Even if we were great speakers, the impact of using broadcast methods for implementation is to increase passivity, deepen the dependency on the leader who just made a great speech, and reinforce the feeling that the program is buttoned up and predetermined—all characteristics of the day-to-day experience we are trying to overcome.

The other problem with most presentations is that they are so scripted and rehearsed that they are lifeless. Many are written by people other than the speaker, and it shows. And sometimes the executive has been dragged into a studio to videotape a message, which is usually sudden death.

All of these practices are more appropriate for a monarchy than a workplace. Granted some important information gets shared, but the emotional cost is too high and our attention is pointed in the wrong direction. A presentation-based meeting, even with questions thrown in as a bone, carries the message that only the top has something important to say and the employee's job is to sit and listen and politely question. The answers are on the stage and the people are here to seek them.

Implementation based on engagement and participation means that the important conversations are the ones that take place between employees. So when we meet, let the audience talk to each other. We feel connected to the institution more by our relationships with our peers than by our identification with the bosses. Granted everyone in this culture wants to hear from the leader, but in my mind this is more a statement of the problem than a solution. It is our dependence and passivity and willingness to give lip service that is the problem with implementation. Why collude with it? It may be important for the leader to speak, so let the leader talk for fifteen minutes, with no rehearsal or overheads. Let them write their own comments and talk from memory. Then we will know what is really important to them and that is good to know.

I get caught in this same trap all the time. During my brief career as the brand name in empowerment, a large electronics company held a celebration day recognizing the work of teams and the success of its employee participation efforts. I am the speaker and I'm talking about empowerment. Four hundred employees in the auditorium and they rope off the first row for the convenience of top management, who come in late and are ushered in like royalty. To add to the occasion, I am on a stage, five feet above the audience, with a moat of flowers surrounding the podium. I'm looking down at the crowd, bosses in the best seats, while talking about the importance of equality. So much for participation. Plus all those flowers make me think that perhaps I've reached my final resting place.

You may be thinking that the importance of the simple balance between presentation and participation is being overstated. Trust me, it has more meaning than we have realized: As straightforward as the concept is, most of the times when we come together we put great energy on presentation and attend to participation as an afterthought.

Transparency and the Public Expression of Doubt

Freedom of speech and the right to assembly are constitutional guarantees. What is true for the streets, however, is less true for the meeting rooms of our institutions. We all hear the claim in the workplace that if you stand up, you will be shot. We now speak the language of self-management, but it is still difficult for a group of subordinates to call a meeting that excludes their boss. We bear the imprint of the fact that in times past self-management was called mutiny.

Part of our task as consultants is to bring the right of assembly and freedom of speech into our organizations. In practical terms this means creating assemblies where there is an opportunity for all voices and points of view to be heard. Where reality in the words of the audience becomes as important as the reality spoken from the podium—perhaps more important. And where those at the podium tell the truth about failure and uncertainty.

Doing this allows for a restoration of faith that is central to any change or improvement effort. Until we can speak in public our sense of what is real, our doubts and reservations, and past disappointments, we are unable to invest in a different future. If we cannot say no, our yes has no meaning.

Sharing the Platform

People do tell the truth in organizations; it is just that they do it in private. In rest rooms, at water coolers, over a meal or a drink. If honest conversation stays private, the public conversations will be unreal and ultimately discouraging. The same is true in a large group meeting. If all the real discussions take place only in small groups, little faith will be built in the larger community.

The redistribution of power and accountability happens when honest, confronting conversations take place in public settings. There is a political power in having a wide range of viewpoints heard by everybody in the room, especially in larger group assemblies. If we believe the redistribution of power is critical to a shift in accountability, the shift will begin when the public conversations shift.

Up to now we have given the gift of public expression mostly to management. I have been in many meetings in which management has used the podium to "challenge" people. In one meeting the vice president declared during a motivational speech that if he had to grade his organization, he would give them a "C." While clearly this grade was not a pick-me-up for his staff, and you can question the wisdom of his approach, at least he was given the platform to say it.

While somehow management has the right to express their "grade," the reverse is not true. When employees express their complaints, it is called whining or a "bitch" session. If management needs to challenge their staff, fine. But there will be no forward movement until the staff in turn has the opportunity to challenge management. Providing public space for this to happen is the first step in shifting a culture, in implementing a change. And it is the task of the consultant to help make this happen.

The Straight Story

Openness and reciprocity need to occur each time we assemble. It cannot be relegated to sessions we label "team building" or a "large-group intervention." Even when we are implementing a highly technical or business-oriented change, there has to be a relatively public platform for people's concerns to be voiced and viewpoints to be sought. Every technical and business change destabilizes the human system in which it is embedded.

Relationships change, influence shifts, boundaries are threatened, and dialogue, widely held, is the only way to find new stability. Management reassurances don't help. Nobody believes them because it's their job to reassure.

We waste meetings that are designed more to reassure, calm the workers, and tell a story than to have a conversation. They are lost opportunities. The question in people's minds is whether they are getting the straight story. If the speaker does not speak of doubt and uncertainty, and talk about failure if it has occurred, there has been no straight story.

People will also not know whether they are getting a straight story until they have joined in the discussion. Too often in the effort to sell a strategy, problems are softened and positioned to promote confidence and win support. People's trust in management comes down not so much to whether management is right, but to whether it is willing to tell the truth.

The truth spoken in public is a rare commodity in most institutions. The success of an implementation strategy will depend on the quality of the conversation that begins it. And the more public the setting, the more powerful the impact. Change begins at the intersection of freedom of speech and the right of assembly. It is not only good for democracy, but it begins to turn rhetoric into reality.

Placing Real Choice on the Table

The argument for the redistribution of power is that each of us is more likely to care for what we control. If this workplace, this project, this community belongs to another, I will do what is required and work by the book. Under conditions of fear or inducement, I may give a little more. If, however, this workplace or project or community is mine, I am more likely to give all I have, to do whatever is required, to care in a different way.

What makes this project mine grows not out of any logic, but out of my engagement with it. The more I join in its creation and its shape, the greater my accountability for its success. There are few ideas that are better understood and less acted on than this one. Even in this age of self-management and participation, our implementation strategies tend to be packaged long before they are presented. Often the only choice left to people is "How are you going to support this project?"

If we want people to be accountable for implementation, we need to push choice as far down in the organization as possible. We do this for the sake of accountability, not as a social movement.

We also bring choice into the engagement because when I have to decide something, I have to learn about it. Choosing demands a struggle. Seeing both sides. Understanding the complexity of the question. The design challenge is how to put choice on the table without everyone deciding everything, which is paralyzing.

In any change effort, there are opportunities for real choice at many levels of the organization in shaping its vision, standards, training, measures, and accountability. These do not have to be prepackaged and decided before the implementation begins. In fact, better that they are not predetermined. These elements are going to vary from group to group, no matter how much consultants and managers think that consistency is necessary for success. Why not view this variability as an asset rather than as a weakness?

There will always be limits to local choice, but the consultant's task is to support maximum reasonable power at lower levels for the sake of genuine change and implementation. The conventional wisdom is that top management is crucial and vital to the change effort and it is up to them to ultimately define how things will change. That is betting on an empirically fragile, and deeply held, myth. If all the critical decisions are made by management, then the implementation will most likely be politely contentious and cosmetic. Change efforts become the flavor of the month when they are embraced only by the top.

Also we talk a lot about resistance to change. I don't know that people are really resistant to change; I think they are resistant to change being inflicted on them. We get into a cycle in which consultants and managers think people are resistant, so we get more and more clever on how to "handle" it. The more clever we get, the more people know it, sense the cleverness, and defend against it. Redistributing choice and power is a way of avoiding this cycle.

Defining choices, then, is an essential element of designing how people engage each other. It is not that each meeting must decide something, but each meeting must involve serious dialogue about what to do about things such as vision, standards, training, measures, and promises. For important change efforts, the struggle is the solution.

Changing the Conversation

The texture and content of the conversation matter. We know that if this implementation is going to be innovative and compelling, then the meetings to plan and initiate it must also be innovative and compelling. Many of the conversations we typically design to increase participation are too cautious and analytical. We need to go beyond simply having people ask questions of clarification from the leader, or brainstorm ways the implementation might be successful, or discuss what are some of the new roles and skills people will need in the future.

These are relevant questions, but they are not demanding enough. They are mostly very heady, intellectual, left-brain exercises. At some point they may cover relevant content, but they don't evoke strong connection and they leave the personal and affective dimension out of the room. We need ways to invite people to personally engage and take risks that are not typical. Whatever new culture or attitudes we seek for the longer implementation, for day-to-day life, must be designed in—right from the beginning and throughout the effort.

The task of the consultant is to find ways to change the conversation as a means of moving the change along. For the new conversation to have meaning it needs to help employees feel connected to one another in this room at this moment. For this to happen we need to avoid the old subjects and provide dialogue where people can be vulnerable and personal.

Away from Familiar Refrains

Most of our conversations don't have these qualities. They are simply recycling positions we have taken before. We each have a habitual way of explaining and talking about our world, and our discussions are like tapes we replay each time something new is on the table. Here are some of the familiar conversations that keep us stuck in our old routines.

The Culture Made Me Do It   Until we change the culture, there is little we can do. This is a culture in which short-term results are all that count, competition reigns supreme, and it is who you know, not what you know.

Leader Behavior Has to Change   Until the leaders model the new behavior, what can you expect from the lower levels?

The Reward System Has to Change   Until we are rewarded for the new behavior, we will keep pouring old wine into new bottles. Or is it keep pouring new wine into old bottles? Whatever.

Risk and Fear Have to Be Eliminated   If you stand up here, you will be shot. We have to value failure and until we do, it is business as usual.

More Skills Are Required   People are not equipped to make the changes. More training is needed. We need to define the new competencies and until we do . . .

Structure Has to Be Changed   Even if the structure has changed, it did not go far enough. We still have too many or too few levels, too many vice presidents or not enough, the workforce is either too old or too inexperienced.

New Roles Have to Be Defined and Prescribed   What is the new role of middle management? Until we clearly define the new boundaries and who decides what . . .

These are some of my favorites; you have your own. They are conversations of delay, held by people who think the business belongs to someone else. Each is somewhat compelling because it contains some truth. In a different context, each of these things will have to happen. The problem is they all are an expression of helplessness; they say that someone else has to do something before we can become players. Often consultants get seduced into these conversations and proceed to answer the questions, forgetting or ignoring the fact that all employees, with their peers, have the capacity to answer the questions for themselves. Do not take these questions at face value. They are test questions designed to see whether we will cooperate in helping people avoid their own freedom and choice to invest.

Toward a New Conversation

The real cost of our habitual conversations is the cynicism they breed. Not because the questions they raise have not been answered. It is the staleness of the discussion that drains energy. Old conversations become a refuge, a way for us to find safety. Here are some ground rules to stimulate new conversations that require some vulnerability and build connection.

Discuss the Personal Impact the Change Has on Me/Us   Find some way of talking about how individuals feel about what is being proposed. Not how they evaluate it, but what feelings it generates. The intent is to surface doubts and reservations without reinforcing the helplessness.

Discourage Discussion of Anyone Not in the Room   The instinct is to talk about who is missing from the discussion. When we require action from someone not a part of the discussion, we buy some relief for the moment, but that relief is purchased at the cost of our own optimism.

Be Careful About Discussing History   The tendency is to begin with an analysis of what got us here, as if a discussion of the past will explain or soften the future. The antidote to history is to keep asking, "What do we want to create together?" Some history can be useful if it tells a personal story that brings us to the moment. Limit the time and make it personal. Use questions such as "What in your experience impacts your capacity to support this plan?"

Postpone Discussion of Action Plans as Long as Possible   It is ironic that the rush to decide what to do is often a defense against real change. Change is the experience of changing our thinking first, actions second. If we rush to action, we stop learning and make tomorrow a reenactment of yesterday. The rush to lists and planning can be an indirect way of saying no to the deeper intent of implementation.

Discuss What Part We Have Played in Creating the Situation   Owning our contribution to the problem gives hope: If we helped cause it, we can fix it. It triggers guilt for a while, but beyond that is our freedom.

Caring About Place

The places in which we meet carry a message about our intentions as clear as any verbal presentation or agenda. The problem is that we have forgotten how important physical space is in influencing our actions. We know how we are changed when we walk into a church, or a courthouse, or an intimate restaurant or courtyard. There is a spirit, a statement of intent, a congruence between the space and the purpose, that reinforces our own reason for being there. Our work spaces, designed to carry the message of efficiency, hierarchical status, and restraint, fly in the face of engagement.

It is almost impossible to find a room in an office building or a hotel that is suited for dialogue and participation. They are mostly suited for instruction and persuasion. To begin with, most of the tables are rectangular. If you sit on either side of a rectangular table, you cannot see most of the people on your side of the table. It's hard to engage people you cannot see. Putting the tables in a

U shape or a square still blinds us to a third or a fourth of those in the room. Boardrooms are the worst. The tables are fixed and monumental. It clearly was never expected that real conversation would be required.

Beyond the problems with the furniture, training and meeting rooms are primarily designed for persuasion and display, either with the speaker in the room or a speaker in another location. Most of the new money spent to design meeting space goes into electronics and projection equipment. In some cases, rooms designed for fewer than thirty people have over $250,000 in the walls, floors, and ceiling. With this kind of investment in the walls, you are not about to have the seats facing each other.

What does this say about our beliefs about connecting and communicating? Each time the room is arranged for people to interact with the speaker rather than each other, we reinforce passive contact and the values of a bureaucratic culture. It doesn't matter, then, what is said, as the structure of the room carries its own message. We will

spend a fortune on talking to someone we cannot see, and in the process arrange the room so that we all face the front and face the wall. These rooms are artifacts of an industrialized and electronic culture. We are in love with technology in a way that far exceeds our interest in connecting with each other. To say that the technology connects us is a myth. It confuses information exchange with human interaction. There is nothing wrong with the technology; we just exaggerate its usefulness.

In a broader sense, we are culturally blind about the power of the physical place. We are willing to meet in rooms without windows, walls without color or pictures, doors with no moldings. Windows, color, art, and architectural detail bring life and humanity into a setting. If you are in the business of change, running meetings, convening people, it is almost impossible to find a room

for work that is designed for people to feel alive and really talk to each other.

The Auditorium, Cafeteria, Etc. and Other Places That Defy Engagement

The one room in our culture that most symbolizes the patriarchal nature of our ways of bringing people together is the auditorium—especially the corporate auditorium. We have a stage where the speaker is elevated and can be seen by all. We have several hundred seats in rows, bolted to the floor all facing forward. The lighting and the sound system are designed to illuminate and amplify only the speaker. There is usually a podium, which is its own command-and-control system. From these podiums you can control the screen, slides, sound, and computer-generated graphics. The podium has a button to raise and lower itself, so it can be customized to the height of the speaker. You can even control time itself, with clocks for actual time, elapsed time, and time to lift off. For the audience we have house lights and, at best, a remote microphone that can be hand passed for audience questions or comments.

If we convene over fifty people and don't use an auditorium, we move to the cafeteria or a ballroom at a local hotel. Both of these are designed for eating, not for meeting. They are a little more flexible than the auditorium, but if your intent is to bring groups of people together for the sake of engagement, you are fighting the space that is available.

Even when we have some flexibility to arrange the room for participation, we often don't do it. We don't even see that the space given to us interferes with our purpose. If our goal is to have all voices heard, to have peers treat each other as important as the leader, if we want the leader to come off of the pedestal and join the institution simply as a powerful member, you can't have the boss and the consultant standing on a stage talking down to the troops.

The Circle

The physical symbol for participation and engagement is a circle. Round tables put each of us in sight of everyone else. Seats in a circle do the same. Even a room full of round tables has an interactive

effect. Don't worry about having some people with their backs to the front. The action is not in the front of the room; it is at the tables. Eventually we will have whole rooms and buildings designed to hold the circle. Some businesses are there already. Saturn and

Harley-Davidson have understood the importance of the circle in the design of their buildings.

Other organizations are also experimenting with new communal space. The Boeing Company has "visibility" rooms designed to continually display the goals, values, and progress of large projects. A senior executive at Boeing started to experiment with the structure of his visibility room in order to get deeper participation. First he got rid of the large table and had only chairs with a few, low coffee tables to put stuff on. Then he brought in plants, to add some life to the environment. They then noticed that the fluoresent lighting was cold and institutional, so they brought in floor lamps. This, however, was going too far. It started to feel like a living room. Out came the lamps, but the chairs and the plants remained, testament to the intent to design a room for open dialogue and human encounter. Still, isn't it interesting that a living room—a room for living, a room to nurture life—seemed so uncomfortably out of place at work?

The point is not that there is a right design for a room—it is about our consciousness about the importance and power of space. As we become more conscious about the impact of how we physically come together, we will start to redesign our common space. This will require the joint effort of furniture designers, architects, hotel executives, organizational real estate people, and those of us who convene the meetings.

The physical space for our implementation meetings is not just a question of flexibility; it carries a message of habitability, of whether this place was designed for human beings or machines. Most commercial workplaces are designed for machines, or machinelike efficiency. Blank walls, colored in gray or white, remind us that the human spirit has been institutionalized. There is little art or humanity on the walls of the corridors or meeting rooms or reception areas. If there is art, it is usually pictures of company history, products, or buildings. Kind of like the Stalinist art of the Soviet Union, where the only images allowed were the ones that glorified the state. Maybe I am getting carried away, but you get the point.

Whatever the space you are given to work in, you always have a choice. Even in an auditorium, people can talk to each other across the rows, or stand up, or move into the aisles or to the front of the room. If you do have a choice, try just chairs—no tables. You will get some complaints, but they are worth absorbing for the flexibility and the message that the space carries.

The Choice for Accountability

No change, no matter how wise and needed, will help if there is not a widespread and deep sense that each individual must make this work. This is real accountability—the willingness to personally care for the well-being of the institution first, and of my unit and self second. This is a personal choice. The choice for accountability is most likely to happen when people feel attached to each other and have influenced the process.

I have talked throughout this book about how to bring responsibility and accountability into the interaction between ourselves and our client. The skills of expressing our wants, dealing with resistance, navigating the contracting meeting, are all ways of building responsibility. Creating high interaction among your clients is how to bring responsibility into the implementation phase.

If the goal is to build internal commitment, the means is to create connection, tell it all, have new conversations in habitable spaces, and finally to offer people a choice over how they do business. The choice we give people is critical and argues against our wish to package the future. Real commitment always entails the redistribution of power. And this is much more subtle than redoing the matrix describing which people decide, who advises, who offers input, at each point in the work process. A chart of decision rules does not shift power; it restrains it. The distribution of power needs to be present in how we live, not just in how we decide. It especially has to be embodied at those moments when we come together in the same room.

Chapter 17

Some Tools for Engagement

CHANGING THE WAY we engage is nowhere near the whole story, but it is a key leverage point for the consultant. As consultants, we are not around for most of the client's interactions, but if we can help them engage differently when we are around, it will spread into the rest of their working.

Change will occur to the extent we use each particular event as a sample of the way we wish the larger implementation to proceed. Each moment becomes an example of the destination. If you are holding a meeting to discuss a new set of measures for a telephone call center, for example, this meeting on measures needs to encourage all of the major principles of implementation:

- Balanced participation

- Real choice on the table

- Difficult questions dealt with publicly

- Connection and vulnerability built into the conversation

- Physical space based on the circle.

Enough theory. What follows are examples of concrete ways I have come to rely on for engaging people, regardless of the setting or the expectations they have on entering the room. All together, these methods embody all the elements of engagement and lead to flawless implementation, for they confront the emotional work that this phase requires. There is great emphasis on structuring and conducting meetings because the way we meet becomes a metaphor for the way we work together day to day.

Methods You Can Really Use

We draw conclusions about the culture and decide whether to trust it by the experiences we have when the culture is convened. If we want to change the culture toward greater accountability and commitment, we can do it by transforming our gatherings.

Here are practical ways to structure a meeting. Each one embodies most of the five elements of engagement:

- High-intensity participation

- Transparency and the public expression of doubt

- Placing choice on the table

- Changing the conversation

- Co-creating structures to fit purpose

And each structure includes activities that affirm the metaphor of meeting as an expression of culture. The structures, theories, and practices here are powerful in themselves, but even more so as concrete examples that carry the larger message. Having people engage one another this way, either by doing the activities as described here or in some form of your own creation, will build accountability for bringing to life the changes that your client has chosen.

Structure 1. Open with Transparent Purpose and Level Playing Field

Whoever convenes the meeting needs to describe the concerns that began the process, define where the change effort is at this moment, describe what the organization needs from us right now, and give some idea of the structure of this step.

Most of us are familiar with the need for this kind of information. The key is to tell the whole story. This includes weaknesses and failures. Don't protect people from bad news in the name of protecting them from anxiety. Anxiety is the natural state, best handled in the light of day. My only caution is to keep it short and informal. More from the heart than from the head.

What is *not* needed are upbeat motivational blessings or homilies from managers or important sponsors who will not be part of the whole session. To have an executive show up for the beginning, express commitment to the process, and then leave is oxymoronic. To say, "I care, I am committed, and I'm gone," does not play well. It is regal and patronizing behavior, demeaning the proceedings and those who stay.

Structure 2. Renegotiate Expectations About Participation

We go to meetings expecting something to happen *to* us. We are programmed for entertainment and wonder how good a meeting they are going to run. The forms we use to evaluate a meeting ask questions about its leaders: Were they prepared? Were their objectives clear and well met? What was the quality of the visual aids? How many evaluation forms have you filled out that asked you about your contribution to the meeting? Meeting leaders always say, "What we get out of the meeting is up to all of us," but they usually don't mean it—and we don't believe it—and few really act on it.

I was in a bar once and the entertainers began by saying, "We are the Southern County Rounders . . . and you are the audience." I thought that they understood something profound about the relationship between them up front and us in the cheap seats. By naming us they declared that we, the audience, had a job to do also. That we had to join in creating the performance. The passive contract between leader and participant needs to be shifted early and dramatically. Here is a way to do it.

The Activity

After the opening, tell people you want them to answer four questions. The questions confront people with the nature of their participation in the meeting we are about to have. Embedded in the questions is the belief that the participants will create the experience they are about to have. Have them rate each question on a 7 point scale, where 1 is very low and 7 is very high.

- **Question 1.** How valuable an experience do you plan to have in this session or this effort—not what kind of experience you want, but what kind do you plan to have?

The Point People are responsible for their own experience. Therefore they have the capacity to determine, up front, the quality of their experience at each moment. If we are going to have a disappointing experience, then let us name it in the beginning and get about the business of making it come true. In answering this question we are faced with deciding, even in a whimsical way, the success of our own future.

Each step of the way in a consulting project is a sample of the larger culture and the larger effort at implementation. If we can decide the quality of this step, then we can decide the quality of every step. And each person in the room has to be faced with this choice. It does not matter how people answer the question; once they answer it, they have taken a step in making the effort their own.

- **Question 2.** How engaged and active do you plan to be?

The Point This is an investment question. We know that the success of implementation will depend on widespread ownership and care. We care for what we have invested in, complained about, spoken for. This question carries within it a demand for activism. If we say no, we do not plan to participate, we have at least defined that stance for ourselves and surrendered, a little, our instinct to watch and blame others' participation. Plus, if people approach a process with cynicism and reluctance, naming the reluctance is the first step in shifting it.

For those who say they plan to be somewhat or very active, stating it early creates pressure to be true to the intent. And we are asking for the intent early, before the stakes are either clear or in play.

- **Question 3. How much risk are you willing to take?**

The Point

This is a question about learning. All learning, change, and transformation come from stepping toward tension. The important moments of our work have been ones of risk, stress, and anxiety. The institutional instinct is to stay calm, move according to plan, be in control, and, above all, don't be surprised. It is just this instinct that turns human systems into mechanical ones. Much of our reluctance to commit is grounded in our wish for safety.

This question is also a measure of our commitment and, as for the other questions, even the answer "no risk" is a starting point for accountability. When I become willing to be accountable for my own position, I have begun to be accountable for something larger.

- **Question 4. How invested are you in the quality of the experience of those around you? What is your level of concern about the well-being of the larger group.**

The Point

This is a Samaritan question. It is a question of accountability: To be accountable is to care first about the larger institution, then to ask what's in it for me. This is a radical stance in a culture that thinks self-interest is the only interest in town. We have listened to the voice of the economist and thought it was the only voice. We have constructed the workplace as a place of barter. Give only where and when you get. You get yours, 'cause I've got mine.

This question confronts the belief that people will consistently choose in favor of themselves over the larger system. It is the most difficult question for people to answer and therefore the most useful. It gets at the heart of implementation and change. Care for a larger purpose is all we have to invite people to go through the stress, loss, and uncertainty of real change.

These four questions have in them the seeds of what is needed for implementation to take hold. At their center, they begin to renegotiate the contract between the leaders and consultant and the participants. That is why they need to be asked early. True, they are just four questions, but they raise the right issues and trigger the right discussions.

When people have answered the questions, have them share their answers with three people around them. Urge them to be curious with each other. Forget the right answers; there aren't any. The process of simply answering the questions and then having to say the answers out loud changes the culture in the room. It communicates to each participant that something more is required than just to sit in the audience. Even if a person does not want to engage and prefers to be quiet and listen, at least it becomes a choice and not a constraint of the setting.

Having done this many times, I can assure you that something always shifts. There is more life in the room. People ask more questions. Some people get irritated. Some would rather keep talking to their neighbor then return to the speaker. All signs of life.

Structure 3. Rearrange the Room

I want to repeat the core concept mentioned at the beginning of this chapter: Change will occur to the extent we use each particular event as a sample of the way we wish the larger implementation to proceed. For example, in our earlier telephone call center example, the meeting on measures needs to encourage balanced participation, real choice on the table, difficult questions dealt with publicly, and the other major implementation principles. The topic of the meeting may be hard measures of telephone center effectiveness, but for them to have meaning people will have to agree to them and be creative about which measures really relate to better customer service and cost. There needs to be dialogue about how the prior measures worked and what doubts people have about the new ones. And most important, those being measured should have some voice in deciding either what the new measures are or how they are to be used, what is done with variances, and for whose sake we are measuring. All business questions, all dependent on employee commitment and care to really take hold.

These steps not only address the content of the meeting, but, regardless of the particular device you use, are important above and beyond the impact in the moment. You may say why make such a big thing out of a small activity like four questions, or rearranging the room? It is because these particular activities carry the message about the change in vision and culture that we have in mind. I am calling them the means of engagement, but they could easily be called the means of transformation or a change in culture.

So, back to the specifics.

The Theory

This particular meeting is a sample and leading indicator of all future meetings. The room, then, becomes a metaphor for the institutional change we have in mind. If we can change the room, and the way we inhabit it, we can change the institution and the way we inhabit it, also.

The Practice

Explain the Theory to the Group   If we come together to explore a shift in the organization, we need to begin with this room and the space in which this exploration will take place. The task then is for us to rearrange this room to better fit the purpose for which we came. Now, we all did not come for the same purpose. The conveners of the meeting certainly have their purpose, but so does every other person. Some came to listen, some came to meet with their peers, some do not want to be here, some came to speak and be heard.

Give the Group Five Minutes to Physically Rearrange the Room to Fit Their Intent Tell people to move themselves, move the furniture, walk around, decide where they want to be and who they want to be with to best approach the task and achieve their goals. Then be quiet. Avoid eye contact. Leave the room. Do not be helpful. Let them struggle. They will not be sure whether to decide together how to move, or whether to allow a wide range of settings.

After a few moments of what seems like chaos, they will take over the room and it will look more like a makeshift flea market than a meeting to plan their future. Some will sit in circles, some will stay where they were, some will want tables, some not. Some will stay close to the door because they have leaving on their mind. Some may stand around the edges, postponing the commitment of where they plant themselves, or . . . maybe they just feel like standing.

You decide, also, where you want to be. You might want to change the "front" of the room. Move to the middle to continue. Or keep shifting where the front is, where the leader is, who is in charge.

Ask Them Questions About Their Personal Experience Take a few minutes to let them reflect on their individual experience with a few others. Have them consider the inertia in getting moving, deciding who to be with, finding others in the spot where they wanted to be . . . whatever. Let them stay in the new configuration and talk in small groups. Then ask them to share their comments with the whole group.

Ask How the Room Has Changed In what way is it different? Elicit as many viewpoints as possible, even from those who thought the whole thing was a waste of time. Keep in mind that, at the core, what has shifted is the ownership of the room. When they arrived, the convener, or the organization, or even the facilities people who care for the room had arranged the place. The room belonged to those who had set it up, those—in a sense—who came before us. Now this has shifted. The room belongs, at least for this moment or even today, to the whole group.

This shift is profound and may be the whole point of building emotional support for change or implementation. The room becomes a visible expression of how we collectively want to be together. And always a statement about who will create the structures and practices we need to proceed.

The Point

Rearranging the room is a wonderful example of how freedom will create at first its own chaos and confusion, even irritation, and then its own order. It will do so quickly and collectively, and do it in a way that fits the task. We can create things together without all having to do the same thing, think the same way, or even locate ourselves in consistent structures. The ongoing challenge of taking action, what we are calling implementation, is how to keep inventing new structures and practices that fit our intentions. Plus to do this in a way that leaves room for local discretion.

The important point here is that there is not a right structure. There is no right way to arrange a room. Tables or not. Circle or square, or lined up like a chapel. Centralization or decentralization, functional or matrix or geographical organization. Is the leader at the front, behind a podium, on a stage, sitting in a circle? They all can work.

What matters is that everyone is engaged in adapting the structures to the task at hand. When we know that each of us can make the shifts to fit our own purpose and still serve the purpose of the larger organization, then the world has shifted. We no longer need to live by the rules of the economist and engineer. We become the architects, designers, authors of the institution in which we live. We have chosen to be accountable for the institution and no longer have to be held to it.

Structure 4. Create a Platform for Doubt

If doubt and even cynicism cannot be publicly expressed, then internal commitment cannot be offered freely. Some doubts give guidance for improvement, others don't. The engineer in us wants to answer every doubt. When you are building a bridge or airplane, you need to know that all the doubts and questions have been answered. Human systems are not so orderly, and many doubts will go unanswered. It is the expression of doubt that counts, not its resolution. We cannot construct a plan that eliminates all doubts, but we can always acknowledge them. We can acknowledge cynicism and make room for it without being paralyzed by it.

People can trust a system only when they see it can handle conflict and skepticism and not become punishing or collapse. An important task for the consultant is to give permission for the expression of negative feelings and to see that they are responded to in a respectful way. Designing time for public doubts and concern is the way faith in an institution is restored.

The Practice

Any Question Will Do   Break people into teams of six to eight people and ask them to share with each other their doubts or reservations about whatever is the focus of the meeting. A colleague of mine, Kathie Dannemiller, one of the inventors of high-interaction methods of working with large groups, likes to ask people what excites them and what scares them. She also uses two other questions: "What did you hear?" and "What is your reaction?"

Ask Each Group to Report   Do not require agreement or consensus within the teams. We want a wide range of reactions. The main purpose is to support open dialogue, not to decide anything. There is no need for the leaders or consultant to do anything more than listen, maybe clear up questions of fact, and support the expression of doubt.

No Solutions Allowed   This is a time for listening and speaking. Postpone action and recommendations. If we make decisions before there is connection, dialogue, and some commitment, the decisions that we do make will be corrupted by the isolation, caution, and distrust that exist at the beginning of the efforts.

The Point

The way we react to doubt, cynicism, even anger, tells the world whether we want negative feelings spoken or not. Our response becomes either an invitation or refusal for the next discussion. In fact the stronger the negative reaction, the more acknowledgement is required. Many of the skills of dealing with resistance outlined earlier in the book are appropriate here.

Freedom of speech and freedom of assembly do not become real except in moments of conflict and disagreement. The fact that the most alienated people in the organization are given a platform to speak does more to build commitment from those watching the conversation than any compelling presentation or financial incentive program ever can.

Structure 5. What Do We Want to Create Together?

There is no more powerful question than this one. And none more difficult to answer in any meaningful way. It is the question on which real accountability hinges. There are two parts to the question: One is the question of creation, the second is the question of together.

. . . Do We Want to Create? This is the dangerous part of the question. If I answer yes, I am no longer reacting to what has been handed to me. I am now beginning to define a future that ultimately I will be responsible for. Our institutional history has valued reacting and responding over creating and initiating. We have the rhetoric of innovation and initiative, but we are hardly organized to provide it. We use grades in school, appraisals in the workplace, and spin doctors in society to keep us in line and under control.

When we decide that we want to create, we are emotionally joining the organization in defining its future and in that way moving against the culture and our own habit. This may be why when we ask people to define their vision, the first try is quite dull. What you hear is a series of fashion statements fed back to you. People say their vision is continuous improvement, great customer service, a humane workplace, and, of course, economic success. My all-time favorite vision statement was a heartfelt commitment by a quality group to "accurate gauging."

When the question is "What do *we* want to create?" the demand is for an answer that is unique to this group. That is the work: to ask each group to construct a unique future that is right for their function. This is another way we confront people with their freedom. Asking people what they want to create forces the issue, even if the response may initially be pale.

. . . Together?   Do we want to create something together? This is also a difficult one to answer. We may be used to creating something on our own, or in our unit, but when you say, in effect, what can we create together that we cannot create alone, you are asking for another level of collaboration. Most of the time when I have asked groups what they can create together, they return with a list of cooperative actions that each group can do alone.

To create something together, we have to cross boundaries and possibly yield territory. Most change efforts and implementation steps require this, and it is hard to do with any depth. This question opens us to the possibility and faces us with the reluctance of attending to the larger institution first and our own unit second.

The Practice   **Simply Ask the Question, "What Do We Want to Create Together?"**   This task should be done in small groups that are mixed by level and function. You can focus the question on whatever the goal of the meeting is—could be a vision, could be a strategy for changing the measurement system, could be how to communicate with the rest of the organization. Whatever the specific focus, the discussion now is about a joint future.

Collect the Answers in the Larger Group   Let the groups share their ideas. Post them on the wall. Look together at what they have come up with. Discuss common themes. This is the starting point for a co-created future.

Ignore the typical complaints that they will have no place to put their water bottle or notes or elbows. Just use chairs. If they feel too exposed, tell them to cross their legs and arms.

Step 2 *Conversation as usual.* Let them discuss the agenda in whatever fashion they are used to. After ten minutes, ask them how it is going. What are they learning? What has surprised them? What you will mostly hear is that the conversation was business as usual.

Step 3 *Knees nine to twelve inches from your neighbor.* Tell them to sit in a circle with their knees nine to twelve inches from the person to their left and right. Not seven inches, not fourteen inches. Nine to twelve inches. This is a physical way to illustrate the kind of new conversation you want them to experience. It forces the experience of the circle; it gets people close enough so they have to be aware of and see those around them, and it counteracts the instinct to withdraw to the fringe of the action and be an emotional spectator to the game others are creating. Meetings are neither entertainment nor a spectator sport. This structure makes that clear.

Walk around the room to urge them into this configuration. You will notice that this forces them to lean forward and engage. Diabolical, but effective. For those who complain, smile and offer a glazed look. Think of the last meeting you attended and the look will come naturally.

You are going to feel a little foolish being so controlling about something so personal. Live with the feeling. There is something about the specificity of a nine-to-twelve-inch space between each person in a circle that is so absurd it is hard to defend against. It may be just this absurdity that gives an excuse to try a different conversation.

Step 4 *The new conversation.* Now it gets interesting. Tell them that for the next few minutes you want them to have a conversation they have not had before. It has to be related to the purpose of the

A Tip

Sometimes it is hard for people to find the right words to say what is in their minds. Urge them to use language that is theirs alone. If they have heard a phrase before, they cannot use it. If they continue to have trouble finding the words, have each small team create a mural on a piece of flip-chart paper, using images, colors, anything *but* words. The images are always compelling and if posted on the wall bring some life into the room. If you have a long roll of paper, all the teams can create their mural on the same piece of paper. It takes them all one step closer to the idea of creating something together.

Structure 6. Creating a New Conversation

A change in action is preceded by a change in the conversation.[9] Old conversations lead to old actions. The challenge is to have a task-related conversation that people have not had before. Holding onto the old conversation, the old way of naming problems or explaining answers, is a way of seeking safety and maintaining control. We each have our favorite answers: clear roles, clear goals, more structure, less structure, higher standards, more training, better communication—and everybody's favorite theme that someone else has to change before this will work. All of thes᷉ ideas have value, and none of them is that helpful.

Answers that were helpful at one point in time become obst᷉ after a while because they keep us from moving on. They got ᷉ far but, if we hang onto them too tightly, we cannot move f᷉ Old conversations are a way of holding to a position that ᷉ we can defend. We want people to take positions that th᷉ defend. Then we know we are in new territory. Plus, ᷉ born the moment we are surprised by what we say or v᷉

The Activity

Step 1 *First create circles of eight*. Get rid of the tab᷉ sible. Tables are good for leaning and eating, but᷉ is best for surprise and unrest, which is the e᷉

---

[9]Joel Henning has been a teacher of mine in understan᷉ you change the culture by changing the conversation᷉

Some

meeting. But tell them that any hope, change, or growth they might have come for will only occur through a new conversation.

Tell them they have twenty minutes to have a conversation, related to the agenda, they have not had before. If they cannot think of anything new to say, ask them to sit in silence. Better to be quiet than return to a routine that has no meaning. This is the space where we stop digging deeper the hole that we are in.

Step 5 *Stop the conversation.* After ten minutes, stop the talk, and ask them how it is going. Many of the groups will say that it is still the same old conversation. Tell them you understand, but this time you are serious. Have them continue the conversation, but you will be coming around to check on them. Restart the groups. Now walk around and ask each one if it is a new conversation. If it is not new, ask them to be silent until it is.

Step 6 *Reconvene the whole.* Ask, What was different? What did they learn? What new came out of it? If nothing else, the task will bring some life into the room. Even the groups that stayed with the old conversation are now confronted with something new: their own reluctance to move forward rather than their "leaders'" reluctance to change. This puts the attention where it belongs—on all of us.

If this activity does nothing else, it gives hope that each time we come together, we have the capacity to transform our experience. This is how culture changes in the moment, and if we do it often enough, we learn more, risk more, and move more quickly. Change and its cousins, surprise and unrest, are always within our reach. They are just waiting for us to design them into existence.

Structure 7. Choosing Commitment and Accountability

We build capacity when commitment and accountability are chosen. In this modern society we have lost faith in our willingness to choose to be accountable. We think we have to legislate accountability, or we have to "manage accountability," or purchase accountability with incentive schemes. These low-faith strategies create their own dead weight, so we have to keep propping them up over time. They create a cycle in which the more management and legislation, the more resistance and loopholes are created, and this evokes a new wave of management and legislation. This is true of the workplace and the larger culture.

The alternative is to have faith that there are conditions in which people want to be accountable: They want to set high goals, care for the well-being of the larger organization, and know how they are doing. One of those conditions is a crisis. In a crisis the rules are suspended, status and self-interest are put aside, and the task and purpose override habit. The challenge is to find the same willingness without a crisis.

There are two conditions of accountability that support high-commitment implementation strategies. The first is that we need to be accountable to our peers first and our boss second. The second is that we need to commit without negotiation or barter.

Peer Accountability

There is a power among peers that bosses can never approach. For one thing, we have a lifetime of practice in managing bosses. It begins with our parents. As children we may have felt that our parents were in charge, but once we become parents we know that was not true. Parents can give orders and administer consequences, but at the end of the day the child decides when to clean the room or put the dishes away. We work hard at managing and, at times, manipulating those who have power over us. Over the years we become maze-bright. We learn how to handle our parents, teachers, and finally bosses, so that we can do what we want and not have to pay a price for it. When our bosses are upset with us, we have learned how to say "thank you for the feedback" as a way of defending against their disappointment, and not really having to change.

Our peers, however, are less likely to tolerate this sort of maneuvering. They see us more clearly, and they are around more, so they are harder to manipulate. This is one reason being accountable to peers is a more demanding proposition. Also, our interdependence lies with our peers, not our boss. It is their work that is eased when we do well and made difficult when we do poorly. They have to pick up the slack and operationally live with our mistakes. Peers are the ones we are functionally accountable to, no matter who conducts our performance review.

We have begun to recognize this interdependence in our attention to teams, team building, and team pay schemes. The next step is to initiate more formal peer conversations about commitments and consequences. We want to adhere to the principle that accountability needs to be a voluntary act, and this has more power with peers.

Peer accountability also means that it is up to peers to speak for the well-being of the organization. It is not just the bosses' function. Peers need to tell us whether we have committed enough to meet the promises of the unit and larger system. This requirement to think of the interests of the whole system has as much impact on the peers listening to the commitments as on the person making them.

Commitment Without Negotiation

A second element of implementation via consent is to explore what *commitment* and *promise* really mean. We are very much a negotiating culture. We like to bargain for goods and have the concept of *quid pro quo* deeply embedded in our relationships. The ideas about contracting outlined earlier in this book are a good example of this. I want to make a distinction, though, between living up to our contractual agreements and making an emotional or personal commitment.

A personal commitment means that we agree to do something that is not conditional on the response of someone else. That is why the word *promise* is so appropriate. If we make our commitments conditional on the response from another, they are really not commitments; they are contracts or other forms of barter. They become conditional agreements that can be withdrawn if the other side does not deliver. Throughout this consulting process we have been seeking the internal commitment required to get past the rhetoric and cosmetic change that surround us. A commitment is a promise or a pledge to do something. Even in its dictionary definition, there is no mention of anything received by the person making the pledge; it is only about the choice to be made.

If we commit in this spirit, the discussion about how the top needs to change, how other departments and people stand in the way, how systems and practices don't support the change—it all disappears. At the moment of commitment the institution becomes ours to create, and in that act of committing we can find our freedom. We now proceed on our own, and with others we have freely joined. Something has shifted for us and the institution.

There will still be obstacles and disappointment, but they will not breed cynicism, for we were not choosing on the basis of another's action. If there is an affirmation or loss of faith, it will not be in others but in ourselves.

The Activity

Accountability and commitment take form in the promises we are willing to make. The language of promises is quite different from goals and objectives. Strong language, difficult to make. Yet there is something sacred and freely chosen in a promise. Here is an activity that confronts and cements people's will to proceed.

Step 1 *Sit in groups of up to eight people.* The groups should be people who have a future together. A work team or people working together on a project. The boss joins the circle and participates as a member.

Step 2 *People state their promises.* Each person states two kinds of commitments or promises: One is the results they agree to deliver, the second is their actions and behavior that will support the team effort. Remember that these promises are voluntary. There are no weapons on the table, no implied threat of punishment, and virtue alone will be the reward. Have people actually use this language: "The promise I am willing to make is. . . ."

Step 3 *People state the measures that have meaning to them.* This may take more than one conversation, but it is good to begin it. The measures for each person need to fit with those of the others in the group and meet the requirements of the organization. The language to be used is: "The measures I choose and that have meaning to me are. . . ." Enforce the language if you can. It makes a difference.

Step 4 *Peers answer the question, "Is that enough?"* The team decides whether each person's promises and measures are enough to meet the common goals. If not enough is promised, the person is asked for more. If the measures seem too soft, the person is asked for tougher ones. What is important is that all are speaking as owners of the unit. All are forced to think about the whole change or implementation and not just their own piece. The value of this discussion is in the dialogue as much as in the outcome.

Step 5 *The group picks a time to review their commitments.* The promises and measures should be put in writing and copies given to each member. It is best to have the documents be handwritten and signed at the bottom. This way, they are not technological and have some symbolic value. Have the handwritten promises/measures copied and bound and give each member a copy. Every few months, or sooner, the group meets to review them. Making promises to peers can mean unusual and very difficult discussions. It will take a few iterations before people get used to initiating with their peers real questions of performance. There are no formal punishments if people do not meet their targets. The team needs to confront the problem, but they do not need the formal sanctions of pay, probation, and low ratings to have influence on their members. In extreme cases the team and the boss may have to revert to some punitive action, but let that be the last resort instead of being built into every discussion, which is what happens when each subordinate negotiates commitments privately with the boss. These discussions can replace the usual performance review, but that is a bigger and more volatile subject than belongs here.

Structure 8. Positive Feedback

There is a need to bring closure to each meeting that acknowledges the effort and care brought into the room. One good way to finish is to focus on the strengths and value each participant brought to the proceedings. We live in a world that is much more interested in our weaknesses and deficiencies than in our gifts. This is so common that we have even come to believe that it is useful. Not so. Most of us have been working on our deficiencies for much of our life, and look at the progress we have made.

If negative feedback were so useful, we would have it together by now, and we don't. The primary impact of focusing on weaknesses is that it breeds self-doubt and makes us easier to control. That is why it is so compelling and popular. We fear that if everyone really understood their strength and value, the system might not hold together. Everyone might exploit their free agency, become too expensive, and hit the road. Or stay and become unbearable. If they stayed, what would they demand? And as employees, we are so used to looking at our weaknesses that it has become a comfort to us.

As adults, we have harvested all the learning we can from focusing on weaknesses. And we are blind and embarrassed by our strengths, our capacity to forgive ourselves, our affirmation of the value we bring. Despite this, change comes more quickly from capitalizing on our strengths. This is true for an organization as well as for an individual.

The Activity

One of the joys of getting older is that you come to accept yourself as you are, deficiencies and all. You put aside your self-fix-it projects and become more effective because of it. Why wait? Why not institutionalize attention to strengths and capacities? At a minimum it will stimulate another new conversation.

Here is an activity that does just that. I have ended most implementation efforts this way and it rarely disappoints. It is never comfortable, but invariably useful.

Step 1 *Back to the circle (optional at this point: knees nine to twelve inches from your neighbor).* The group is made up of people who have worked together in this session this day. It does not matter whether people have a long or short history with each other.

Step 2 *Name the value each has brought to the session.* Focusing on one person at a time, take three minutes for each person. The rest of the group states what strengths the person embodies and what value was brought to this meeting. Be specific. Everyone does not have to speak, but each has to have a full three minutes in the sun.

Step 3 *Embarrassed Listening.* This is a new skill you can add to active listening. When you receive feedback on your value and gifts, maintain eye contact, take a breath, and say, "Thank you. I like hearing that." It may be the most honest thing you have said all day. Then let the group know when you cannot stand it any longer by saying "next" or simply pointing if that is easier.

Checklist #9. Preparing for Implementation

Here are some reminders on working the elements of engagement into the implementation process.

1. What will you do during each implementation event to tilt the balance away from presentation and more toward participation?

2. How are you planning to provide the space for people to voice their concerns and opinions? What will you do to promote openness and telling the truth?

3. Consider how you may be able to help define choices for the client. How could you help open opportunities for real choice at many levels of the organization? How can you structure time for serious dialogue on how things will change?

4. What will you do to help people get unstuck from the same old conversations and begin new ones about the hopes and doubts the proposed change generates?

5. How will you bring the power of place into your design for each event?

Mixing Metaphor and Methodology

These structures and activities are both methodology and a metaphor of a more universal possibility. Each symbolizes the larger intent and in that way has more meaning than its momentary effect. Implementation is not a universal, clear path stretched out before us. It is more complex than the phases of contracting and discovery, for it is more particular to each situation. The practices I have described are more a menu or a starting point than a series of steps, and each is an example of how to treat engagement as the central issue in implementation. We all wish for a simpler path, as if decision were followed immediately by action, so we could see corrective action taken and then measure. This rational, problem-solving conception of how ideas get embodied into a living system presents a world that does not exist.

The world we live in is a political system, driven as much by the wish for safety, predictable territory, and a home-cooked meal as by analysis and reason. If something different and more adventurous is being forced on us, then we need methods that build relationships, that encourage local choice and more distributed governance, that value the importance of assembly, free speech, and the common purpose that these things foster.

This mind-set is what a consultant is in a unique position to offer. We are not so embedded in the culture that we cannot see it, nor are we so different from our clients that we cannot help them change it. If, however, we simply become a reflection of the way they have always brought their ideas to fruition, we will have left little behind.

Checklist #10. Reviewing an Implementation Event

Here are some questions to ask yourself after an implementation meeting. Use them to assess your own learning from each meeting and to prepare for the next one.

1. What was the outcome?

2. How was it like or different from what you expected?

3. How did people choose to engage in the process? How active were they? What kind of risk taking did you observe?

4. What happened when you rearranged the room? (Or did you?)

5. What doubts and reservations were expressed? How was the discussion handled—A rush to agreement? A search for solutions? or Was it possible for the group to postpone decision making?

6. How did the group determine what they wanted to create together?

7. What did people do to make new conversations occur? How did you help? What did they learn?

8. What promises were people willing to make? Were they enough?

9. What did you do to end the meeting so that each participant's effort and contributions were acknowledged?

10. What effect on your relationship with the client did this event have?

11. What would you do differently next time?

Chapter 18

Ethics and the Shadow Side of Consulting

CONTRARY TO POPULAR BELIEF, consulting is the world's oldest profession. The first consultant was the Serpent in the Garden of Eden. Amidst a scene of unprecedented peace and tranquility, the Serpent, with the encouragement of top management, took it upon himself to assume an advisory role with Eve. When Eve followed his advice and picked the low-hanging fruit, the consequences were grave and long-lasting. So in addition to what some have called Original Sin, we now have the concept of Original Advice. We still feel the chill of this ancestral shadow cast over our work.

I raise the ethical side of consulting with some reluctance as the term "ethics" is one I like to avoid. Living in a glass house, talking about ethics can put the speaker in a position of judgment and righteousness that is false and hypocritical. Not the intent here; this chapter is meant more as confession than sermon, for there is a moral line in the consulting role that we have all stepped on or crossed.

Being clear about the dark side of consulting has a practical as well as a moral side. It makes a difference in the quality of our work, for when we get caught in our own self-interest or our need to assume a central or inflated role, our client feels it and withdraws from us for reasons rarely spoken.

I personally experience a shadow on the work because calling myself a consultant all these years has carried with it a certain uneasiness. There was a time on an airplane when I answered the question of what I did by saying I was a child photographer. Nice conversation stopper. When people ask you what you do for a living, and you decide to answer truthfully, as soon as you say "consultant," you see their eyes glaze over as they search for a gentle way of asking whether you have ever had an honest job. Whatever their statement, I usually make light of the profession, thinking that if I can tell the jokes about consultants first, I will finesse the discomfort and ward off the other's cynical comments.

Twenty years ago, I began this book with my usual jokes about consulting, my favorite defense against criticism that contains the truth. I left them in the revised edition because, if anything, people's trust in the integrity of consultants has eroded even further. A popular magazine has a regular column about the exploiting nature of consultants. The business press has written about the cost and questionable value of many large consulting efforts, and about the inability of consultants to live according to their own advice. In November 1997 the *Wall Street Journal* reported that a well-known consultant and author confessed to revising his theories almost at the peak of their popularity; he found that in his passion for new structures, he had left people out of his thinking. Nobody's perfect.

So why this deteriorating confidence in consulting, even in the midst of enormous growth of the industry? I think the cynicism aimed at consultants is more about our ethics than about our competence or contribution. In the effort to avoid the discomfort associated with unflattering views of the profession, we maintain our sense of humor, but mostly deny our own culpability in deserving the culture's questions about our utility and value.

My intent in this chapter is to explore what might be deserved in the world's skepticism about whether consulting really brings the value that it promises. When consultants deny their own questions about both the value and the legitimacy of our stances in working with clients, we are feeding the cynicism and making the next generation of work more difficult.

The Promise

Part of the problem is that the promise of consulting is a commitment to care and to service. We promise to act in the interest of another, the client. When we can hold to that promise, we probably add real value and become legitimate. It is just hard to meet such a standard. What follows is an attempt to explore what interferes with our capacity to serve, even in the face of our best intentions.

Although most of the heat about the profession is about external consultants, the same conflicts exist with internal consultants and staff groups. The concern is certainly more urgent with external consultants, but it also applies to those who consult within an organization. Staff groups are under great pressure to do the bidding of top management and often find it difficult to hold to their own values and beliefs. In this way they carry much the same burdens as external consultants. It is not accidental that internal staff groups are labeled "overhead items" or that staff groups are an early target of cost reductions and outsourcing.

Many internal staff groups also operate as virtual consulting businesses: They are self-funding, bill out their services, and experience the same tension between serving their own interests and doing what is best for their clients. And with the increasing cost pressure on most organizations, many are even free to extend their services to other, outside clients.

The Commercialization of Service

One fundamental tension in consulting work is between delivering service and the economics of the consulting unit. When a service becomes a business first and a service second, something fundamental about the work is changed. Most of us did not begin our consulting work with the business in mind: We were attracted to a set of ideas and trained in a set of skills. We also wanted to make a living. It wasn't until we became successful that we got caught between commerce and care.

There is an inherent strain between the economic demands of a consulting practice and the care and service we wish to offer in the interest of the client. Care comes when we can customize our service for each client, when something new is created with each client. The consultant's promise is most accurately fulfilled when the person selling the work is the person doing the work. This way the client knows exactly who will be doing the work after the decision to proceed. Care is delivered when we build the capacity of the client to design their own changes and the client is not dependent on the consultant. In a practice based on care, each client becomes important, and the marketing strategy is basically to do good work.

Consulting becomes commercialized when the service gets standardized and becomes a product to be marketed. The economics of a service business drive you in the direction of standardized or packaged service. Salaries are the major cost item, and one way to reduce labor costs is to make the service predictable. It takes a very experienced, and therefore high-cost, consultant or staff person to be able to create a strategy and service for each particular client. It takes a lot of experience for one person to be able to conceptualize the project, sell the project, manage the project, and do the work. One way to solve this dilemma is to, in effect, package the service so lower cost, less experienced people can manage and do the work. Then you only need highly experienced people in the front end of the project, doing the selling.

Many consulting firms and internal staff groups divide themselves into those who sell the work, those who manage the work, and those who do the work. As the overhead costs of the consulting unit come under more pressure, the drive to build sales and make repeat sales within each client organization becomes intense. At some point, the success of the practice gets measured by standard business criteria—annual growth, margin, earnings, return on capital. At this point, commerce has become dominant over care.

The shift from care to commerce can occur in any size firm or staff unit. It often just happens to us, rather than being something we planned. It happens when what we do works, and it happens in many professions. Physicians, architects, and lawyers, for example, often find themselves driven more by the economics than the professional objectives of their practice.

The inherent pressure is to make a business out of a profession. We worry about how to create growth opportunities so we can keep good people. We believe we need a large group to offer a full range of services and to take on really big change efforts, and it takes money to support more services. Plus the culture places a high premium on economic success. But the commercialization of our profession is more a mind-set than a requirement of growth. It is a question of purpose and focus, and that is why it becomes an ethical question.

Growth Can Undermine Service

The growing marketplace for consulting services has intensified the problem and also changed the industry. For example, in the large accounting firms, consulting services used to be a second cousin—something done because the client demanded it or the consultants themselves got restless with the more routine financial work they had been doing too long. There were the large consulting companies, but they were primarily experts in a particular aspect of business, such as marketing, regulatory requirements, or technical innovation. Services aimed at information systems and changing organization culture were not really on their radar screen.

Much of the growth of consulting has been riding the wave of the information explosion combined with the downsizing of industry. Most large organizations have found it more profitable to shrink and merge and outsource jobs; this mentality dominated the Eighties and Nineties and shows no sign of abating. This creates the challenge of how fewer people can do more work, and the consulting industry has been the beneficiary of this movement.

There has also been growth in the consulting services business because of the interest in quality improvement, better customer service, and changing cultures toward more team-oriented and involved workplaces. All of these goals are worthy, but what I want to explore is how the commercialization of our services has subverted their intent. I have picked four examples—you might come up with different ones—each of which has noble intent, is widely accepted, and has generally under-delivered on its promise.

The areas are *reengineering, performance management, leadership development,* and *change management.* Each of these areas of practice has power and relevance. Their intent is inarguable. Something shifted, though, when they become commercialized and popular. Here is a snapshot of what has been occurring.

The Reengineering Wave . . . Promising Magic

Reengineering is a good example of an idea that became the rage and consulting firms that made promises to the point they were unsustainable. After a good run, the work has fallen of its own weight. Left behind is a residue of something less than goodwill.

We might say that the clients did not adequately implement what the consultants recommended, but that argument is too one-sided.

The idea that organizations should be structured according to the customer-driven work process rather than by discipline-driven vertical silos makes sense. It is a way to break up the bureaucracies that have made organizations unable to give customers a unique, quick, anytime-anywhere response. Popularized by Michael Hammer through his book and presentations, reengineering brought what used to be called "socio-technical systems redesign" into the mainstream. The idea had been around for a long time, but Hammer renamed it, expanded it, and made a market for it by connecting the methodology to the new customer environment.

It reached a point where whatever change we had in mind was called reengineering. Every department thought it was reengineering itself. I even heard individuals say they were in the process of reengineering themselves. The energy was more about becoming modern than becoming better. Reengineering became synonymous with restructuring and was sold by the large accounting and consulting firms with promises of a 30 to 50 percent return on the investment.

The bloom is now off the rose. A large fashion company spent $600 million in consulting fees alone to restructure itself and bring up-to-date information technology to its business. After years of investment, a leader of this company acknowledged publicly that the effort had not been successful and eventually 2,500 employees were reassigned, retired, or laid off to help, in effect, finance the venture.

The dark side of reengineering, which threatens the whole profession, is that the promises made to sell the work either were never fulfilled or could finally be achieved only by eliminating jobs on a wide scale. The goal of restructuring the work process for the sake of the customer was more often than not unrealized. In fact many of the users of reengineering are now undoing its efforts because they found the concept unworkable. Some have even sued to get their money back.

Reengineering is a good example of two larger problems: how consultants take advantage of what is in vogue and how we pursue covert purposes. When an idea is fashionable it becomes, almost by definition, a cosmetic solution. When consultants offer a service primarily because clients want it, we have chosen commerce over care. If we were strictly a business you would say, What's the problem? Customer is always right. We only gave them what they asked for. Being also a service function, though, means that something more is due the client.

Clients have a right to expect the consultant to decide whether what the client is willing to buy will deliver what the client really needs. If the client manager asks for a service that will not help, or may even be harmful, then when does the consultant say no and turn away the work? It is a tough thing to do, especially for internal consultants.

The other questionable edge to consulting is a form of double-dealing, for example, when force reductions are packaged as organization improvement. Reengineering had some of this quality. Who can argue with restructuring for the sake of the customer? Organizations went through a long process of interviews, redesign teams, and extensive selling and training for the new system, when the real net result of the effort was the elimination of jobs with little real change in culture or function.

Performance Management . . . Let Me Do It for You

In a culture in which profitability and efficiency have become the priority, accountability becomes everyone's favorite word. We think that there is a relationship between holding ourselves and others more accountable and increasing performance. If we can just tighten our accountability grip, the organization would deliver more. This illusion creates a market for methodologies and consultant services that promise better gripping power.

There are consulting firms that guarantee concrete results in return for a fee. If you don't see the results, you don't pay the fee. This is the ultimate in performance consulting. How could a consultant make this kind of guarantee? Simple. Take over that segment of the business that you promise to improve. The consultant becomes a surrogate manager, and the line management clears the way and effectively steps aside. The people in the unit live under the power of the consultant, and generally the consultant delivers on the "performance improvement" by closer controls and ending with fewer people doing more jobs.

This is not really consulting. It is something we might call "insourcing": bringing into the organization, on a temporary basis, surrogate managers who are willing to take a difficult stand, reduce head count, confront people in a way that the permanent, resident management is unwilling to do.

Even if the job needed to be done, the use of consultants in this way undermines the legitimacy of the consultant role. Consulting is no longer educational, advisory, or capacity building. Line managers cast the consultant in the role of the Serpent in order to protect their own good image with their own people. When we go along with this, it may be good for our business, but hard on the service dimension of the profession.

There are milder forms of performance consulting, the main problems of which have more to do with taking measurements than with taking charge. There is a resurgence of the belief that anything you cannot measure does not exist. And internal staff groups are under more and more pressure to be more business oriented and return-on-investment minded than in the past. Hard to argue with in theory.

The risk is that staff groups will no longer be in the business of cultural change or confronting the culture with aspects of its own blindness. Performance consulting will drive staff groups to be more like the culture that surrounds them. This will reinforce services that treat only symptoms and seek acceptance at the cost of some greater impact than the consultant or staff group has the potential to make.

There is great pressure for this in the human resource area. The HR function comes under siege because much of its value is hard to quantify. In periods when people concerns are in remission, the push to "rationalize" HR almost leads to its elimination. There has to be a way for qualitative services to demonstrate their value without sacrificing the power of their unique perspective.

Leadership Development . . . Entertainment Tonight

Another economic growth area of consulting comes from our love for leadership. We have been in search of leaders since the late Seventies. Before that we were in search of managers. We now have a leadership industry fueled more by training and presentations than by consulting. The industry is led by authors and ex-chief executive officers who, in many cases, have found more meaning teaching leadership than providing it. The headliners come not only from private industry, but also from politics, sports, and the government.

The high end of the leadership industry is probably more accurately called the "edutainment" industry, for its emphasis is more on entertainment than on learning. At the top the pay is good, the hours are reasonable, and the expectations are pretty low. No one asks about the financial return to the organization as a result of a celebrity presentation. They just wish the celebrity could have stayed around longer. From edutainment to the one-or two-week immersion events, the number of leadership courses offered within companies and as public conferences has grown rapidly. I have even been the beneficiary of this trend.

One large company required a week of training for the top two thousand executives. Forty sessions run for fifty executives at a time. Monday was globalization, Tuesday was finance, Thursday was product innovation, and Friday was a talk with the top. Wednesday was a day on empowerment, and I had written a book on the subject. So I showed up as the centerfold of the week and talked about creating an empowered workforce, a subject of greatest interest to myself and those sitting in the back of the room who sponsored the program.

Most of the participants were there to get their ticket punched. Some were very interested, some seemed somewhat engaged in what they were learning, most were going through the motions. I finally withdrew from the program and as a postscript to the experience, I received from the support staff a special goodbye present. The four people who handled the secretarial and logistical duties for the program gave me a T-shirt. In gold letters on the back were the words "Empowered My Ass." A little crude perhaps, but an apt commentary on the impact of the effort.

All of the emphasis on leadership these days is disturbing because it holds on to the belief that organizations are the creation of those who run them and will forever live in their shadow. Training its leaders becomes the centerpiece strategy for improving the organization. There is little evidence that training leaders has any impact on organizational change, and there is little accountability for the investment made in leader training.

This is in sharp contrast to the scrutiny given training at lower levels, which really is a form of elitism. Train supervisors for two hours a week for six weeks and we are asked to defend the investment. Send the top management team to a university for four weeks, and the question of value received is limited to asking the participating managers whether they liked the program. Four weeks in Cambridge, Charlottesville, Evanston, Palo Alto—what's not to like?

Change Management . . . Contrast Between Intention and Form

Faced with increasing competition and a loss of customers, managers decided in the Eighties that what was needed was a change in culture. Pressures for better quality and sharper customer focus added to the traditional pressures for cost reduction and accountability. We needed workplaces in which people acted as owners of the institution, employees felt empowered and involved, change was welcomed, and fear was driven out.

To achieve these goals, managers brought in consultants to end command-and-control and bring in more participation. Bosses were to become coaches, employees would now be called associates; all were to work in teams, even across functions. It reached the point where employees were to evaluate their bosses, just as college students have been evaluating their teachers.

All of this was a large undertaking, which created a logical need for consulting help. In many ways this culture change effort fed the interest in reengineering and leadership and performance consulting. The ethical question arises from the disparity between the claims and the reality. The promise of culture change was essentially that a shift in power was needed: Teams close to the work had to have more control over how the work was done and how money was spent.

Much of the consulting that accompanied this, however, was done in a way that undermined a true resurgence of worker power and choice. To begin with, we believed that the workers were presently incapable of exercising more choice without intensive training. They had to be given empowerment tools. They had to be taught to work in teams. They had to be persuaded that they should act in ways that serve the well-being of the business. And it was the consulting companies that owned these tools and methods of persuasion, which they sold through a series of training and consulting products to the employees, albeit paid for by the organizations.

The consultants' marketable tools were not limited to training products. There were major projects to define the new competencies that would be required in the new age. There were new assessment and measurement products that would help gauge the progress of the change effort. There were major communications programs to publicize and explain the new culture both to employees and to the outside world.

The questions I want to raise about these efforts are not really about their effectiveness, even though the reports are mixed on how much of a given culture actually changed, depending on who you talk to. If you talk to the top management who sponsored the effort or the internal and external consultants who implemented it, they think the effort was very successful and the culture has indeed shifted.

But if you talk to employees in most companies that made the investment, you generally find fear is still a daily part of their lives; they work in some teams, but individualism is still the dominant mode of operation; and while they may have more budget and spending authority than before, top management is still very much in control and patriarchy is alive and well.

The question of whether the culture has shifted becomes almost a projection exercise for the person asking. Whatever you want to see, you can find evidence to support it. What is more disturbing to me is the way that the consultants and managers approached the task of making organizational changes. Whenever the change effort serves to build the business of the service provider more than the client, or when the change effort serves to simply reinforce the existing culture and belief systems about control and power, then the work is open to question. Here are the practices to question:

They Are the Problem; They Need to Change, We Don't

In defining the lower levels, and often middle management, as the "problem," change management reinforces the patronizing and imperial attitudes of management. There is collusion between consultant and top management in deciding that it is the rest of the organization that needs changing. There is the widespread illusion that top management either doesn't need to change or all they need is a quick study, so they get a half-day version of the training that takes other employees three days to absorb.

There sometimes is recognition—or at least rhetoric—that the top needs to change also, and many top teams have worked on their own relationships as part of a strategy to bring more teamwork to the organization. But most of the time the thinking is that the real change needs to take place at lower levels. When consultants affirm this belief and become its main economic beneficiaries, we are on thin ice.

The dilemma was most evident in the reengineering rage. Very few reengineering efforts began by focusing on the job of the person signing the check. Very few efforts resulted in reducing the number of jobs at the level where the project was commissioned. When the promise was to restructure the work around core processes, the real impact was usually to rationalize a reduction in force.

Using Assessment as a Way to Market Services

In many cases consultants are engaged to define a problem or to assess "training needs." Too often it turns out that the training *needs* identified are best met by the training *services* and *programs* offered by these same consultants. This fit between diagnosis and prescription is in fact a business strategy for many consulting firms. Some even give away the assessment as a loss leader for future business.

To make the strategy credible, the consultants offer a false customization of their product. The assessment or training product stays constant, but is cosmetically altered to look like a unique offer to each customer. No matter how "customized" or "tailored," each training program is only superficially different from the last, and the consulting firm is the economic beneficiary of their own supposedly objective analysis.

Colluding with Cosmetic Change

In the early Nineties the Association for Quality and Participation found that 73 percent of large companies surveyed said they had an employee involvement program, but these programs had impacted only 13 percent of the jobs within those companies. This spread defines the gap between promise and reality. The growth in employee involvement occurred at the same time organizations were eliminating levels of management and reducing the labor force as a means to greater productivity.

While employee participation and culture change were genuine in some companies such as Ford and Harley-Davidson, for many companies they were a way to put an attractive face on the real objective of contraction and belt tightening. Consultants became an ingredient in the cosmetics. There is an intolerable strain between an institutional promise of participation, or empowerment, or caring for the customer, and a consulting change process that uses language like "driving down change," or "taking the vision and drilling it down through the organization." What you end up with is high-control management, shoulder to shoulder with high-control consultants "selling" and "installing" participative restructuring, empowerment, and the illusion that people are the "number one asset of the institution."

If an organization believes in high control, speaks high control, and hires consultants to tighten it all up, this is well and good. When consultants sell services to create high-involvement packages that mask the reality that business will continue as usual, then we deserve the arrows we receive.

Who Takes Credit?

Assessing the value of a professional service is difficult. The wish is to attribute to the consulting effort direct cost savings or improvement in performance. Although the need to prove our value is important, when consultants take credit, it is most often an exaggeration of our role and inflation of its worth. Unless the consultant has become a surrogate manager and taken over the management task, no credit accrues; organizational results are earned by those living in the system.

As a side comment, consultants are predisposed by role and personality to self-inflation. In fact, the role almost demands arrogance. Clients want someone to lean on, someone who seems to have answers to unsolvable problems. Plus, when meeting a new client, the consultant has maybe an hour to make contact with the people, read the situation, make suggestions, define a plan, and negotiate general price and terms. Not a job for the meek.

Plus, if you find a consultant who also likes to conduct training, give presentations at conferences, and write books, you have found a person who likes the spotlight and usually partakes in all the protestations of humility that make it all plausible. With all this, the instinct to take credit is even more understandable.

The reality, though, is that the risks of change—and its payoffs—belong to the line organization. Courage, will, and the persistence to see a change through are required of the managers and employees, not of consultants. We may contribute greatly at key points, but when we list their cost savings and performance improvement in our brochures and publicity, we in some way have overstated our role at the expense of the client. This is true even when they give us their permission to use their results for our own benefit.

Seller Beware

When I reflect on the ethical snares we face, the most surprising one is the willingness of line managers to follow the fashions and buy what is popular. When one high-profile company and executive starts claiming victory with a new approach, the approach is transformed from service into fashion. No matter that reengineering author Michael Hammer states that 70 percent of reengineering efforts will fail, everybody wants one. Maybe each organization is arrogant enough to believe that it will be among the 30 percent that succeed, but most are wrong. Many of the largest consulting efforts never deliver on their promise. Once the fashion parade begins, though, there is no stopping it, and we consultants participate and profit from it.

Every organization claims it desires to be number one, a leader in its field, a center of innovation and creativity. Yet, when it comes time to experiment with a new strategy, management wants to know where else this idea has worked. If some other high-profile company has done it, we will do it. If we are to be the first, let us wait. Consultants benefit from this caution by offering safety.

Consulting firms make a living by giving legitimacy to a manager's efforts to sell an idea internally. Or to play the bad cop in pushing unpopular decisions, rationalizing cutbacks, implementing get-tough, back-to-basics strategies. It is the timidity of our captains of industry that drives these uses of consultants, but we need to own the nature of our participation.

Owning the Shadow— Some Thoughts on What to Do

For each profession, what began as a calling at some point became a business. We enter our professions because that is the work we want to do. As we succeed, we get pulled from the work itself and get drawn into managing the work. The pressure to sustain and succeed pushes our attention from how to deliver quality service to how to build a successful business. The tension between the two is inevitable. It is a paradox that has no simple answer.

Consulting is also a service, and so customers are likely to project qualities on you that you do not possess. In a sense, the client looks for hope where little exists. Seeking a consultant has an element of seeking a super-someone, be it man or woman. So there is a willingness from the client to demand and expect more than we may be able to offer.

In the face of this, there are some steps, or at least ways of thinking that will at a minimum raise our consciousness about our contribution to the cynicism and doubt that infect the consulting industry. At best we may find a way of working where the longing that brought us into the work can be realized.

Say No As Often As You Say Yes

Consultants should make their own decisions on which projects to accept. We should say no to projects as often as we say yes. There are many reasons to back away from business. Clients often want us to treat a symptom. They think training or restructuring will solve their problem, when it will only postpone resolution. Say no when the chemistry between you and the client is not good. Be careful when the client has expectations of you that you cannot fulfill. Say no to a five-dollar solution for a fifty-dollar problem.

Stay True to Your Worth

Stop measuring the success of your internal staff consulting work by the size of your staff, the volume of work you can generate, or the approval rating of top management. If you are an external consultant, don't judge your practice by the sales volume of your business, return on equity, or margins. Setting high growth targets for your business will force you and others to take marginal business. It will push new services into the marketplace before they are fully developed. Your ambition will also be sensed by the client, and although they might say yes today, they will feel used over time.

Start measuring your work by the optimism and self-sufficiency you leave behind. Consulting is fundamentally an educational and capacity-building function. You need to be economically self-sufficient, true, but that is not the point. You are successful when the clients feel more accountable for their own system, more able to learn by themselves in the future, more confident and powerful in creating an organization they believe in. These are qualitative measures, but they are knowable if we pay attention.

Grow on Your Own Terms

Accept the fact that the work you have chosen will most likely and appropriately remain a boutique business. Professional practice is the point, not the size of the practice. For external consultants, decide how much money you need to live on and how many days you are willing to work, peg your rates to that equation, and avoid conversations with other consultants in which they will ask how busy and successful you are.

If there is more demand for your services than you can handle, give the business away. Build a network of people who do what you do and you respect and send the business to them. Don't take a finder's fee, or talk about mergers and partnerships that are driven by economic opportunity. If this seems bizarre and counter-cultural to you, it means you are on the right track.

Show How Everybody Counts

The whole system is your client. All parts of it need to be supported, to learn, and to be fully informed. Ensure that the client manager making the decision to hire you is as vulnerable to the effects of the change effort as others at lower levels of the organization. If a project begins as a way to control or change others, it will be very difficult to turn its focus back to where it began. Real change has to be chosen, it is a voluntary act. If we are in the business of joining with the top to change others, we have become an agent of top management—and a part of the problem. We have become a stealth operation that will eventually undermine trust and make it harder the next time around.

Ask whether you would be willing for all members of the client organization to be witnesses to the selling and planning conversations you have with the client—a fresh-air test to the promises we make and the plans we develop. Meeting this test would change many of the conversations. It would be harder to blame people not in the room and harder to plan for the transformation of others.

Leave It All Behind

Commit yourself to the concepts of "home schooling" and building capacity. Clients have the capacity to learn and create for themselves the future they thought they needed a consultant to provide. Your job is fundamentally an educator, not a problem solver. You may have to problem solve in the short run, but over time you need to develop ways for people to learn about your expertise. Be a support system for your clients' self-sufficiency.

And, Finally, Forgive

In thinking about these conflicts and paradoxes, forgiveness is required. No one can fully live according to his or her beliefs. That is why we are called humans. In fact that is why, in the first consulting act, God suggested to the Serpent that he chat with Eve. By eating the apple, she and Adam lost their paradise and gained their humanity and all the freedom and flaws that go with it.

What we can do with our freedom is tell the truth, at least to ourselves, about the choices we make. If we take business because we need the money, so be it. If we over-promise because that is the only way things will move forward, if we seek too much approval from the top, if we are swept along with a fad and find ourselves mimicking the language of others—all of these are forgivable.

What is hard to forgive is self-delusion and positioning ourselves as a cut above our clients and others who do our work. This is pride and hubris and it seems to come with our working papers. It is our own awareness and courage to see who we are that enables us to offer the service and care that is the best of the profession. And maybe some day I will be less embarrassed by my choice of work and, better yet, can stop telling bad consultant jokes.

Chapter 19

The Heart of the Matter

CONSULTING IS PRIMARILY a relationship business. No matter how research-based or technical the project, it will always reach a point at which the success of the work will hinge on the quality of the relationship we have with our client. This relationship is the conduit through which our expertise passes.

The way we contact and engage people around our expertise is an applied art and takes a hundred forms. At times it is one-to-one coaching with an individual or team. Or it can be working with a group on strategy or technology, or running a training session. Underlying all the ways we work with clients is a set of beliefs about relationships and learning that ultimately define our practice.

While this book is threaded with thoughts about good, or flawless, consulting practice, I want to take a moment to be explicit about its foundational concepts. When I am lost, unsure how to proceed, which is most of the time, I return to a few ideas that ground me again and again and serve to reassure. Each of these ideas has as much to do with the heart as the head; in fact, finding and sustaining this connection may be the whole point. Consulting cannot be done well without genuine caring for the client, and the challenge is to find ways to embody our care in the way we do the work. Our care is expressed partly in our behavior and style, but it is also a matter of how we structure critical elements of the learning and change process.

In a sense, our job is to be a "learning architect." At our best, we design social settings that lead to insight, resolution of differences, and change. What follows are some ideas that support conditions under which learning and change are more likely to happen. None is fail-safe, each contains elements of adventure, all flow against the stream of the conventional wisdom and the dominant culture. That is what makes them useful.

Choosing Learning over Teaching

While we usually claim that we are in the business of helping our clients learn, most traditional educational or consulting efforts are more about teaching than learning. If you ask who is really learning at any meeting, communication session, or training event, the answer is usually the person in charge.

The dominant models for learning come from our educational system. If you look at most of our classrooms, the teacher stands in front, and students line up behind or around tables, facing the front. The agenda, the objectives, the method of learning are all specified by the teacher. The teacher is in effect the supervisor of learning. Similarly in consulting, the consultant is expected to be the change manager. Even change agent. The task of the client is to absorb what the consultant has to offer.

The classroom or consulting project run on this model is based on the need for predictability and control. Our need is to make the teacher or consultant central to the learning. It is partly a question of pedagogy and our desire to prescribe for others what we wish them to do. But we are not the only ones lured into an all-eyes-front approach. This classroom or meeting model is also demanded by the learners. If you decide to invite your client to define the agenda, create the learning process, and evaluate their own performance, you will probably face a revolt. Clients are so conditioned to be passive in the teaching/learning process that, given the choice to manage their own learning, they will pass and turn the floor back to the consultant.

The result is that the teacher or consultant conspires with the participant or client to keep the teacher/consultant central and the student/client reactive. And one effect is that too often the consultant is the one who learns the most. Some of this is inevitable, for when we are forced to explain ourselves or teach others, we invest in the subject matter in a way that the client is not required to do. But some of it comes from our need to control what is presented and to specify what is learned and accepted. The symbol of this for me is the way we do much of our training. We have a passion for modeling tapes in training, for example. They promise a right way, they make the way explicit by headlining the learning points, and they pretend that what needs to be learned is predictable before the training event begins.

The cost is that we rarely see people engage their full capacity to learn. Just as Tim Gallwey, author and creator of the Inner Game method of learning, has suggested: In most training and instruction, there is a great deal of teaching and very little learning. In teacher-centered formats, the real learner is the trainer, and the participant is engaged in a sophisticated form of imitation and absorption.

The real learning is in the act of *creating* the modeling tape, the headlined points, and the lesson plan. It is in the struggle to create that we find value. It is in the effort to understand and create ideas and practices that the learning resides.

Learning As a Social Adventure

To bring value to the participant or the client, we need to design our efforts to support learning at the expense of teaching. This means we need to build elements of surprise, discovery, and not knowing into our interaction with the client. We need to allow risk in the room, raise the stakes, engage in caring confrontation, offer strong support, ensure affirmation of what each of us knows. These are what create learning.

Packaging an answer, as we do with our tapes and programs, interferes with learning. Granted, packaged consultation or training is faster, more digestible, more visible and predictable, and therefore more saleable; it is a good short-term business strategy. But, over time, it is like the alcoholic's hair-of-the-dog cure for a hangover. If high-control, predetermined thinking is the client's problem, we cannot fix it with high-control, predetermined answers.

If learning and change are truly our intent, a slower, more demanding, and more deliberative approach is required. We have to value struggle over prescription, questions over answers, tension over comfort, and capacities over needs and deficiencies.

The Struggle Is the Solution

Most persistent problems that call for consultation have no clear right answer. This means we have to get used to facing the paradoxical nature of the workplace and the human beings we find there. Think about how you deal with situations where two opposing viewpoints are both true. Do we need more control, or less? More centralization, or more local control? Do people need more of quick fix and fashion. And if a consultant cannot pose these questions, who will?

Insight Resides in Moments of Tension

To value struggle, entertain maddening questions, and live with paradox in the service of thinking differently is hard. Really hard. Our instinct is to move toward comfortable subjects. To reach for the habitual way of working. If we consultants propose questions about meaning and demand an extended period of reflection, we will be blamed for not being practical, action-oriented, step-minded.

If we view this tension as a flaw in the process, we will jump ship at the first salvo and retreat into comfort. Many of my mistakes have occurred when I got anxious about the process and reverted to the safe harbor of action plans and lists. Once the actions were listed, we all breathed a sigh of relief and smiled at the familiar feel of milestones in our hands. That was the good news.

When I would look back at those times, though, the changes that came out of those efforts were always disappointing. Follow-through was weak, optimism quickly faded, and even the effort to push the changes along left most people feeling that nothing had changed. We just had more action items on our plate. I let those clients down by yielding to the tension too easily. If I had persisted with the difficult questions longer, asked for more rethinking of the basics, I would have served the client better.

Another source of tension might simply be the strained relationships among those in the room. If resolving this strain were easy, they would have done it before we got there. We are often faced with tension that is historical and tenacious. Everyone feels it, but no one wants to name it. Do we dive into it or manage around it?

Here is a recent example that still rolls around in my mind. I facilitated a meeting of eleven agencies that had come together to better cooperate with each other. Good cause, and big event to even all be in the room together. Halfway through the meeting, after getting acquainted and hearing some ideas on possible mutual interests, the momentum for action and agreement started to build. I had planned for more open dialogue, more discussion of differences, more reflection, more time in mixed groups getting connected.

I felt the pressure build, the co-planners huddled with me in the corner, and I yielded on the original plan. We broke people into their natural teams and asked them to come back in an hour with ideas on what this whole group could do together that their organizations could not accomplish separately. Seemed reasonable—that is why we were there. At the end of the hour, the teams reported. To a team, each reported what that team alone might do to move its agenda forward. They were not prepared to cross boundaries, to yield on the positions they had come to the meeting with, or to trust each other in new ways. A group that had been convened to seek new cooperation devolved into their history of firm boundaries and negotiation.

The tension that was expressed in the desire to get to an action plan was really a defense against the deeper conversation about ways they were apart and the caution they felt in yielding positions that would be required for significant movement to occur. And the worst part was that I had colluded with them out of my own anxiety about being practical and useful. I tried to recover the next morning, but it was too late; the moment had passed, the energy that might have led to a shift had been drained.

The door to new ways of thinking does not open easily, and it is the tension in the room that actually becomes the key. The tension points to where the resistance or doubt resides. Discussing the tension makes insight and resolution possible. If we can see the tension as energy and go toward it, big insights will follow. If we manage around it, we risk losing the day as I did.

When the tension surfaces, it needs to be named—and discussed and acknowledged. The consultant has to push the discussion into the difficult areas. We have to ask ourselves when we will be in a better position to move ahead. When will be a better time to discuss failure, conflict between individuals and groups, feelings of futility and doubt? More structure is not what is needed at these moments; it is courage that is in short supply. By naming the tension and supporting a discussion of what it means, we gain some learning about the emotional part of work.

This is what learning requires and what clients need from us. It is the patriarchal culture that wants to keep a lid on feelings, which is what running from the tension is about. The key is understanding that the expression itself is what is valuable, not the answer or resolution. If we can support both sides in expressing things they find hard to discuss, then the decisions made afterward will be of a different nature.

Capacities Bear More Fruit Than Deficiencies

Another element of change is the choice whether to focus on what is missing or on what is present. I once thought that my service as a consultant was to identify problems, and so I dedicated myself to figuring out what was missing. After capitalizing on weaknesses for years, I have changed my focus to seeing what gifts are there and where capacities lie.

There is a practical side to this choice. We should accept that we have harvested the yield available in the deficiency field. Why pursue a path of diminishing marginal returns? We already have the product of a lifetime of working on deficiencies. A lot more effort will yield few more results.

In terms of strategic work with clients, John McKnight has articulated a wonderful case that focusing on deficiencies or needs only reinforces the power of the expert at the expense of the client or employee. In his language, it turns *citizens*, people with rights and power, into *consumers*, people with weaknesses and needs. He believes that in this shift from citizen to consumer, the one who benefits is the service provider—in our case, the consultant.

Focusing on deficiencies is also a question of how we treat the human spirit. Are we here to remind each other of what is missing or of what is possible? If what you see is what you get, then look for the strength and you will find it. The problem with looking at strengths is that we are not used to it, and we don't know what to say, so we feel embarrassed. And we have dealt with weaknesses for years, so it is easy for us to decide not to change them. But to search for the divine in each of us, or in our communities, would confront us in ways that most of us are not prepared for.

Finally, if we persist in looking at needs and weaknesses, it becomes a political gambit. An expression of power. The one who defines the conversation and the needs is the one in charge. When we institutionalize the talk of weaknesses in others, it is a way of maintaining control over what we are talking about. We position ourselves above the fray, uniquely able to see what is wrong. When we look at what is missing in other people or other organizations, we put them in a lesser position, even if we do so with the claim that we just want to be helpful. Our attitude implies that they have work to do and we do not. We are the parents lovingly looking at the child.

This becomes a comfortable stance for the consultant, for we can stand next to the critics, joining them in their favored position. It is a way of being sheltered by their halo. It also affirms that we are needed. But comfort is only the easiest way, not the most fruitful. Better for us to be present by virtue of choice rather than by need, and let our gift be to affirm the best in what we see.

We Are Responsible for One Another's Learning

Everything that happens in the room is every person's business. This is a radical thought. Why? Because we have such a history of competition that it has become the air we breathe. In our first exposure to institutional life, at school, our success came at the expense of others. I needed to get a "D" so someone else could get an "A." If I got the "A," then it needed to be balanced by another's failure. If you don't believe this, think what would happen if a teacher gave all "A's." The teacher would have a problem. What happens if a boss thinks everyone is an outstanding performer? Think again, boss.

This is not a moral stance against competition; it is a question of how competition affects learning. Competition with our peers breeds isolation and leads to holding tightly to what we have. Good, perhaps, for our ambition, but hardly for our institutions. If learning requires risk and not knowing, it will not happen if we see others as strangers with their own problems—problems that we do not share. The fact that so much of the culture thinks that individual competition is the key to motivation is a measure of how much our thinking has been defined by a marketplace mentality and its love of scarcity.

It always surprises me when I hear managers speak for the well-being of the whole and then see them participate in fostering competition among the parts. The challenge of organizational life is to connect people in common effort. Understanding my interdependence with all others connects me to the whole. And when each is responsible for the learning of the whole, then each shares a deeper sense of purpose with all members. Accepting this challenge demands cooperation and a willingness to acknowledge our connectedness. No small feat, but worth trying, for it is a significant way to ensure lasting learning.

If our goal as consultants is learning and change, we need to act as if all are responsible for it. This simple shift in thinking leads us to be more inclusive and to see that learning needs to come from all directions. If we are working in systems that breathe competition, we may not be able to change that, but at a minimum we can refuse to reinforce it.

Culture Changes in the Moment

This is a tricky and potentially very powerful idea. In every encounter with the client, we hear concern about what will happen tomorrow. We rarely end a meeting without someone expressing doubts about whether their agreements will last and their optimism endure. In the first hour of our training sessions, someone will ask whether the world will be any different when we leave the session.

My response is that if we want to see change, we had better not wait to leave this session for it to happen. How can we have hope in tomorrow if today is not different? Each moment has to carry within it an element of the destination. This is why the way we come together is so important. It offers hope—at this minute—about how the future might look. It leads us to give great attention to how we design this moment, this meeting.

The moment also instructs us in methods. If we learn to watch what is happening now, this reflection will tell us what works and what doesn't. As a discovery method, it is understanding the universe in a grain of sand. It is understanding the organizational culture in the nature of this meeting or conversation. If you see nothing happening, either you are not watching or maybe there is "no thing" happening. To witness the absence of life, or action, or dialogue is as descriptive of a system as seeing the presence of something. If we would trust the moment we would learn the power of reflection.

Also we would see that we can implement the future without having to wait for it. How long does change take? Well, are we ready to begin it at this moment? Want to bring trust, honesty, more or less structure, cooperation between units, clearer focus, alignment into the organization? Now is the time to begin. Our action plan is what we do in the next hour. Not what we say, but *what we do together.* This meeting becomes the tablet on which the future is written. Each intention of cultural change needs to find expression in the present or it loses its credibility.

The moment only fails us when what we have in mind is a change in someone else. Those "someone elses" cannot be changed in the moment if they are not in the room. If they are not in the room, they cannot be party to the change. So why are we focusing on them anyway? Why do we always think that some other group is the problem? Why is it that, in thirty years of training, I have never had the right group in the room? Whoever is in the room is always the wrong person. Whoever gets the training asks whether others have received it yet. If I say they have, then they say it didn't take.

If I say they haven't, then they ask, why do you expect us to change if they won't?

Changing the moment into a preview of tomorrow also requires us to forsake the past, to let go of our guilt or resentment. Victims do not do well in the moment, and we have all been wounded. We create little room in organizational life for forgiveness—of ourselves and others. I have seen few learning exercises that are about forgiveness. Maybe this is one of the reasons we are so focused on weaknesses; they remind us of our unfinished business with our own history. If we have not forgiven the past we will keep trying to fix it. Changing the moment, giving it importance, honoring it as a prediction of the future may be the way to heal the wounds and urge us into choosing optimism.

If Change Is So Wonderful, Why Don't You Go First?

Another heart-of-the-matter notion is that change, transformation, and hope are all self-inflicted. Change faces us with human questions, and dealing with them is so dependent on hope. Hope is found in our own integrity and willingness to participate in what we have chosen for the larger system. We colonize each other when we define others as the problem. And the higher in the institution we go, the more we are cut off from our own need to change.

When we run an organization or achieve real success, we begin to think of ourselves as a finished product. The institution expects so much, and the employees project so strongly on its management, that people at the top begin to believe their own press. They begin to think there is no room for them not to know. They are the godfather, and their lot is to dispense justice to others, not to be the ones who strive for justice within themselves.

If you look at the great leaders through history, you see a consciousness of their own limitations that was essential to their greatness. From Confucius, Buddha, and Christ, to Lincoln, Gandhi, and Martin Luther King—all touched lives because of their presence more than their position. They became archetypes for the right use of power, and one source of their power was their own humility.

Power used to distance ourselves from our prescriptions is power abused. In seeking a partnership with school administrators and communities, Bob Chase, president of the National Education Association, often said that the union had to be the one to blink first. It is an observation that we would be wise to take to heart. It would make us credible and offer an antidote to the patriarchy embedded in our strategies of change.

But don't think that leaders are alone in thinking others should be the ones to change. The love of patriarchy is as strong in employees as in management. As consultants we once thought that as soon as management changed, employees would follow. Not necessarily so. Employees create bosses. If we create high-control bosses, we consider ourselves entitled, and entitlement means that we are not the problem: Something is due us, and we owe nothing. We hold to the safety of our dependency, just as the boss does, and each of us thinks the other needs to be fixed.

The Final Question Is One of Faith

All of these beliefs trust that there is a movement toward learning that has its own energy and own intention. The world will provide the events that will force movement. Life provides the disturbance. We do not have to induce change, or drive it, or guide it. All we have to do is join it. The consultant is as much a learner as any client. We in fact are often more changed by our consultation than the client, and this is as it should be.

In the end it is our authenticity, the way we manage ourselves, and our connection to our clients, that is our methodology, our marketing strategy, and the fruit of our labor. The fact that we show up with a briefcase, a resume, and a conceptual framework is more a function of habit than necessity. It will be enough if we simply show up. And that is the heart of the matter.

Appendix

Another Checklist You Can Use

NOW THAT YOU HAVE FINISHED reading this book, you should have a good grasp of consulting concepts and skills. You have also seen how specific skills and techniques must be brought to bear in a methodical, sequential fashion during the preliminary events to heighten the probability of successful implementation. And you have seen that knowing what to do (the product of the discovery phase) is quite a different matter from finding the right way to do it (in the implementation phase).

So why another checklist? To help make this book easily accessible and useful to you as a *continuing* reference on how to do consulting. Suppose you have an appointment to see a prospective client and want to quickly refresh your understanding of what to do in contracting. Turn to the section on contracting here, and use it as an outline of what to cover in your meeting, what to pay attention to.

This appendix is divided into seven parts—overview, contracting, data collection and discovery, feedback, implementation, resistance, and ethical practice. The checklist in each section is an outline of main points or a summary of the business of that phase and the skills required. You can simply read through the checklists to refresh your knowledge and understanding of the material in the book from time to time. Or you may use them to check off some of the points you may not be completely sure about, that you want to learn more about, or that you want to practice further. The checklists also function as a topic index, giving page numbers of text if you want to review a particular point in more detail.

Before You Negotiate Your Next Contract, Remember . . .

	Chapters 4, 5, 6	**Page**
2. Elicit the client's expectations of you		58
3. State clearly and simply what you want from the client		58
4. Say no, or postpone a project that in your judgment has less than a 50/50 chance of success		50
5. Probe directly for the client's underlying concerns about exposure and vulnerability		50
6. Discuss directly with the client why the contracting meeting is not going well when it isn't		58
☐ A contract is an explicit agreement of what the consultant and client expect from each other and how they are going to work together.		55
☐ There are two key concepts in contracting:		55
• Mutual consent: Both sides enter the agreement freely and by their own choosing		55
• Valid consideration: Each party to the contract receives something of value		56
☐ Most of your contracts should contain these elements:		59
1. The boundaries of your analysis		60
2. Objectives of the project		60

Before You Go into the Data Collection and Discovery Phase of Your Next Project, Remember . . .

☐ The business of the data collection/ discovery phase is:

189

1. Doing layers of analysis

2. Understanding the political climate

3. Resurfacing resistance to sharing information

4. Seeing the interview as an intervention

☐ The specific skills involved in discovery are to be able to:

187

1. Distinguish between the presenting problem and the underlying problem

2. Elicit and describe both the technical/ business problem and how the problem is being managed

3. Ask questions about the client's own personal role in causing or maintaining the presenting or target problem

4. Ask questions about what others in the organization are doing to cause or maintain the presenting or target problem

5. Plan the data collection jointly with the client

6. Involve the client in interpreting the data collected

7. Recognize the similarity between how the client manages *you* and how they manage their own organization

	Chapters 10, 11, 12	Page

8. Condense the data into a limited number of issues

9. Use language that is understandable to people outside your area of expertise

☐ The purpose of discovery is to get action, not do research.   175, 176

☐ Your goal is to develop a clear and simple picture of what is causing and maintaining the client's problem, including a description of the technical/business problem the client has asked for help on and a description of how that problem is being managed.   179

☐ Concentrate on four things beyond the technical considerations: 177

1. Keep simplifying, narrowing, reducing your inquiry so it focuses more and more on the next steps the client can take.   177

2. Use everyday language.   177

3. Give a great deal of attention to your relationship with the client. Include the client at every opportunity in deciding how to proceed. Deal with resistance as it arises.   178

4. Treat data on how the client organization is functioning as valid and relevant information. Also assess how the problem you are exploring is being managed.   178

	Chapters 10, 11, 12	Page
☐ How the problem is being managed is key.		194
☐ Understanding how the problem is being managed requires looking at such dimensions as:		194
1. Clarity of objectives		194
2. Subgroup competition and cooperation		194
3. Support		194
4. Evaluation of performance		194
5. Sex roles		194
6. Status differences		195
7. Authority and power		195
8. Decision-making effectiveness		195
9. Norms for individual behavior		195
10. Management information		195
11. Leadership style		195
12. Conflict		195
13. Domination		195
14. Attitudes about this project and your involvement		195
☐ To plan a data collection meeting, use Checklist #5.		203
☐ To review what happened in a data collection meeting, use Checklist #6.		206

	Chapters 10, 11, 12	**Page**
1. Design learning experiences for others		215
2. Convene and bring people together		215
3. Help people question their current reality and envision their future		215
4. Confront people with their freedom and responsibility through interactive activities		215

	Chapters 13, 14	**Page**

Before You Go into the Feedback Phase of Your Next Project, Remember . . .

☐ The business of the feedback phase is:		228
1. Funneling data		228
2. Presenting personal and organizational data		228
3. Managing the feedback meeting		228
4. Focusing on the here and now of the meeting		228
5. Don't take it personally		228
☐ The specific skills involved in feedback are to be able to:		245
1. Confront the client with all relevant data collected, even if it wasn't part of your original assignment		245
2. Give descriptive rather than evaluative feedback		245
3. Feed data back to the client about personal behavior in handling the target problem		245

When You Encounter Resistance, Remember . . .

**Before You
Go into the
Implementation
Phase of Your
Next Project,
Remember . . .**

☐ There are two aspects of implementa-   249
tion: (1) the technical work, using your
particular expertise, and (2) the question of building support for the business
or technical change you are planning.

☐ There is a difference between seeing   248
implementation as a matter of installation or as a matter of engagement. Installation sees change as an engineering
process and addresses the tangibles,
such as technical changes, work processes, and structure. Engagement
acknowledges that any change also
requires a shift in many intangibles,
such as relationships, faith, commitment.

☐ Many of the ways consultants try to change   250
institutions actually create defenses against
change. Our mistake in implementation
is to over-invest in, or even misuse, such
legitimate mechan-isms as

     1. Vision and leadership

     2. Standards

     3. Rewards

     4. Training

5. Measurement

	Chapters 15, 16, 17	**Page**

☐ Implementation is more complex than contracting or discovery, for it is more particular to each situation. There is no universal, clear-cut path to follow. Even so, the most successful implementation efforts invariably build relationships, encourage local choice and more distributed governance, and promote common purpose. The consultant is in a unique position to introduce this mind-set to the client.

303

☐ To prepare for implementation, use Checklist #9.

302

☐ To review the implementation process, use Checklist #10.

304

	Chapters 18, 19	**Page**

To Create an Ethical Practice, Remember . . .

☐ All consulting has its shadow side—attitudes and practices that engender doubt and cynicism. Possible ways to confront and accept the shadow are:

307

1. Say no as often as you say yes — 324

2. Stay true to your worth — 324

3. Grow on your own terms — 325

4. Operate as if everyone counts — 325

5. Leave it all behind — 326

6. Forgive — 326

Suggestions for Further Reading

Alexander, Christopher. *The Timeless Way of Building.* New York: Oxford University Press, 1979.

Argyris, Chris. *Flawed Advice and the Management Trap: How Managers Can Know When They're Getting Good Advice and When They're Not.* New York: Oxford University Press, 1999.

Argyris, Chris. *Knowledge for Action, A Guide to Overcoming Barriers to Organizational Change.* San Francisco: Jossey-Bass, 1993.

Axelrod, Richard H. *Terms of Engagement: Changing the Way We Change Organizations* (working title). San Francisco: Berrett-Koehler, forthcoming Spring 2000.

Bellman, Geoffrey M. *The Consultant's Calling: Bringing Who You Are to What You Do.* San Francisco: Jossey-Bass, 1992.

Biech, Elaine. *The Business of Consulting: The Basics and Beyond.* San Francisco: Jossey-Bass/Pfeiffer, 1999.

Blake, Robert R., and Jane S. Mouton. *Consultation.* Reading, Mass.: Addison-Wesley, 1976.

Block, Peter. *The Empowered Manager: Positive Political Skills at Work.* San Francisco: Jossey-Bass, 1987.

Block, Peter. *Stewardship: Choosing Service over Self-Interest*. San Francisco: Berrett-Koehler, 1993.

Briskin, Alan. *The Stirring of Soul in the Workplace*. San Francisco: Berrett-Koehler, 1998.

Bunker, Barbara Benedict, and Billie T. Alban. *Large Group Interventions: Engaging the Whole System for Rapid Change*. San Francisco: Jossey-Bass, 1996.

Clapp, Neale. *Work Group Norms: Leverage for Organizational Change*. Part I: Theory. Part II: Application. Plainfield, N.J.: Block Petrella Associates, 1979.

Dannemiller, Kathleen, et al. *Unleashing the Magic* (working title). San Francisco: Berrett-Koehler, forthcoming 2000.

Dannemiller, Kathleen, et al. *How to Unleash the Magic: A Fieldbook* (working title). San Francisco: Berrett-Koehler, forthcoming 2000.

Gallwey, W. Timothy. *The Inner Game of Tennis* (rev. ed.). New York: Random House, 1997.

Henning, Joel P. *The Future of Staff Groups: Daring to Distribute Power and Capacity*. San Francisco: Berrett-Koehler, 1997.

Illich, Ivan, John McKnight, Irving K. Zola, Jonathan Caplan, and Harley Shaiken. *Disabling Professions*. New York and London: Marion Boyars Publishers, 1987.

Koestenbaum, Peter. *Leadership: The Inner Side of Greatness—A Philosophy for Leaders*. San Francisco: Jossey-Bass, 1991.

Maurer, Rick. *Beyond the Wall of Resistance: Unconventional Strategies That Build Support for Change*. Austin, Texas: Bard Press, 1996.

McKnight, John. *The Careless Society: Community and Its Counterfeits*. New York: BasicBooks, 1995.

Oshry, Barry. *Seeing Systems: Unlocking the Mysteries of Organizational Life.* San Francisco: Berrett-Koehler, 1995.

Palmer, Parker J. *The Courage to Teach: Exploring the Inner Landscape of a Teacher's Life.* San Francisco: Jossey-Bass, 1998.

Schein, Edgar H. *Process Consultation Revisited: Building the Helping Relationship.* Reading, Mass.: Addison-Wesley/Longman, 1999.

Steele, Fritz. *Consulting for Organizational Change.* Amherst, Mass.: University of Massachusetts Press, 1975.

Walton, Richard E. *Interpersonal Peacemaking: Confrontations and Third-Party Consultation.* Reading, Mass.: Addison-Wesley, 1969.

Weisbord, Marvin. *Discovering Common Ground: How Future Search Conferences Bring People Together to Achieve Breakthrough Innovation, Empowerment, Shared Vision, and Collaborative Action.* San Francisco: Berrett-Koehler, 1993.

Weisbord, Marvin, and Sandra Janoff. *Future Search: An Action Guide to Finding Common Ground in Organizations and Communities.* San Francisco: Berrett-Koehler, 1995.

Wheatley, Margaret J., and Myron Kellner-Rogers. *A Simpler Way.* San Francisco: Berrett-Koehler, 1996.

Whitmore, John. *Coaching for Performance: People Skills for Professionals.* London: Nicholas Brealey, 1996.

About the Author

SINCE THE PUBLICATION of the first edition of *Flawless Consulting*, Peter Block has written two additional books: *The Empowered Manager: Positive Political Skills at Work* (1987) and *Stewardship: Choosing Service over Self-Interest* (1993).

Peter received a B.S. degree in business administration from the University of Kansas and a master's degree in industrial administration from Yale University. He is the creator of the Staff Consulting Skills Workshops, which teach consulting skills to people in the staff role in areas such as engineering, systems analysis, finance, and personnel. The workshops are offered by Designed Learning and have been conducted in public seminars and internally for hundreds of organizations in the United States and around the world. Designed Learning can be reached at (908) 889-0300 or www.Designedlearning.com.

Active in supporting the Association for Quality and Participation, he has joined with AQP to create The School for Managing and Leading Change, a unique, nine-month program for public- and private-sector teams to learn how to redesign their workplaces. For information on the school, call (513) 381-1959 or visit the Website at www.aqp.org.

He has received several national awards for outstanding contribution in the field of training and development, including the American Society for Training and Development Award for Distinguished Contributions, the Association for Quality and Participation President's Award, and *Training* magazine's HRD Hall of Fame.

Designed Learning, founded by Peter Block is *The Center for Consulting Competence.* We support Training, HR, Information Systems, Quality, Engineering and other staff groups in their efforts to transform themselves into consulting organizations. Our workshops transfer powerful consulting concepts, skills and expertise to staff professionals. Our expertise is in successfully navigating the day-to-day problems facing staff groups transitioning to and operating as consulting units. With us, they develop the expertise that builds the capacity of their clients for marketplace success.

Flawless Consulting—**Two hands-on, skill-building workshops for internal and external consultants!** The *only* consulting skills workshops developed by *Flawless Consulting* author, Peter Block.

Learn how to establish and maintain collaborative working relationships with clients, which result in positive outcomes for the business.

Consulting Skills Workshop I—*The Fundamentals of the Contract*
- Apply a Simple Powerful Process for Managing Consulting Relationships
- Raise and Deal with Client Concerns about Control and Vulnerability
- Practice the Skills and Competencies to Create a Consulting Contract

Consulting Skills Workshop II—*Getting Others to Act on What They Know*
- Discover the Underlying Dimensions of the Situation
- Create Feedback Statements which Enable Clients to Act
- Respond Constructively to Client Resistance to Difficult Feedback

Other Designed Learning workshops and consulting:
- Advanced Consulting Skills—*Developing Offers that Promise to Build Real Capacity in Client Organizations*
- Reinventing Staff Groups—*Creating Consultative Organizations*
- Choosing Accountability—*Bringing Hands, Mind and Heart to Work*
- Building Capacity—*Deepening Customer Service by Distributing Power*
- Conversations—*Creating Powerful Sustainable Change at the Local Level*
- Managing Differences & Agreement—*Making Conflict Work for You*
- The Business of Consulting—*The Basics and Beyond*
- Staff Unit Development—*A Unique Strategy for Transforming Staff Groups*

For more information contact:
Designed Learning Inc.
313 South Avenue, Suite 202
Fanwood, NJ 07023
Phone: (908) 889-0300
Email: Info@DesignedLearning.com

DESIGNED LEARNING
The Center For Consulting Competence

Fax: (908) 889-4995
Website: www.Designedlearning.com